Praise for
Loving What Is

"Byron Katie has rocked my world and shaken loose my mind more thoroughly than any other spiritual teacher I've ever encountered, living or dead. Using her simple process called The Work, I have managed to liberate myself from thoughts and beliefs that had brought me years of suffering and that I had honestly feared would never leave me."
—Elizabeth Gilbert, author of *Eat, Pray, Love*

"A spiritual innovator for the new millennium."
—*Time* magazine

"Katie's laserlike tough love burns away all illusions."
—*The Times* (London)

"Good Lord! Where did Byron Katie come from? She's the real McCoy. Her work is amazingly effective—a simple, straightforward antidote to the suffering we unnecessarily create for ourselves. She asks us to believe nothing but provides a surprisingly effective and simple way to cut through the tangle of delusions we wrap ourselves in. Just reading the exchanges in *Loving What Is*, I can admit things I didn't want to admit and stop torturing myself in ways I didn't realize I was doing."
—David Chadwick, author of *Crooked Cucumber: The Life and Zen Teaching of Shunryu Suzuki*

"Suppose you could find a simple way to embrace your life with joy, stop arguing with reality, and achieve serenity in the midst of chaos. That is what *Loving What Is* offers. It is no less than a revolutionary way to live your life. The question is: Are we brave enough to accept it?"
—Erica Jong, author of *Fear of Flying*

"Byron Katie is an immeasurable gift to the world."

—Martha Beck, author of *Finding Your Own North Star*

"*Loving What Is* is filled with the essence of wisdom. Katie's Work is a wonderful, transformative practice for anyone interested in spiritual growth."

—Lama Surya Das, author of *Awakening the Buddha Within*

"Byron Katie's Work is a great blessing for our planet. The root cause of suffering is identification with our thoughts, the 'stories' that are continuously running through our minds. Byron Katie's Work acts like a razor-sharp sword that cuts through that illusion and enables you to know for yourself the timeless essence of your being. Joy, peace, and love emanate from it as your natural state. In *Loving What Is,* you have the key. Now use it."

—Eckhart Tolle, author of *The Power of Now*

Loving What Is

Four Questions That Can Change Your Life

BYRON KATIE

with Stephen Mitchell

Second Edition

HARMONY

BOOKS • NEW YORK

Copyright © 2002, 2021 by Byron Katie and Stephen Mitchell

Published in the United States by Harmony Books, an imprint of Random House,
a division of Penguin Random House LLC, New York.
harmonybooks.com

Harmony Books is a registered trademark, and the Circle colophon is a trademark of
Penguin Random House LLC.

An earlier edition of this work was published by Harmony Books, an imprint of
Random House, a division of Penguin Random House LLC, in 2002.

Library of Congress Cataloging-in-Publication Data
is available upon request.

ISBN 978-0-593-23451-8
Ebook ISBN 978-0-593-23452-5

Printed in the United States of America

Book design by Andrea Lau
Cover design by Anna Bauer Carr, based on the original design by
Jenny Wunderly and Andy Bernstein
Cover photographs by (front) Susan Carpendale and
(back) Andre2013/iStock/Getty Images Plus

10 9 8 7 6 5

Revised Edition

To Adam Joseph Lewis and to Michael

Contents

Preface to the Second Edition

For this second edition of *Loving What Is,* I have clarified and added a few passages, and I have replaced some of the dialogues with seven new ones.

When I discovered The Work—when it discovered me—I realized that reality is always good, whatever form it appears in. Every experience is supplied by a friendly universe. Every experience is a gift. It's falling down; it's getting up; it's your everyday chores; it's the smell of fresh strawberries, the smell of a dead mouse; it's the death of a loved one; it's your husband falling in love with another woman; it's everything that happens in your life, whether you believe that it's good or bad. People with questioned minds see the apparently bad as good, because they no longer live in the world of opposites, the world in which there is any thought powerful enough to override the true nature of things. They have realized this goodness so deeply that they can live it every moment of their lives.

I sometimes call reality "God," because it rules. In my life I trust God's will, and I don't have to guess what it is. Whatever happens is God's will. Whether I live or die, whether my husband and children live or die, whether I am rich or poor, sick or well, whether there is war or peace, health or pandemic, sunshine or hurricane or earthquake, that is God's will, and therefore it's my will. I'm in love with reality, and reality includes everything: both sides of everything. My arms are open to it all.

I experience reality as something so benevolent, so beautiful, so pure, that there is no word for it. I don't have a problem calling it "God." It exists wherever I turn my eyes (and even saying "exists" is saying too much). When I first realized this, I was amazed. I was ecstatic, and I still am. "God, God, God"—that was the song singing through me. That's the song I still sing. There is nothing that doesn't fit into this kindness, this radical abundance. And who of right mind wouldn't be devoted to it? That's where I find myself—on my knees internally, at its feet, without reservation, unceasingly grateful, unceasingly awake to what I have realized. God, for me, is the beloved, the goodness and purity of the world. And to know reality as goodness without limit is to know the true nature of yourself as well.

Everything is fair, everything is right, everything is beautiful, and if you see anything in your life as unfair, you realize that it's your next opportunity to question what you're believing and remove yourself from ignorance. Anything that would darken your awareness is simply the next thing to question. The truth sets you free, but that truth has to be yours, not the world's. The world's truth is secondhand. I had to act from my own truth. I realized that the world was as I believed it to be, and when I questioned what I believed, I experienced a world of all-penetrating kindness and beauty.

This is the *what* of spiritual practice. And the *how*? The *how* is The Work. When The Work is alive in you, there's nothing else you need. Whenever there is anything unclear in your life, all you have to do is question your stressful thoughts. The Work is mental hygiene, the technology of going inside and finding your own answers. All the wisdom that has ever existed becomes alive in you. You discover that all your anger, all your sadness, have just been a misunderstanding.

The wisdom of the ages lives inside you. It lives immovably within the illusion of suffering. The only requirement is to question anything that would compete with the living answer. You're always being answered, but your mind is so full of concepts and assumptions that often there's no space available for you to notice. So you need to get very still, ask sincerely, stay rooted in the question, and settle for nothing less than the authentic.

Sometimes you don't even have to ask or seek or knock. If your mind is open, even for a moment, the answer can slip in. All it takes is a mind that is empty of concepts just long enough to recognize the answer it's giving itself. When I woke up to reality, I was simply witnessing. The ego didn't override what I was shown. The door was opened, and I hadn't even knocked. It was beyond a physical body. It was prior to existence as I understood it. I witnessed how all existence is created, and that was the joke, that was the laughter that poured out of this mouth, the laughter between worlds, an ecstatic response to the joyous nature of reality. It came out of nowhere, and it returned there instantly, and there was no coming or going. It was the key to my heart: the kindest, truest, most intimate experience. Authenticity is self-evident. We naturally trust it with all our heart.

When you wake up to reality, life becomes effortless, because there's no fear left in you. Your mind can't project a future. You don't have to know what to do; you just do it. You realize that you're not the doer, that the creative mind, the wisdom of the universe, is what's running the show. *God* is another name for the nameless: reality, the kind, the loving, the immovable. There's nothing you can do about it, and whenever you argue with it, you hurt yourself. It's not waiting for your invitation or your permission. It's always there. It's perfect. It's yours from the beginning of time.

Introduction

by Stephen Mitchell

The more clearly you understand yourself and your emotions,
the more you become a lover of what is.
—Baruch Spinoza

The first time I watched The Work, I realized that I was witnessing something truly remarkable. What I saw was a succession of people—young and old, educated and uneducated—who were learning to question their thoughts, the thoughts that were most painful to them. With the lovingly incisive help of Byron Katie (everyone calls her Katie), those people were finding their way not only toward the resolution of their immediate problems but also toward a state of mind in which the deepest questions are resolved. I have spent a good part of my life studying and translating the classic texts of the great spiritual traditions, and I recognized something very similar in process here. At the core of these traditions—in works such as the Book of Job, the Tao Te Ching, and the Bhagavad Gita—there are an intense questioning about life and death and a profound, joyful wisdom that emerges as an answer. That wisdom, it seemed to me, was the place Katie was standing in, and where these people were headed.

As I watched from my seat in a crowded community center, five men and women, one after another, were learning freedom through the very thoughts that had caused their suffering, thoughts such as "My husband betrayed me" or "My mother doesn't love me enough." Simply by asking four questions and listening to the answers they found inside themselves, those people were opening their minds to profound, spacious, life-transforming insights. I saw a man who had been suffering for decades from anger and resentment toward his alcoholic father light up before my eyes within forty-five minutes. I saw a woman who had been almost too frightened to speak, because she had just found out that her cancer was spreading, end the session in a glow of understanding and acceptance. Three out of the five people had never done The Work before, yet the process didn't seem to be more difficult for them than it was for the other two, nor were their realizations any less profound. They all began by realizing a truth so basic that it is usually invisible: the fact that (in the words of the Greek philosopher Epictetus) "we are disturbed not by what happens to us, but by our thoughts about what happens." As soon as they grasped that truth, their whole understanding changed.

Before people have experienced The Work of Byron Katie for themselves, they often think that it is too simple to be effective. But its simplicity is precisely what makes it so effective. Over the past two years, since Katie and I first met (we are now married), I have done The Work many times, on thoughts I hadn't even been aware of. And I've watched more than a thousand people do it in public events across the United States and Europe, on the whole gamut of human problems: from major illnesses, the deaths of parents and children, sexual and psychological abuse, addictions, financial insecurity, professional problems, and social issues, to the usual frustrations of daily life. Again and again, I have seen The Work quickly and radically transform the way people think about their problems. And as their thinking changes, their problems disappear.

"Suffering is optional," Katie says. Whenever we experience a stressful feeling—anything from mild discomfort to intense sorrow, rage, or despair—we can be certain that there is a specific thought causing our reaction, whether or not we are conscious of it. The way to end our stress is to investigate the thinking that lies behind it, and anyone can do this, alone, with a computer, a smart phone, or a piece of paper and a pen. The Work's four questions, which you will see in context later in this introduction, reveal where our thinking isn't true for us. Through this process—Katie also calls it "inquiry"—we discover that all the concepts and judgments that we believe or take for granted are distortions of things as they really are. When we believe our thoughts instead of what is really true for us, we experience the kind of emotional distress that we call suffering. Suffering is a natural alarm, warning us that we're attaching to a thought; when we don't listen, we come to accept the suffering as an inevitable part of life. It's not.

The Work has striking similarities with the Zen koan and the Socratic dialogue. But it doesn't stem from any tradition, Eastern or Western. It is American, homegrown, and mainstream, having originated in the mind of an ordinary woman who had no intention of originating anything.

To realize your true nature, you must wait for the right moment and the right conditions. When the time comes, you are awakened as if from a dream. You understand that what you have found is your own and doesn't come from anywhere outside.
—Buddhist sutra

The Work was born on a February morning in 1986 when Byron Kathleen Reid, a forty-three-year-old woman from a small town in the high desert of southern California, woke up on the floor of a halfway house.

In the midst of an ordinary life—two marriages, three children, a successful career—Katie entered a ten-year-long downward spiral into rage, paranoia, and despair. For two years she was so depressed that she could seldom manage to leave her house; she stayed in bed for weeks at a time, doing business by telephone from her bedroom, unable even to bathe or brush her teeth. Her children would tiptoe past her door to avoid her outbursts of rage. Finally, she checked in to a halfway house for women with eating disorders, the only facility that her insurance company would pay for. The other residents were so frightened of her that she was placed alone in an attic room.

One morning, a week or so later, as she lay on the floor (she had been feeling too unworthy to sleep in a bed), she woke up without any concept of who or what she was. "There was no me," she says.

> All my rage, all the thoughts that had been troubling me, my whole world, *the* whole world, was gone. At the same time, laughter welled up from the depths and just poured out. Everything was unrecognizable. It was as if something else had woken up. *It* opened its eyes. *It* was looking through Katie's eyes. And it was so delighted! It was intoxicated with joy. There was nothing separate, nothing unacceptable to it; everything was its very own self.

When Katie returned home, her family and friends felt that she was a different person. Her daughter, Roxann, who was sixteen at the time, says:

> We knew that the constant storm was over. She had always yelled at me and my brothers and criticized us; I used to be scared to be in the same room with her. Now she seemed completely peaceful. She would sit still for hours on the win-

dow seat or out in the desert. She was joyful and innocent, like a child, and she seemed to be filled with love. People in trouble started knocking on our door, asking her for help. She'd sit with them and ask them questions—mainly, "Is that true?" When I'd come home miserable, with a problem like "My boyfriend doesn't love me anymore," Mom would look at me as if she knew that wasn't possible, and she'd ask me, "Honey, how could that be true?" as if I had just told her that we were living in China.

Once people understood that the old Katie wasn't coming back, they began to speculate about what had happened to her. Had some miracle occurred? She wasn't much help to them; it was a long time before she could describe her experience intelligibly. She would talk about a freedom that had woken up inside her. She also said that through an inner questioning, she had realized that all her old thoughts were untrue.

Shortly after Katie got back from the halfway house, her home began to fill with people who had heard about her and had come to learn. She was able to communicate her inner inquiry in the form of specific questions that anyone who wanted freedom could apply on his own, without her help. Soon she began to be invited to meet with small gatherings in people's living rooms. Her hosts often asked her if she was "enlightened." She would answer, "I'm just someone who knows the difference between what hurts and what doesn't."

In 1992, she was invited to Northern California, and The Work spread very fast from there. Katie accepted every invitation. She has been on the road almost constantly since 1993, demonstrating The Work in church basements, community centers, and hotel meeting rooms, in front of small and large audiences. And The Work has found its way into all kinds of organizations, from corporations, law firms, and therapists' offices to hospitals, prisons, churches, and schools. It is now popular in other parts of the world where Katie has traveled. All across the United States and Europe there are groups of people who meet regularly to do The Work.

Katie often says that the only way to understand The Work is to experience it. But it's worth noting that inquiry fits precisely with current research into the biology of mind. Contemporary neuroscience identifies a particular part of the brain, sometimes called "the interpreter," as the source of the familiar internal narrative that gives us our sense of self. Two prominent neuroscientists have recently characterized the quirky, undependable quality of the tale told by the interpreter. Antonio Damasio, the director of the Brain and Creativity Institute at the University of Southern California, described it this way: "Perhaps the most important revelation in human split-brain research is precisely this: that the left cerebral hemisphere of humans is prone to fabricating verbal narratives that do not necessarily accord with the truth." And Michael Gazzaniga, the director of the SAGE Center for the Study of Mind at the University of California, Santa Barbara, wrote, "The left brain weaves its story in order to convince itself and you that it is in full control. . . . What is so adaptive about having what amounts to a spin doctor in the left brain? . . . The interpreter . . . is really trying to keep our personal story together. To do that, we have to learn to lie to ourselves." These insights, based on solid experimental work, show that we tend to believe our own press releases. Often when we think we're being rational, we're being spun by our own thinking. That trait explains how we get ourselves into the painful positions that Katie recognized in her own suffering. The self-questioning she discovered uses a different, less known capacity of the mind to find a way out of its self-made trap.

After doing The Work, many people report an immediate sense of release and freedom from thoughts that were making them miserable. But if The Work depended on a momentary experience, it would be far less useful than it is. The Work is an ongoing and deepening process of self-realization, not a quick fix. "It's more than a technique," Katie says. "It brings to life, from deep within us, an innate aspect of our being."

The deeper you go into The Work, the more powerful you realize it is. People who have been practicing inquiry for a while often say, "The Work is no longer something I do. *It* is doing *me*." They describe how, without any conscious intention, their mind notices each stressful thought and undoes it before it can cause any suffering. Their internal argument with reality has disappeared, and they find that what remains is love: for themselves, for other people, and for whatever life brings. The title of this book describes their experience: loving what is becomes as easy and natural as breathing.

Considering that, all hatred driven hence,
The [mind] recovers radical innocence
And learns at last that it is self-delighting,
Self-appeasing, self-affrighting,
And that its own sweet will is Heaven's will.
        —*William Butler Yeats*

I have waited until now to introduce the four questions to you, because they don't make much sense out of context. The best way to meet them is to see how they function in an actual example of The Work. You'll also meet what Katie calls the "turnaround," which is a way of experiencing the opposite of what you believe is true.

The following dialogue with Katie took place before an audience of about two hundred people. Mary, the woman who is sitting opposite Katie on the stage, has filled out a one-page Worksheet that asked her to write down her thoughts about someone who upsets her. The instructions are: "Allow yourself to be as judgmental and petty as you really feel. Don't try to be 'spiritual' or kind." The pettier we can be when writing, the more likely it is that we'll benefit from

The Work. You'll see that Mary hasn't held back at all. She is a forceful woman, perhaps forty years old, slim, attractive, and dressed in expensive-looking exercise clothes. At the beginning of the dialogue, her anger and impatience are palpable.

A first experience of The Work, as a reader or onlooker, can be uncomfortable. It helps to remember that all the participants—Mary, Katie, and the audience—are on the same side here; all of them are looking for the truth. If Katie ever seems to be mocking or derisive, you'll realize, upon closer examination, that she's making fun of the thought that is causing Mary's suffering, never of Mary herself.

Toward the middle of the dialogue, when Katie asks, "Do you really want to know the truth?," she doesn't mean her truth or any abstract, predetermined truth but Mary's truth, the truth that is hidden behind her troubling thoughts. Mary has entered the dialogue in the first place because she trusts that Katie can help her discover where she is lying to herself. She welcomes Katie's persistence.

You'll also notice right away that Katie is very free in her use of terms of endearment. One CEO, before a workshop that Katie gave to his top executives, felt that he had to issue a warning: "If she holds your hand and calls you 'sweetheart' or 'honey,' please don't get excited. She does this with everyone."

Mary [*reading the statements from her Worksheet*]: *I hate my husband because he drives me crazy—everything about him, including the way he breathes. What disappoints me is that I don't love him anymore, and our relationship is a charade. I want him not to be needy, not to be dependent on me, to be more successful, to not want to have sex with me, to get in shape, to get a life outside of me and the children, to not touch me anymore, and to be powerful. My husband shouldn't fool himself that he's good at our business. He should create more success. My husband is a wimp. He's needy and lazy. He's fooling himself. I refuse to keep living a lie. I refuse to keep living my relationship as an imposter.*

Katie: Does that pretty well sum it up? *[The audience bursts into laughter, and Mary laughs along with them.]* By the sound of the laughter, it seems as though you speak for a lot of people in this room. So let's start at the top and see if we can begin to understand what's going on.

Mary: *I hate my husband because he drives me crazy—everything about him, including the way he breathes.*

Katie: Your husband drives you crazy—is it true? *[This is the first of the four questions: Is it true?]*

Mary: Yes.

Katie: Okay. What's an example of that, sweetheart? He breathes?

Mary: He breathes. When we're doing conference calls for our business, I can hear his breath on the other end of the telephone, and I want to scream.

Katie: So his breath drives you crazy—is that true?

Mary: Yes.

Katie: Can you absolutely know that that's true? *[The second question: Can you absolutely know that it's true?]*

Mary: Yes!

Katie: We can all relate to that. I hear that it really is true for you. In my experience, it can't be your husband's breath that's driving you crazy; it has to be your *thoughts* about his breath that are driving you crazy. So let's take a closer look and see if that's true. What are your thoughts about his breath on the phone?

Mary: That he should be more aware that he's breathing loudly during a conference call.

Katie: How do you react, what happens, when you believe that thought? *[The third question: How do you react, what happens, when you believe that thought?]*

Mary: I feel like I want to kill him.

Katie: So what's more painful—the thought you attach to about his breathing or his breathing?

Mary: The breathing is more painful. I'm comfortable with the thought that I want to kill him. *[Mary laughs, and so does the audience.]*

Katie: You can keep that thought. That's the beautiful thing about The Work. You can keep all your thoughts.

Mary: I've never done The Work before, so I don't know any of the "right" answers.

Katie: Your answers are perfect, sweetheart. Don't rehearse. So he's breathing on the phone, and you have the thought that he should be more aware, and he's not. What's the next thought?

Mary: It brings up every terrible thought I have about him.

Katie: Okay, and he's still breathing. He should stop breathing into the phone on the conference call—what's the reality of it? Does he?

Mary: No. I've told him to stop.

Katie: And he still does it. That's reality. What's true is always what's happening, not the story about what *should* be happening. He should stop breathing on the phone—is it true?

Mary *[after a pause]*: No. It's not true. He's doing it. That's what's true. That's reality.

Katie: So how do you react when you think the thought that he should stop breathing on the phone and he doesn't?

Mary: How do I react? I want out. It feels uncomfortable because I know I want out and I know I'm not going anywhere.

Katie: Let's move back to inquiry, honey, rather than moving further into your story, your interpretation of what's happening. Do you really want to know the truth?

Mary: Yes.

Katie: Okay. It helps if we stick to one written statement at a time. Can you see a reason to drop the thought that he should stop breathing on the phone? *[This is an additional question that Katie sometimes asks.]* For those of you new to The Work, if you hear that I'm asking Mary to drop her story, let me make it very clear: I'm not. This is not about getting rid of thoughts or about overcoming, improving, or surrendering them. None of that. This is about realizing for yourself internal cause and effect. The question is simply "Can you *see a reason* to drop this thought?"

Mary: Yes, I can. It would be a lot more enjoyable to do conference calls without this thought.

Katie: That's a good reason. Can you find a stress-free reason to keep this thought, this lie, that he should stop breathing on the phone? *[This is a second additional question.]*

Mary: No.

Katie: Who or what would you be without that thought? *[The fourth question: Who or what would you be without the thought?]* Who would you be while you're on a conference call with your husband if you didn't have the ability to think that thought?

Mary: I'd be much happier. I'd be more powerful. I wouldn't be distracted.

Katie: Yes, sweetheart. That's it. It's not his breathing that is causing your problem. It's your *thoughts* about his breathing, because you haven't investigated them to see that they oppose reality in the moment. Let's look at your next statement.

Mary: *I don't love him anymore.*

Katie: Is that true?

Mary: Yes.

Katie: Okay. Good. I hear that, and do you really want to know the truth?

Mary: Yes.

Katie: Okay. Be still. There's no right or wrong answer. You don't love him—is that true? *[Mary is silent.]* If you had to answer honestly either yes or no, right now, and you had to live forever with your answer—your truth or your lie—what would your answer be? You don't love him—is that true? *[There is a long pause. Then Mary begins to cry.]*

Mary: No. It's not true.

Katie: That's a very courageous answer. If we answer it that way, with what's really true for ourselves, we think that there may be no way out. "Is it true?" is just a question! We're terrified to answer the simplest question honestly, because we project what that may mean in the imagined future. We think we have to do something about it. How do you react when you believe the thought that you don't love him?

Mary: It makes my whole life a stupid charade.

Katie: Can you see a reason to drop this thought that you don't love him? And I'm not asking you to drop the thought.

Mary: Yes, I can see a reason to drop it.

Katie: Can you think of one stress-free reason to keep the thought?

Mary *[after a long pause]*: I think if I keep my story, then I can keep him from wanting to have sex all the time.

Katie: Is that a stress-free reason? It seems stressful to me.

Mary: I guess it is.

Katie: Can you find one stress-free reason to keep that thought?

Mary: Oh, I see. No. There aren't any stress-free reasons to keep the story.

Katie: Fascinating. Who would you be, standing with your husband, without the thought that you don't love him?

Mary: It would be great. It would be fabulous. That's what I want.

Katie: I'm hearing that *with* the thought, it's stressful. And *without* the thought, it's fabulous. So what does your husband have to do with your unhappiness? We're just noticing here. So "I don't love my husband"—turn it around. *[After the four questions comes the turn-around.]*

Mary: I do love my husband.

Katie: Feel it. It has nothing to do with him, does it?

Mary: No. It really doesn't. I do love my husband, and you're right, it doesn't have anything to do with him.

Katie: And sometimes you think you hate him, and *that* doesn't have anything to do with him, either. The man's just breathing. You tell the story that you love him, or you tell the story that you hate him. It doesn't take two people to have a happy marriage. It only takes one: you! There's another turnaround.

Mary: I don't love myself. I can relate to that one.

Katie: And you may think that if you divorce him, then you'll feel good. But if you haven't investigated your thinking, you'll attach these same concepts onto whoever comes into your life next. We don't attach to people or to things; we attach to uninvestigated concepts that we believe to be true in the moment. Let's look at the next statement on your Worksheet.

Mary: *I want my husband not to be needy, not to be dependent on me, to be more successful, to not want to have sex with me, to get in shape, to get a life outside of me and the children, and to be more powerful.* Those are just a few.

Katie: Let's turn that whole statement around.

Mary: I want me not to be needy. I want me not to be dependent on him. I want me to be more successful. I want me to want to have sex with him. I want me to get in shape. I want me to get a life outside of him and the children. I want me to be more powerful.

Katie: So he shouldn't be needy—is it true? What's the reality of it? Is he?

Mary: He's needy.

Katie: "He shouldn't be needy" is a lie, because the guy is needy, according to you. So how do you react when you believe the thought "He shouldn't be needy" and in your reality he is needy?

Mary: I just want to run away all the time.

Katie: Who would you be in his presence without the thought "He shouldn't be needy"?

Mary: What I just understood is that I could be with him in a space of love, instead of just having my defenses up. It's like if I notice any bit of neediness, I'm out of there. I've got to run. That's what I do with my life.

Katie: When he's acting needy, in your opinion, you don't say no honestly. You run away or want to run away instead of being honest with yourself and him.

Mary: That's true.

Katie: Well, it would have to be. You have to call him needy until you can get some clarity and honest communication going with yourself. So let's be clear. You be him and be very needy. I'll take the role of clarity.

Mary: Mr. Needy comes in and says, "I just had the best phone call. You've got to hear about it. It was this guy and he's going to be fabulous in the business. And I had another call . . ." You know, he just goes on and on. Meanwhile, I'm busy. I've got a deadline.

Katie: "Sweetheart, I hear that you had a wonderful phone call. I love that, and I would also like you to leave the room now. I have a deadline to meet."

Mary: "We have to talk about our plans. When are we going to Hawaii? We have to figure out what airlines . . ."

Katie: "I hear that you want to talk about our plans for Hawaii, so let's discuss this at dinner tonight. I really want you to leave the room now. I have a deadline to meet."

Mary: "If one of your girlfriends called, you would talk to her for an hour. Now you can't listen to me for two minutes?"

Katie: "You could be right, and I want you to leave the room now. It may sound cold, but it's not. I just have a deadline to meet."

Mary: I don't do it like that. Usually I'm mean to him. I just seethe.

Katie: You *have* to be mean, because you're afraid to tell the truth and say no. You don't say, "Sweetheart, I would like you to leave. I have a deadline," because you want something from him. What scam are you running on yourself and on him? What do you want from him?

Mary: I am never straightforward with anybody.

Katie: Because you want something from us. What is it?

Mary: I can't stand when somebody doesn't like me. I don't want disharmony.

Katie: So you want our approval.

Mary: Yes, and I want to maintain harmony.

Katie: Sweetheart, if your husband approves of what you say and what you do, then there is harmony in your home—is that true? Does it work? Is there harmony in your home?

Mary: No.

Katie: You trade your integrity for harmony in the home. It doesn't work. Spare yourself from seeking love, approval, or appreciation—from anyone. And watch what happens in reality, just for fun. Read your statement again.

Mary: *I want my husband not to be needy.*

Katie: All right. Turn it around.

Mary: I want me not to be needy.

Katie: Yes, you need all this harmony. You need his approval. You need his breathing to change. You need his sexuality to change for you. Who's the needy one? Who is dependent on whom? So let's turn the whole list around.

Mary: I want myself not to be needy, not to be dependent . . .

Katie: On your husband, perhaps?

Mary: I want myself to be more successful. I want myself to not want to have sex with me.

Katie: That one could be really legitimate if you sit with it. How many times do you tell the story of how he has sex with you and you hate it?

Mary: Constantly.

Katie: Yes. You're having sex with him in your mind and thinking how terrible that is. You tell the story, over and over, of what it's like having sex with your husband. That story is what's repelling you, not your husband. Sex without a story has never repelled anyone. It just is what it is. You're having sex, or you're not. It's our thoughts about sex that repel us. Write that one out, too, honey. You could write a whole Worksheet on your husband and sexuality.

Mary: I get it.

Katie: Okay, turn the next statement around.

Mary: I want me to get in shape. But I *am* in shape.

Katie: Oh, really? How about mentally?

Mary: Oh. I could work on that.

Katie: Are you doing the best you can?

Mary: Yes.

Katie: Well, maybe he is, too. He's supposed to be in shape—is that true?

Mary: No. He's not in shape.

Katie: How do you react when you believe the thought that he should be in shape and he's not? How do you treat him? What do you say? What do you do?

Mary: Everything is subtle. I show him my muscles. I don't ever look at him with approval. I don't ever admire him. I don't ever do anything kind in that direction.

Katie: Okay, close your eyes. Look at yourself looking at him that way. Now look at his face. *[There is a pause. Mary sighs.]* Keep your eyes closed. Look at him again. Who would you be, standing there with him, without the thought that he should be in shape?

Mary: I would look at him and see how handsome he is.

Katie: Yes, angel. And you'd see how much you love him. Isn't that fascinating? This is very exciting. So let's just be there a moment. Look at how you treat him, and he still wants to go to Hawaii with you. That's amazing!

Mary: What's amazing about this guy is that I am so horrible and mean and he loves me without conditions. It drives me nuts.

Katie: He drives you nuts—is that true?

Mary: No. So far it's been my thinking that drives me nuts.

Katie: So let's go back. "He should get in shape"—turn it around.

Mary: *I* should get in shape. I should get my thinking in shape.

Katie: Yes. Every time you look at him and are repulsed, get your thinking in shape. Judge your husband, write it down, ask four questions, and turn it around. But only if you are tired of the pain. Okay, honey, I think you've got it. Just continue through the rest of the statements on your Worksheet in the same manner. I love sitting with you. And welcome to inquiry. Welcome to The Work.

Step aside from all thinking,
and there is nowhere you can't go.
          —Seng-ts'an (the Third Founding Teacher of Zen)

In *Loving What Is,* Katie has given you everything you need in order to do The Work by yourself or with others. The book will guide you, step by step, through the whole process, and along the way it will show you many people doing The Work directly with Katie. These one-on-one dialogues, in which Katie brings her clarity to the most complicated human problems, are examples—dramatic examples, some of them—of how ordinary people can find their own freedom through inquiry.

                              Stephen Mitchell
                              January, 2002

The Work is merely four questions; it's not even a thing. It has no motive, no strings. It's nothing without your answers.

These four questions will join any program you've got and enhance it. Any religion you have—they'll enhance it. If you have no religion, they will bring you joy. And they'll burn up anything that isn't true for you. They'll burn through to the reality that has always been waiting.

Byron Katie

How to Read This Book

The purpose of this book is your happiness. The Work has worked for thousands of people, and *Loving What Is* will show you exactly how to use it in your own life.

You begin with the problems that irritate or depress you. The book will show you how to write them down in a form that is easy to investigate. Then it will introduce the four questions and show you how to apply them to your problems. At that point, you'll be able to see how The Work can reveal solutions that are simple, radical, and life changing.

There are exercises that will teach you how to use The Work with increasing depth and precision and show you how it can function in every situation. After doing The Work on the people in your life, you'll learn how to do it on the issues that cause you the most pain—money, for example, illness, injustice, self-hatred, or the fear of death. You'll also learn how to recognize the underlying beliefs that hide reality from your eyes and how to work with the self-judgments that upset you.

Throughout the book, there will be many examples of people just like you doing The Work—people who believe that their problems are unsolvable, who are sure that they have to suffer for the rest of their lives because a beloved child died or because they live with someone they no longer love. You will meet a man who is tormented by jealous thoughts, a woman living in fear about her investments in the stock market, people terrorized by their thoughts about childhood trauma or just trying to get along with a difficult co-worker. You'll see how they came to find a way out of their suffering; and perhaps through them and the practical insights on the pages ahead, you'll find a way out of your own.

Everyone learns The Work in his or her own way. Some learn the process primarily by watching how the dialogues unfold. (I encourage you to read them actively, looking inside yourself for your own answers as you read.) Others learn The Work by doing it: inquiring into whatever is troubling them at the time, with laptop, smart phone, or pen and paper in hand. I suggest that you read chapter 2, and possibly chapter 5 as well, in order to absorb the basic instructions. You might then read each dialogue in sequence—but only if this feels helpful. If you feel like skipping around and going to the dialogues whose topics particularly interest you, that's fine. Or you might prefer to follow the thread of instructions as they continue throughout the book and dip into a dialogue only now and then. I trust that you'll do whatever works best for you.

We are entering
the dimension where
we have control:
the inside.

1

A Few Basic Principles

What I love about The Work is that it enables you to go inside and find your own happiness, to experience what already exists within you, unchanging, immovable, ever-present, ever-waiting. No teacher is necessary. You are the teacher you've been waiting for. You are the one who can end your own suffering.

I often say, "Don't believe anything I say." I want you to discover what's true for you, not for me. Still, many people have found the following principles to be helpful for getting started in The Work.

Noticing When Your Thoughts Argue with Reality

The only time we suffer is when we believe a thought that argues with what is. When the mind is perfectly clear, what is is what we want.

If you want reality to be different than it is, you might as well try to teach a cat to bark. You can try and try, and in the end the cat will look up at you and say, "Meow." Wanting reality to be different than it is, right now, is hopeless. You can spend the rest of your life trying to teach a cat to bark.

Yet if you pay attention, you'll notice that you believe thoughts like this dozens of times a day: "People should be kinder," "Children

should be well behaved," "My neighbors should take better care of
their lawn," "The line at the grocery store should move faster," "My
husband (or wife) should agree with me," "I should be thinner (or
prettier or more successful)." These thoughts are ways of wanting
reality to be different than it is, right now. If you think this sounds
depressing, you're right. All the stress that we feel is caused by arguing with what is.

After I woke up to reality in 1986, people often referred to me as
the woman who made friends with the wind. Barstow is a desert
town where the wind blows a lot of the time, and everyone hates it;
people even move away from there because they can't stand the wind.
The reason I made friends with the wind—with reality—is that I
discovered that I didn't have a choice. I realized that it's insane to
oppose it. When I argue with reality, I lose—but only 100 percent of
the time. How do I know that the wind should blow? It's blowing!

People new to The Work often say to me, "But it would be dis-
empowering to stop my argument with reality. If I simply accept
reality, I'll become passive. I may even lose the desire to act." I answer
them with a question: "Can you really know that that's true?" Which
is more empowering, "I wish I hadn't lost my job" or "I lost my job;
what intelligent solutions can I find right now?"

The Work reveals that what you think shouldn't have happened
should have happened. It should have happened because it did happen, and no thinking in the world can change it. This doesn't mean
that you condone it or approve of it. It just means that you can see
things without resistance and without the confusion of your inner
struggle. No one wants their children to get sick, no one wants to be
in a car accident; but when these things happen, how can it be helpful to mentally argue with them? We know better than to do that, yet
we do it because we don't know how to stop.

I am a lover of what is, not because I'm a spiritual person but
because it hurts when I argue with reality. We can know that reality
is good just as it is, because when we argue with it, we experience

tension and frustration. We don't feel natural or balanced. When we stop opposing reality, action becomes simple, fluid, kind, and fearless.

Staying in Your Own Business

I can find only three kinds of business in the universe: mine, yours, and God's. (Anything that's out of my control, your control, and everyone else's control, I call God's business.)

Much of our stress comes from mentally living out of our own business. When I think, "You need to get a job," "I want you to be happy," "You should be on time," "You need to take better care of yourself," I am in your business. When I'm worried about earthquakes, floods, war, or when I will die, I am in God's business. If I am mentally in your business or in God's business, the effect is separation. I noticed this early in 1986. When I mentally went into my mother's business, for example, with a thought like "My mother should understand me," I immediately experienced a feeling of loneliness. And I realized that every time in my life I had felt hurt or lonely, I had been in someone else's business.

If you are living your life and I am mentally living your life, who is here living mine? We're both over there. Being mentally in your business keeps me from being present in my own. I am separate from myself, wondering why my life doesn't work.

To think that I know what's best for anyone else is to be out of my business. Even in the name of love, it is pure arrogance, and the result is tension, anxiety, and fear. Do I know what's right for *me*? That is my only business. Let me work with that before I try to solve your problems for you.

If you understand the three kinds of business enough to stay in your own business, it can free your life in a way you can't even imagine. The next time you're feeling stress or discomfort, ask yourself whose business you're in mentally, and you may burst out laughing!

That question can bring you back to yourself. And you may come to see that you've never really been present, that you've been mentally living in other people's business all your life. Just to notice that you're in someone else's business can bring you back to your own wonderful self.

And if you practice it for a while, you may come to see that *you* don't have any business, either, and that your life runs perfectly well on its own.

Meeting Your Thoughts with Understanding

A thought is harmless unless we believe it. It is not our thoughts but the *attachment* to our thoughts that causes suffering. Attaching to a thought means believing that it's true, without inquiring. A belief is a thought that we've been attaching to, often for years.

Most people think they *are* what their thoughts tell them they are. One day I noticed that I wasn't breathing—I was being breathed. Then I also noticed, to my amazement, that I wasn't thinking—that I was actually being thought and that thinking isn't personal. Do you wake up in the morning and say to yourself, "I think I won't think today"? It's too late: you're already thinking! Thoughts just appear. They come out of nothing and go back to nothing, like clouds moving across the empty sky. They come to pass, not to stay. There is no harm in them until we attach to them as if they were true.

No one has ever been able to control his or her thinking, although people may tell the story of how they have. I don't let go of my thoughts; I meet them with understanding. Then *they* let go of *me*.

Thoughts are like the breeze or the leaves on the trees or the raindrops falling. They appear like that, and through inquiry we can make friends with them. Would you argue with a raindrop? Raindrops aren't personal, and neither are thoughts. Once a painful concept is met with understanding, the next time it appears, you may find it interesting. What used to be the nightmare is now just interesting. The next time it appears, you may find it funny. The time after that, you may not even notice it. This is the power of loving what is.

Becoming Aware of Your Stories

I often use the word *story* to talk about thoughts or sequences of thoughts that we convince ourselves are real. A story may be about the past, the present, or the future; it may be about what things should be, what they could be, or why they are. Stories appear in our minds hundreds of times a day—when someone gets up without a word and walks out of the room, when someone doesn't smile or doesn't return a phone call, or when a stranger *does* smile; before you open an important letter or when you feel an unfamiliar sensation in your chest; when your boss invites you to come to his office or when your partner talks to you in a certain tone of voice. Stories are the untested, uninvestigated theories that tell us what all these things mean. We don't even realize that they're just theories.

Once, as I walked into the ladies' room at a restaurant near my home, a woman came out of the single stall. We smiled at each other, and, as I closed the door, she began to sing and wash her hands. "What a lovely voice!" I thought. Then, as I heard her leave, I noticed that the toilet seat was dripping wet. "How could anyone be so rude?" I thought. "And how did she manage to pee all over the seat? Was she standing on it?" Then it came to me that she was a man—a transvestite, singing falsetto in the women's restroom. It crossed my mind to go after her (him) and let him know what a mess he'd made. As I cleaned the toilet seat, I thought about everything I'd say to him. Then I flushed the toilet. The water shot up out of the bowl and flooded the seat. And I just stood there laughing.

In that case, the natural course of events was kind enough to expose my story before it went any further. Usually it doesn't; before

I found inquiry, I had no way to stop this kind of thinking. Small stories bred bigger ones; bigger stories bred major theories about life, how terrible it was, and how the world was a dangerous place. I ended up feeling too frightened and depressed to leave my bedroom.

When you're operating on uninvestigated theories of what's going on and you aren't even aware of it, you're in what I call "the dream." Often the dream becomes troubling; sometimes it even turns into a nightmare. At times like these, you may want to test the truth of your theories by doing The Work on them. The Work always leaves you with less of your uncomfortable story. Who would you be without it? How much of your world is made up of unexamined stories? You'll never know until you inquire.

Looking for the Thought Behind the Suffering

I have never experienced a stressful feeling that wasn't caused by attaching to an untrue thought. Behind every uncomfortable feeling, there's a thought that isn't true for us: "The wind shouldn't be blowing," "My husband should agree with me." We have a thought that argues with reality, then we have a stressful feeling, and then we act on that feeling, creating more stress for ourselves. Rather than understanding the original cause—a thought—we try to change our stressful feelings by looking outside ourselves. We try to change someone else, or we reach for sex, food, alcohol, drugs, or money in order to find temporary comfort and the illusion of control.

It is easy to be swept away by some overwhelming feeling, so it's helpful to remember that any stressful feeling is like a compassionate alarm clock that says, "You're caught in the dream." Depression, pain, and fear are gifts that say, "Sweetheart, take a look at what you're thinking right now. You're living in a story that isn't true for you." Caught in the dream, we try to alter and manipulate the stressful feeling by reaching outside ourselves. We're usually aware of the feeling before the thought. That's why I say the feeling is an alarm clock that lets you know there's a thought that you may want to do The Work on. And investigating an untrue thought will always lead you back to who you really are. It hurts to believe you're other than who you are, to live any story other than happiness.

If you put your hand into a fire, does anyone have to tell you to move it? Do you have to decide? No: when your hand starts to burn, it moves. You don't have to direct it; the hand moves all by itself. In the same way, once you understand, through inquiry, that an untrue thought causes suffering, you move away from it. Before the thought, you weren't suffering; with the thought, you're suffering; when you recognize that the thought isn't true, again there is no suffering. That is how The Work functions. "How do I react when I think that thought?" Hand in the fire. "Who would I be without it?" Out of the flames. We look at the thought, we feel our hand in the fire, and we naturally move back to the original position; we don't have to be told. And the next time the thought arises, the mind automatically moves from the fire. The Work invites us into the awareness of internal cause and effect. Once we recognize this, all our suffering begins to unravel on its own.

Inquiry

I use the word *inquiry* as synonymous with The Work. To *inquire* or to *investigate* is to put a thought or a story up against the four questions and the turnarounds (explained in the next chapter). Inquiry is a way to end confusion and to experience internal peace, even in a world of apparent chaos. Above all else, inquiry is about realizing that all the answers we ever need are always available inside us.

Inquiry is more than a technique. It brings to life, from deep within us, an innate aspect of our being. When practiced for a while, inquiry takes on its own life within you. It appears whenever thoughts appear, as their balance and mate. This internal partnership leaves you free to live as a kind, fluid, fearless, amused listener, a student of yourself, and a friend who can be trusted not to resent, criticize, or hold a grudge. Eventually, realization is experienced automatically, as a way of life. Peace and joy naturally, inevitably, and irreversibly make their way into every corner of your mind, into every relationship and experience. The process is so subtle that you may not even have any conscious awareness of it. You may only know that you used to hurt and now you don't.

You're either attaching to your thoughts or inquiring. There's no other choice.

2

The Great Undoing

The one criticism of The Work I consistently hear is that it's just too simple. People say, "Freedom can't be this simple!" I answer, "Can you really know that that's true?"

Judge your neighbor, write it down, ask four questions, turn it around. Who says that freedom has to be complicated?

Putting Your Mind into Words

The first step in The Work is to identify the thoughts that are causing your stress and to write them down. These thoughts can be about any situation in your life, past, present, or future—about a person you dislike or worry about, a situation with someone who angers or frightens or saddens you, or someone you're ambivalent or confused about. Write your judgments down, just the way you think them. Use short, simple sentences. Use a blank sheet of paper, or you can go to https://thework.com, to the section called "How to Do The Work," where you'll find a Judge-Your-Neighbor Worksheet to download and print. Or, if you don't have time for a full Worksheet, you can fill out a One-Belief-at-a-Time Worksheet. You can also use The Work mobile app, available for 99 cents on the same web page.

Don't be surprised if you find it difficult at first to fill out the

Worksheet. For thousands of years, we have been taught not to judge; but let's face it, we still do it all the time. The truth is that we all have judgments running in our heads. Through The Work we finally have permission to let those judgments speak out, or even scream out, once we've written them down. We may find that even the most unpleasant thoughts can be met with unconditional love.

I encourage you to write about someone whom you haven't yet totally forgiven, someone you still resent. This is the most powerful place to begin. Even if you've forgiven that person 99 percent, you aren't free until your forgiveness is complete. The 1 percent you haven't forgiven them is the very place where you're stuck in all your other relationships (including your relationship with yourself).

If you are new to inquiry, I strongly suggest that you not write about yourself at first. When you start by judging yourself, your answers come with a motive and with solutions that haven't worked. Judging someone else, then inquiring and turning it around, is the direct path to understanding. You can judge yourself later, when you have been doing inquiry long enough to trust the power of truth.

If you begin by pointing the finger of blame outward, the focus isn't on you. You can just let loose and be uncensored. We're often quite sure about what other people need to do, how they should live, whom they should be with. We have 20/20 vision about other people but not about ourselves.

When you do The Work, you see who you are by seeing who you think other people are. Eventually you come to see that everything outside you is a reflection of your own thinking. You are the story-teller, the projector of all stories, and the world is the projected image of your thoughts.

Since the beginning of time, people have been trying to change the world so that they can be happy. This hasn't ever worked, because it approaches the problem backward. What The Work gives us is a way to change the projector—mind—rather than the projected. It's like when there's a piece of lint on a projector's lens. We think there's a flaw on the screen, and we try to change this person and that person, whomever the flaw appears to be on next. But it's futile to try to change the projected images. Once we realize where the lint is, we can clear the lens itself. This is the end of suffering and the beginning of a little joy in paradise.

People often ask me, "Why should I judge my neighbor? I already know that it's all about me." I say, "I understand. And please trust the process. Judge your neighbor, and follow the simple directions." Here are some examples of people you may want to write about: mother, father, wife, husband, child, sibling, partner, neighbor, friend, enemy, roommate, boss, teacher, employee, co-worker, teammate, salesmen, customers, men, women, authorities, God. Often, the more personal your choice is, the more potent The Work can be.

Later, as you become skilled in The Work, you may want to investigate your judgments about issues such as death, money, your health, your body, your addictions, and even your self-criticisms. (See chapter 6, "Doing The Work on Work and Money"; chapter 7, "Doing The Work on Self-Judgments"; and chapter 11, "Doing The Work on the Body and Addictions.") In fact, once you're ready, you can write about and inquire into any uncomfortable thought that appears in your mind. When you realize that every stressful moment you experience is a gift that points you to your own freedom, life becomes very kind.

How to Fill In a Worksheet

Please avoid the temptation to continue without writing down your judgments. If you try to do The Work in your head, the mind will outsmart you. Before you're even aware of it, it will be off and running into another story to prove that it's right. But though the mind can justify itself faster than the speed of light, it can be stopped through the act of writing. Once the mind is stopped on paper or on a screen, your thoughts will remain stable and inquiry can easily be applied.

Write down your thoughts without trying to censor them. Sit with your pen and paper—or your laptop, tablet, or phone—and just wait. The words will come. The story will come. And if you really want to know the truth, if you're not afraid to see your story written down, the ego will write like a maniac. It doesn't care; it's totally uninhibited. This is the day the ego has been waiting for. Give it its life. It has been waiting for you to stop just once and really listen to it. It will tell you everything, like a child. Then, when the ego is fully expressed, you can inquire.

I invite you to contemplate for a moment a situation where you were angry, hurt, sad, or disappointed with someone. Be as judgmental, childish, and petty as you were in that situation. Don't try to be wiser or kinder than you were. This is a time to be totally honest and uncensored about how you felt in that situation. Allow your feelings to express themselves as they arise, without any fear of the consequences.

People who have been doing The Work for a while get pettier and pettier on their Worksheets when they try to find the sticking-points that are left. As problems dissolve, beliefs just get more subtle, more invisible. They're the last little children calling out, "Yoo-hoo! Here I am! Come and find me!" The more you do The Work, the more uncensored you become and the pettier you like to get, because it becomes hard to find something that upsets you. Eventually, you can't find a problem. That's an experience I hear from thousands of people.

Write down the thoughts and stories that are running through you, the ones that really cause you pain—the anger, the resentment, the sadness. Point the finger of blame first at the people who have hurt you, the people who have been closest to you, the ones you're jealous of or whom you can't stand or who have disappointed you: "My husband left me," "My partner infected me with AIDS," "My mother didn't love me," "My children don't respect me," "My friend betrayed me," "I hate my boss because he treats me unfairly," "I hate my neighbors because they're ruining my life." Write about what you read this morning in the newspaper about people dying or losing their homes through pandemic or recession. Write about the checker at the grocery store who was too slow or the driver who cut you off on the freeway. Every story will be a variation on a single theme: "This shouldn't be happening," "I shouldn't have to experience this," "God is unjust," "Life isn't fair."

People new to The Work sometimes think, "I don't know what to write. Why should I do The Work anyway? I'm not angry at anyone. Nothing's really bothering me." If you don't know what to write about, wait. Life will give you a topic. Maybe a friend didn't call you back when she said she would, and you're disappointed. Maybe when you were five years old, your mother punished you for something you didn't do. Maybe you become upset or frightened when you read the newspaper or think about the suffering in the world.

Write down the part of your mind that is saying these things. You can't stop the story inside your head, however hard you try. It's not possible. But when you write down the story, just the way the mind is telling it, with all your suffering and frustration and rage and sadness, then you can take a look at what's swirling around inside you. You can see it brought into the material world in physical form. And finally, through The Work, you can begin to understand it.

When a child gets lost, he may feel sheer terror. It can be just as frightening when you're lost inside the mind's chaos. But when you enter The Work, it is possible to find order and learn the way back home. It doesn't matter what street you walk down, there's something familiar; you know where you are. You could be kidnapped and someone hides you away for a month and then throws you blindfolded out of a car, but when you take off the blindfold and look at the buildings and streets, you begin to recognize a phone booth or a grocery store, and everything becomes familiar. You know what to do to find your way home. That is how The Work functions. Once the mind is met with understanding, it can always find its way back home. There is no place where you can remain lost or confused.

The Judge-Your-Neighbor Worksheet

After my life changed in 1986, I spent a lot of time in the desert near my home, just listening to myself. Stories arose inside me that had been troubling mankind forever. Sooner or later, I witnessed every concept, it seemed, and I discovered that even though I was alone in the desert, the whole world was with me. And it sounded like this: "I want," "I need," "They should," "They shouldn't," "I'm angry because," "I'm sad," "I'll never," "I don't want to." Those phrases, which repeated themselves over and over in my mind, became the basis for the Judge-Your-Neighbor Worksheet. The purpose of the Worksheet is to help you put your painful stories and judgments into writing; it's designed to draw out judgments that otherwise might be difficult to uncover.

The judgments you write on the Worksheet will become the material that you'll use to do The Work. You'll put each written statement—one by one—up against the four questions and let each of them lead you to the truth.

Here is an example of a completed Judge-Your-Neighbor Worksheet. I have written about my second husband, Paul, in this example (included here with his permission); these are the kinds of thoughts that I used to believe about him before inquiry found me. As you read, you're invited to replace Paul's name with the name of the appropriate person in your life.

1. In this situation, who angers, confuses, saddens, or disappoints you, and why?
   I don't like (I am angry at or saddened, frightened, confused, etc., by) (name) <u>Paul</u> *because* <u>he doesn't listen to me.</u>

2. In this situation, how do you want him/her to change? What do you want him/her to do?

   I want (name) Paul to see that he is wrong. I want him to stop lying to me. I want him to see that he is killing himself.

3. In this situation, what advice would you offer him/her? "He/she should/shouldn't . . ."

   (Name) Paul *should* take a deep breath. He should calm down. He should see that his behavior frightens me. He should know that being right is not worth another heart attack.

4. In order for *you* to be happy in this situation, what do you need him/her to think, say, feel, or do?

   I need (name) Paul *to* hear me when I talk to him. I need him to take care of himself. I need him to admit that I am right.

5. What do you think of him/her in this situation? Make a list. (It's okay to be petty and judgmental.)

   (Name) Paul *is* unfair, arrogant, loud, dishonest, way out of line, and unconscious.

6. What is it about this situation that you don't ever want to experience again?

   I don't ever want Paul to lie to me again. I don't ever want to see him ruining his health again.

Tips

Statement 1: Be sure to identify what most upsets you in that situation about the person you are writing about. As you fill in statements 2 through 6, imagine yourself in the situation that you have described in statement 1.

Statement 2: List what you wanted him or her to do in this situation, no matter how ridiculous or childish your wants were.

Statement 3: Be sure that your advice is specific, practical, and detailed. Clearly articulate, step by step, how he or she should carry out your advice; tell him or her exactly what you think he or she should do. If he or she followed your advice, would it really solve your problem in statement 1? Be sure that your advice is relevant and doable for this person (as you have described him or her in statement 5).

Statement 4: Did you stay in the situation described in statement 1? If your needs were met, would that take you all the way to "happy," or would it just stop the pain? Be sure that the needs you have expressed are specific, practical, and detailed.

Inquiry: The Four Questions and the Turnarounds

1. Is it true? (Yes or no. If no, move to question 3.)
2. Can you absolutely know that it's true? (Yes or no.)
3. How do you react, what happens, when you believe that thought?
4. Who or what would you be without the thought?

And

> Turn the thought around. Then find examples of how each turnaround is true for you in this situation.

Now, using the four questions, let's investigate the statement from number 1 on the Worksheet: *Paul doesn't listen to me.* As you read along, think of someone you haven't totally forgiven yet or someone who just wouldn't listen to you.

1. Is it true? As you consider the situation again, ask yourself, "Is it true that Paul doesn't listen to me?" Be still. If you really want to know the truth, the honest yes or no from within will rise to meet the question as you recall the situation in your mind's eye. Let the mind ask the question, and wait for the answer that surfaces. (The answer to question 1 or 2 is just one syllable long; it's either yes or no. Notice if you experience any defense as you answer. If your answer includes "because . . ." or "but . . . ," this is not the one-syllable answer you are looking for, and you're no longer doing The Work. You're looking for freedom outside yourself. I'm inviting you into a new paradigm.)

2. Can you absolutely know that it's true? Consider these questions: "In that situation, can I absolutely know that it's true that Paul isn't listening to me? Can I ever really know when someone is listening or not? Am I sometimes listening even when I appear not to be?"

3. How do you react, what happens, when you believe that thought? How do you react when you believe that Paul doesn't listen to you? How do you treat him? Be still; notice. For example: "I feel frustrated and sick to my stomach; I give him 'the look'; I interrupt him; I punish him; I ignore him; I lose my temper. I start talking faster and louder, and I try to force him to listen." Continue your list as you witness the situation and allow the images in your mind's eye to show you how you react when you believe that thought.

Does that thought bring peace or stress into your life? What images do you see, past and future, and what physical sensations arise as you witness those images? Allow yourself to experience them now. Do any obsessions or addictions begin to appear when you believe that thought? (Do you act out by using any of the following: alcohol, drugs, credit cards, food, sex, television, etc.?) Also, witness how you treat yourself in this situation and how that feels. "I shut down. I isolate myself, I feel sick, I feel angry, I eat compulsively, and for days I watch television without really watching. I feel depressed, separate, resentful, and lonely." Notice all the effects of believing the thought "Paul doesn't listen to me."

4. Who or what would you be without the thought? This is a very powerful question. Picture yourself standing in the presence of the person you have written about when he or she is doing what you think he or she shouldn't be doing. Consider, for example, who you would be without the thought "Paul doesn't listen to me." Who would you be in the same situation if you didn't believe that thought? Close your eyes and imagine Paul not listening to you. Imagine yourself without the thought that Paul doesn't listen to you (or that he even *should* listen). Take your time. Notice what is revealed to you. What do you see now? How does that feel?

Turn it around. The turnarounds are an opportunity to experience truths that are the opposite of what you believe. One statement turned around can bring many revelations. Inquiry can set you free from the painful ways of seeing a situation that you innocently believe to be true. The turnarounds can be a powerful gateway into a kinder, more self-realized life.

Sometimes a statement can be turned around in many ways. Sometimes there are only one or two turnarounds. Open your mind, expand yourself, and see what turnarounds fit your situation. Try on each turnaround as if you are trying on a new pair of shoes. You don't want to pay for the shoes and walk out of the store if you haven't tried them on first. Find examples, in your situation, where the turnaround is just as true as or truer than the original statement.

The original statement, "Paul doesn't listen to me," when turned around, becomes "I don't listen to myself." Is that turnaround as true or truer? In that situation were you listening to yourself? Slow down and identify examples of how you weren't listening to yourself in that same situation with Paul. For me, one example is that in that situation accusations were flying out of my mouth. I was so focused on proving I was right that I couldn't be listening to myself.

Another turnaround is "I don't listen to Paul." Find examples of how you weren't listening to Paul, from *his* perspective, in that situation. Are you listening to Paul when you're thinking about him not listening to you?

A third turnaround is "Paul does listen to me." For example, he put out the cigarette he was smoking. He might light another one in five minutes, but in that situation, even as he was telling me that he didn't care about his health, he was apparently listening to me. For this and for each turnaround you discover, always find authentic examples of how the turnaround is true for you in the situation you have written about.

After meditating on each of your turnarounds, you would continue a typical inquiry with the next statement written on the Worksheet—in this case "I want Paul to see that he is wrong"—and then with every other statement on the Worksheet.

The turnarounds are *your* prescription for health, peace, and happiness. Can you give yourself the medicine that you have been prescribing for others?

Your Turn: The Worksheet

Now you know enough to try The Work. First relax, get very still, close your eyes, and wait for a stressful situation to come to mind. Fill in the Judge-Your-Neighbor Worksheet as you identify the thoughts and feelings that you were experiencing in the situation you have chosen to write about. Use short, simple sentences. Remember to *point the finger of blame or judgment outward*. You may write from your point of view as a five-year-old or at any age in your life. Please do *not* write about yourself yet.

You can find an extended Worksheet, created by Maria Canci, complete with lists of emotions, at https://thework.com/extended -worksheet/.

1. In this situation, who angers, confuses, saddens, or disappoints you, and why? (Remember: be harsh, childish, and petty.)
   I don't like (I am angry at, or saddened, frightened, confused, etc., by) (name) because _____

   _____

   _____.

2. In this situation, how do you want him/her to change? What do you want him/her to do?

I want (name) to _____

_____

_____.

3. In this situation, what advice would you offer him/her? "He/she should/shouldn't . . ."

(Name) should (shouldn't) _____

_____

_____.

4. In order for *you* to be happy in this situation, what do you need him/her to think, say, feel, or do? (Pretend it's your birthday and you can have anything you want. Go for it!)

I need (name) to _____

_____

_____.

5. What do you think of him/her in this situation? Make a list. (Don't be rational or kind.)

(Name) is _____

_____

_____.

6. What is it about this situation that you don't ever want to experience again?

I don't ever want _____

_____

_____.

[Note: Sometimes you may find yourself upset without knowing why. There is always an internal story, but occasionally it can be hard to find. If you feel blocked with the Judge-Your-Neighbor Work-sheet, see "When the Story Is Hard to Find," page 252.]

Your Turn: The Inquiry

One by one, challenge each statement on the Judge-Your-Neighbor Worksheet with the four questions. Then turn around the statement you're working on and allow yourself time in the inner stillness to find examples of how each turnaround, in that situation, is as true as or truer than the original statement. (Refer to the example on pages 17–18. You can also find help at thework.com or in The Work App, which includes a tutorial with me.) Throughout this process, explore being open to possibilities beyond what you think you know. There's nothing more exciting than discovering the don't-know mind and what it will reveal to you.

The Work is meditation. It's like diving into yourself. Contemplate the questions, drop down into the depths of yourself, listen, and wait for what shows itself to you. The answer will find your question if your mind is open. No matter how closed down, depressed, confused, or hopeless you may be, the gentler polarity of mind will meet the polarity that is confused because it hasn't yet been enlightened to itself. You may even begin to experience revelations about yourself and your world, revelations that will transform your life forever.

Take the time now to give yourself a taste of The Work. Look at the first statement that you have written on your Worksheet. Now ask yourself the following questions:

1. Is it true? When asking the first question, take your time. The answer is either yes or no. (If it's no, move to question 3.) The Work is about discovering what is true from the deepest part of yourself. It may not coincide with anything you've ever considered before. But when you experience your own answer, you'll know it. Just be gentle, sit with it, and let it take you deeper in.

There are no right or wrong answers to these questions. You are listening for *your* answers now, not other people's and not anything you have been taught. This can be very unsettling at first, because you're entering the unknown. As you continue to dive more deeply, allow the truth within you to rise and meet the question. Be gentle as you give yourself to inquiry. Let this experience have you completely.

2. Can you absolutely know that it's true? This is an opportunity to go deeper into the unknown, to find the answers that live beneath what we think we know. All I can tell you about this realm is that what lives beneath the nightmare is a good thing. Do you really want to know the truth?

If your answer to question 2 is yes, you can simply move on to the next question. But you may find it useful to pause and rewrite your statement in order to uncover your interpretation of it. Often it is the interpretation, which may be hidden from you, that causes you pain. For a detailed explanation of rewriting, see "When You Think That It's True," pages 147–150.

3. How do you react, what happens, when you believe that thought? How do you treat yourself, how do you treat the person you've written about, when you think that thought? What do you do? Be specific. Make a list of your actions: What do you say to that person when you think that thought? How do you live when you believe that thought? List how each reaction feels physically inside you. Where do you feel it? How does it feel (tingling, hot, etc.)? What is the self-talk that goes on in your head when you believe that thought?

4. Who or what would you be without the thought? Close your eyes and wait. Imagine yourself just for a moment without the thought. Imagine that you didn't have the ability to think the thought as you stand in the presence of that person (or in that situation). What do you see? How does it feel? How is the situation different? List the possibilities for living your life without this concept. For example, how would you treat that person differently in the same situation without the thought? Does this feel kinder inside you?

Turn It Around

To experience the power of the turnarounds, find opposites of the original statement on your Worksheet. Often a statement can be turned around to the self, to the other, and to the opposite. First, write it as if it were about you. Where you have written someone else's name, put yourself. Instead of "he" or "she," use "I." For example, "Paul doesn't listen to me" turns around to "I don't listen to myself." Find one, two, or three authentic examples of how this turnaround is as true as or truer than your original statement. Then continue with "I don't listen to Paul." Another type is a 180-degree turnaround to the extreme opposite: "Paul does listen to me." Let yourself fully experience each turnaround as you consider the situation you are meditating in. Ask yourself if any of your turned-around versions seem as true as or truer than your original thought, and see if specific examples come to mind. For example, name the ways in which *you* don't listen to *yourself* in that specific situation. Name the ways in which *you* don't listen to *Paul* in that situation. Name the ways in which Paul *does* listen to you in that situation. This is not about blaming yourself or feeling guilty. It's about discovering alternatives that can bring you peace.

You may come to see three or four or more turnarounds for one statement. Or there may be just one that feels true for you. (The turnaround for statement number 6 on the Worksheet is different from the usual turnaround. We take the statement and replace "I don't ever want to . . ." with "I am willing to . . ." and then "I look forward to . . .") See "The Turnarounds," "The Three Kinds of Turnarounds," "The Turnarounds in Action," and "The Turnaround for Statement 6," pages 154–162, for help with turnarounds.

For each turnaround, go back and start with the original statement. For example, "He shouldn't waste his time" may be turned around to "I shouldn't waste my time," "I shouldn't waste his time," and "He *should* waste his time." Note that "I should waste my time" and "I should waste his time" are not valid turnarounds; they are turnarounds of turnarounds, rather than turnarounds of the original statement.

Consider whether or not the turned-around statement is as true as or truer than your original statement. For example, let's play with the statement "Paul should be kind to me." The turnaround "I should be kind to myself" does fit for me; it does seem as true as or truer than the original statement, because when I think that Paul should be kind to me and he's not, I get angry and resentful, and I cause myself a lot of stress. This is not a kind thing to do. If I were kind to myself, I wouldn't have to wait for kindness from others. "I should be kind to Paul"—that, too, is at least as true for me as the original statement. When I think that Paul should be kind to me and I get angry and resentful, I treat Paul very unkindly, especially in my mind. Let me begin with myself and act as I'd like Paul to act and as my turnaround, which came out of my own wisdom, has guided me to do. As for "Paul shouldn't be kind to me," that is certainly truer than its opposite. He shouldn't be kind in that situation, because he isn't. That's the reality of it.

The Inquiry Continued

Now it's time for you to apply the four questions and the turnarounds to the rest of your judgments, one at a time. Read all the sentences you have written on your Judge-Your-Neighbor Worksheet. Then, one by one, investigate each statement by asking yourself:

1. Is it true?
2. Can I absolutely know that it's true?
3. How do I react, what happens, when I believe that thought?
4. Who or what would I be without the thought?

And

> Turn it around. Then try on examples of how each turnaround is
> true for you in that situation.

When you're questioning your stressful thoughts, it's important
to be as still as possible. Close your eyes. Ask to be shown the answer,
and mean it. The point is not to stop, not to settle for the familiar
answers that the ego is only too happy to supply. The authentic answer may be very different from what you think you know. It will rise
from a stillness that's deeper than thought. If thoughts distract you
during your inquiry, keep moving your attention back to the stillness. That's where the answer to the question will come from.

But whether it's noticed or not, the answer lives inside you. It
lives immovably within the illusion of suffering. The only requirement is to notice, to question anything that would compete with the
living answer. You're always being answered, but your mind is so full
of concepts that there's no space available to notice.

So you get very still, you ask sincerely, you stay in the question,
and you settle for nothing less than the genuine. You witness from
that place beyond help as you have understood it to be. Don't be
frightened by the answer. Allow the unknown to bring you through—
not what you *think* you know.

If your first experience of The Work doesn't seem to work for
you, that's okay. Just move on to the next chapter, or try filling out a
Worksheet on a different person and come back to this one later.
Don't worry about whether The Work is working or not. You're just
beginning to learn how to do it. It's like riding a bike; all you need to
do is keep wobbling on. You'll get a better feel for it as you read the
dialogues that follow. And you won't necessarily be the first to notice
that it's working. You may find, as many people have, that it doesn't
seem to have any effect now, but you have already shifted in ways you
can't feel yet. The Work can be very subtle and profound.

Everyone is a mirror
image of
your own thinking
coming back at you.

3

Entering the Dialogues

In reading the dialogues in this book, it's important to understand that there is no essential difference between what a facilitator does (in these examples, it happens to be me) and what a person doing The Work alone does. You are the teacher and healer you've been waiting for. This book is designed to help you do The Work by yourself. It's not necessary to work with a facilitator, though that can be very powerful. It can also be useful to watch someone else do The Work with a facilitator and, as you watch, to look inside for your own answers. Participating in this way helps you learn how to question yourself.

Many of the following chapters contain edited transcripts of conversations taped during workshops that I have given in America and Europe. At a typical workshop, several participants volunteer to sit with me, one by one, in front of the audience and read what they have written on their Judge-Your-Neighbor Worksheet. Then they are guided into the power of the four questions and the turnarounds, and thus into their own self-induced realizations.

I have discovered that in every language and in every country I have visited, there are no new stories. They're all recycled. The same stressful thoughts arise in each mind one way or another, sooner or later. That's why anyone's Work can be your Work also. Read these dialogues as if the Worksheets had been written by you. Don't just read the workshop participants' answers. Go inside and discover your own. Get as emotionally involved and as close to them as you can. Discover where and when you have experienced what you're reading about.

You'll notice that I don't always ask the four questions in the order you've learned. I sometimes vary the usual order; I may leave out questions, zeroing in on just one or two; and sometimes I skip the questions entirely and go directly to the turnarounds. Even though the usual order of the questions works well, eventually it may not be necessary to ask them in order. You don't have to begin with "Is it true?" You can start with any question; "Who or what would you be without the thought?" might be the first one, if that feels right. Just one of these questions can set you free if you inquire deeply from within. After you do The Work for a while, the questions will become internalized. But until this happens, the deepest shifts happen when you ask all four questions in the suggested order and then apply the turnarounds. That's why I strongly recommend that those new to The Work stay with this form.

Sometimes I also invite people to consider two subsidiary questions: "Can you see a reason to drop that thought?" and "Can you find one stress-free reason to keep the thought?" These are follow-ups to the third question, "How do you react, what happens, when you think that thought?" They can be very useful.

When I feel it's appropriate, I'll help someone find the story that is the real cause of the suffering and that may be hidden from his or her awareness. This may involve looking more deeply at the original statement to find the statement behind it. Or it may involve shifting the inquiry from the written statements to a painful statement that they've just spontaneously made. (When you do The Work on your own and a new painful thought or deeper story appears, you may want to write it down to include in your inquiry.) Sometimes I'll share my own answer to a question or I'll tell a personal story. Please

understand that I'm speaking from my own experience and that my
answers are not intended as suggestions for how *you* should live.

The Work does not condone any harmful action. To see it as
justifying anything that is less than kind is to misinterpret it. If you
find anything in the following pages that sounds cold, uncaring, un-
loving, or unkind, I invite you to be gentle with it. Breathe through
it. Feel and experience what arises in *you*. Go inside yourself and
answer the four questions. Experience inquiry for yourself.

Read these dialogues as if they were your own. Go inside for
your own answers. Get as emotionally involved and as close to them
as you can. Discover where and when you have experienced what
you're reading about. If you can't relate to one of the following examples, try substituting someone who is significant in your life. For
example, if the participant's issue is with a friend, and you substitute
the word *husband, wife, lover, mother, father,* or *boss,* you may find
that his Work turns out to be your Work. We think we are doing The
Work on people, but actually we're working on our *thoughts* about
people. (You can write an entire Worksheet on your mother, for example, and later find that your relationship with your daughter has
dramatically improved because you were attached to the same
thoughts about her, though you weren't aware of it.)

The Work enables you to go inside and experience the peace
that already exists within you. That peace is unchanging, immovable,
and ever-present. The Work takes you there. It's a true homecoming.

(Note: To help you follow the process of inquiry, the four questions are printed in **boldface** in the dialogues in chapter 4.)

If I had a prayer,
it would be this:
"God, spare me
from the desire for
love, approval, or
appreciation. Amen."

4

Doing The Work on Couples and Family Life

My experience is that the teachers we need most are the people we're living with now. Our spouses, parents, and children are the clearest spiritual masters we could hope for. Again and again, they will show us the truth we don't want to see, until we see it.

After I returned home from the halfway house in 1986 with a radically different understanding of the world and of myself, I found that nothing my husband or my children did could upset me. Inquiry was alive inside me, and every thought I had was met by a wordless questioning. When Paul did something that would have angered me before, and the thought "He should . . ." appeared in my mind, all I felt was gratitude and laughter. The man might have been walking on the carpets with mud all over his shoes, or dropping his clothes everywhere, or shouting at me, waving his arms, his face red, and if "He should . . ." appeared in my mind, I just laughed at myself, because I knew what it led to; I knew it led to "I should . . ." "He should stop screaming"? *I* should stop screaming, mentally, about him, before I remind him to take off his muddy shoes.

I remember sitting on the living room couch with my eyes closed, and Paul came into the room and saw me, and he stormed up to me, shouting "Jesus Christ, Kate, what the hell is the matter with you?" It was a simple question. So I went inside and asked myself, "What the hell *is* the matter with you, Katie?" It wasn't personal. Could I just find an answer to that question? Well, there had been one instant when I'd had the thought that Paul shouldn't have been shouting, though the reality was that he *was* shouting. Ah. *That's* what was the matter with me. So I said, "Sweetheart, the matter with me is that I had the thought that you shouldn't be shouting, and it didn't feel right. Thank you for asking. Now it feels right again."

During those first few months, my children would seek me out and tell me what they really thought of the woman they'd known as their mother—things they would have been punished for saying before. For example, Bobby, my older son, trusted me enough to say, "You always favored Ross over me. You always loved him the most." (Ross is my younger son.) And I was finally the mother who could listen. I went inside with it and got still. "Could this be true? Could he be right?" And since I had invited my children to speak honestly, because I really wanted to know the truth, I found it. So I was able to say, "Honey, I see it. You're right. I was very confused." I felt such love for him as my teacher who had lived through all that pain and such love for the woman who had thought she preferred one child over another.

People often ask me if I had a religion before 1986, and I say yes—it was "My children should pick up their socks." That was my religion, and I was totally devoted to it, even though it never worked. Then one day, after The Work was alive in me, I realized that it simply wasn't true. The reality was that day after day, they left their socks on the floor, after all my years of preaching and nagging and punishing them. I saw that *I* was the one who should pick up the socks if I wanted them picked up. My children were perfectly happy with their socks on the floor. Who had the problem? It was me. It was my thoughts about the socks on the floor that had made my life difficult, not the socks themselves. And who had the solution? Again, me. I realized that I could be right or I could be free. It took just a few moments for me to pick up the socks, without any thought of my children. And an amazing thing began to happen: I realized that I loved picking up their socks. It was for me, not for them. It stopped being a chore in that moment, and it became a pleasure to pick them up and see the uncluttered floor. Eventually, my children noticed my pleasure and began to pick up their socks on their own, without my having to say anything.

Our parents, our children, our spouses, and our friends will continue to press every button we have, until we realize what it is that we don't want to know about ourselves yet. They will point us to our freedom every time.

My Husband's Affair

Marisa was obviously upset when she came up onstage to sit with me; her lips were quivering, and she looked as if she was on the brink of tears. Watch how powerful inquiry can be if someone sincerely wants to know the truth, even though she is in great pain and thinks she has been terribly wronged.

Marisa [reading from her Worksheet]: I'm angry at David—that's my husband—because he keeps saying he needs time to sort things out. I want David to express what he is feeling when he's feeling it, because I'm tired of asking. And I'm too impatient to wait.

Katie: So husbands should express what they're feeling—**is that true?**

Marisa: Yes.

Katie: And what's the reality on this planet?

Marisa: Well, basically they don't.

Katie: So how do I know that husbands *shouldn't* express their feelings? They don't. [The audience and Marisa laugh.] Sometimes. That's reality. "Husbands should express their feelings" is just a thought that we believe without a single piece of evidence. **How do you react**

when you believe this lie? Can you hear where I'm coming from when I call it a lie? It's *not* true that he should express his feelings, because the truth is that he doesn't, in your experience. This doesn't mean that he's not going to fully express his feelings in ten minutes or in ten days. But the reality is that right now, it's not true. So **how do you react when you think this thought?**

Marisa: I'm angry and hurt.

Katie: Yes. And how do you treat him when you believe the thought that he should express his feelings, and he doesn't?

Marisa: I feel like I'm prying, I'm demanding something.

Katie: I would drop the "I feel like." You pry and demand.

Marisa: But I . . . Oh! . . . Yes. That's exactly what I do.

Katie: And how does it feel when you pry and demand?

Marisa: It doesn't feel good at all.

Katie: Can you see a reason to drop the thought? And please don't try to drop it. My experience is that you *can't* drop a thought, because you didn't make it in the first place. So the question is simply "Can you *see a reason* to drop the thought?" Often, very good reasons can be found in your answer to question 3, "How do you react when you think that thought?" Each stressful reaction—anger, for example, or sadness or distancing—is a good reason to drop the thought.

Marisa: Yes, I can see a reason.

Katie: Give me a stress-free reason to believe the thought that husbands should express their feelings.

Marisa: A stress-free reason?

Katie: Give me a stress-free reason to believe this.

Marisa: I really don't know how to . . .

Katie: Give me a reason that doesn't cause you pain or stress to believe the thought "My husband should express his feelings to me." How many years have you been married?

Marisa: Seventeen.

Katie: And for seventeen years, according to you, he hasn't expressed his feelings. Give me a stress-free reason to believe the thought. *[Long pause.]* It could take you a while to find one.

Marisa: Yes. I can't find a stress-free reason.

Katie: And **who would you be,** living with this man, **if you didn't believe this lie?**

Marisa: I would be a happier person.

Katie: Yes. So what I'm hearing is that your husband is not the problem.

Marisa: Yes. Because I'm the one who pries and demands.

Katie: You're the one who believes this lie that hurts so much. I hear from you that if you didn't believe it, you'd be happy. And when you do believe it, you pry and demand. So how can your husband be the problem? You're trying to alter reality. This is confusion. I'm a lover of reality. I can always count on it. And I love that it can change, too. But I'm a lover of reality just the way it is now. So read that statement again, about what you want him to do.

Marisa: I want David to express what he is feeling when he's feeling it.

Katie: Turn it around: "I want me . . ."

Marisa: I want me to express my feelings. But that's what I do all the time!

Katie: Yes, exactly. That's for you to live. It's your way, not his.

Marisa: Ah. I see.

Katie: You're the one who should express her feelings, because you do. He shouldn't express his, because he doesn't. You go through the house prying and demanding, fooling yourself with this lie that your way is better. How does it feel to pry?

Marisa: It doesn't feel good at all.

Katie: And you're feeling bad in his name. You're blaming it on him.

Marisa: Exactly. I see what you're saying.

Katie: You feel bad and believe that *he's* doing it. And all the time, it's your own misunderstanding. All right, let's look at the next statement.

Marisa: *I'm tired of asking. And I'm too impatient to wait.*

Katie: You're too impatient to wait—**is that true?**

Marisa: Yes.

Katie: And *are* you waiting?

Marisa: I guess I am.

Katie: I would drop the "I guess."

Marisa: I *am* waiting. Yes.

Katie: You're too impatient to wait—**is that true?**

Marisa: Yes.

Katie: And *are* you waiting?

Marisa: Yes. And I don't know how to stop it.

Katie: So you're too impatient to wait—**is that true?** *[A very long pause.]* You *are* waiting! You're *waiting*! I heard it from your own lips!

Marisa: Oh! I see! . . . Yeah.

Katie: Got it?

Marisa: Yes.

Katie: Yes. You're *not* too impatient to wait. You're hanging in there. Seventeen years, eighteen years . . .

Marisa: Yes.

Katie: So **how do you react when you think the thought** that you're too impatient to wait? How do you treat *him* when you believe that lie?

Marisa: I don't treat him well. I close off to him. I scream at him sometimes or cry and threaten to leave him. I say some pretty nasty things.

Katie: So give me a stress-free reason to believe this lie.

Marisa: There isn't any.

Katie: Who would you be in your home **if you didn't believe this lie?**

Marisa: I guess I would enjoy the fact that I do love him and not get caught up in the rest of it.

Katie: Yes. And the next time you speak to him, you may want to say, "You know, sweetheart, I must love you a lot, because I *am* patient. I've been fooling myself. I've been telling you I'm too impatient to wait, and it's not true."

Marisa: Yes.

Katie: That's what I love about integrity. Each time we go inside, that's where it is. It's a sweet place to live in. So let's **turn it around.** "I'm too impatient to wait"—what is the extreme opposite of that, the 180-degree turnaround?

Marisa: I'm *not* too impatient to wait.

Katie: Yes. Isn't that as true or truer?

Marisa: It's truer. Definitely truer.

Katie: Let's look at your next statement.

Marisa: I'm going to read it, because I wrote it. *David shouldn't think that I'll wait forever. [Laughs.]* Which I *have* been doing, of course.

Katie: So he shouldn't think that—**is it true?**

Marisa: Of course not.

Katie: No. He has all the proof that you *will* wait.

Marisa [*smiling and nodding her head*]: Yes.

Katie: So **how do you react when you think this?** You know what I love, sweetheart? The thoughts that used to send us into deep depression—these same thoughts, once understood, send us into laughter. This is the power of inquiry.

Marisa: It's amazing!

Katie: And it just leaves us with "You know, honey, I love you." Unconditional love.

Marisa: Yeah.

Katie: And it's nothing more than clarity. So **how do you react when you believe the thought** that he shouldn't think you'll wait forever?

Marisa: I'm fooling myself if I believe what I wrote.

Katie: Yes. And it's very painful to live a lie. We're like children. We're so innocent. The whole world would tell you that you're right to be impatient.

Marisa: I certainly believed it up until today.

Katie: But when you go inside, you can see what's really true. It makes sense that no one else can cause you pain. That's *your* job.

Marisa: Yes, it's a lot easier to blame it on the other person.

Katie: Well, but is that true? Maybe it's easier *not* to. And it's the truth that sets us free. I came to see that there was nothing to forgive, that *I* was the one who caused my own problems. I found just what you're finding. Let's look at your fourth statement.

Marisa: *I need David to stop saying that he doesn't want to hurt me when he keeps doing things that hurt me.*

Katie: He wants to hurt you—**can you really know that that's true?**

Marisa: No. I can't really know that.

Katie: He wants to hurt you—go inside and see if it's true.

Marisa: I don't know how to answer this. He *says* he doesn't.

Katie: I would believe him. What other information do you have?

Marisa: His actions.

Katie: He wants to hurt you—**can you absolutely know that that's true?**

Marisa: No.

Katie: And **how do you react when you believe this?** How do you treat him?

Marisa: I don't treat him well. I basically lay on the guilt.

Katie: Basically, you act as if you want to hurt him.

Marisa: Oh! I see . . . I see.

Katie: So of course you would project that he wants to hurt you. The truth is that *you* want to hurt *him*. You're the projector of it all, the storyteller of it all.

Marisa: Is it that easy, really?

Katie: Yes, it is.

Marisa: Wow!

Katie: If I think that someone else is causing my problem, I'm insane.

Marisa: I see. So . . . we cause our own problems?

Katie: Yes, but only all of them. It's just been a misunderstanding. Your misunderstanding. Not theirs. Not ever, not even a little. Your happiness is your responsibility. This is very good news. How does it feel when you live with a man and believe that he wants to hurt you?

Marisa: It feels terrible.

Katie: So give me a stress-free reason to believe the thought that your husband wants to hurt you.

Marisa: I can't think of one.

Katie: **Who would you be,** living with your husband, **if you didn't believe this thought?**

Marisa: I'd be a very happy person. I can see that so clearly now.

Katie: "He wants to hurt me"—**turn it around.**

Marisa: I want to hurt myself. Yes. I understand that.

Katie: Is that as true or truer?

Marisa: Truer, I think.

Katie: That's how we are. We don't know another way, until we do. That's what we're here for this evening: We sit together, and we find another way. There's another turnaround: "He wants to hurt me . . ."

Marisa: I want to hurt him. Yes. That's truer, too.

Katie: And there's still another turnaround. "He wants to hurt me"—what's the 180-degree turnaround?

Marisa: He *doesn't* want to hurt me.

Katie: He could be telling you the truth. That's just as possible. Okay, I'd like to go back. You want to hurt your husband—is that really true?

Marisa: No. No, I don't.

Katie: No, sweetheart. None of us would ever hurt another human being if we weren't confused. That's my experience. Confusion is the only suffering on this planet. How does it feel when you hurt him?

Marisa: It doesn't feel good at all.

Katie: Yes. And that feeling is a gift. It lets you know that you've moved from your integrity. Our thoughts say, "Oh, I shouldn't hurt him." But we don't know how to stop. Have you noticed?

Marisa: Yes.

Katie: It just goes on and on. So through self-realization—the way we're experiencing it here—through these realizations, the doing changes. I was the same as you. I couldn't change. I couldn't stop hurting my children and myself. But as I realized what was true for me, with the questions alive inside me, the doing changed. The problems stopped. *I* didn't stop them; they stopped. It's just that simple. Now, what has he done? You said that his actions prove that he wants to hurt you. What's an example of that? Where's your proof?

Marisa: To put it simply, he had an affair, and he told me about it five months ago. The feelings they had for each other are still very much there, and they still talk and see each other. Those are the actions.

Katie: Okay. Now watch the two of them in your mind. Can you see them?

Marisa: I've seen them many times.

Katie: Now look at your husband's face. Look at him looking at her. Now look at him for just a moment without your story. Look at his eyes, look at his face. What do you see?

Marisa: Love for her. And happiness. But also hurt, because they're not together. He wants to be with her.

Katie: Is that true? Can you absolutely know that it's true?

Marisa: Not absolutely. No, I can't.

Katie: Who's he with?

Marisa: Oh! He's with me.

Katie: "He wants to be with her"—**is that true?**

Marisa: Umm . . . he . . .

Katie: Who's he with?

Marisa: Okay. Yes. I see what you're saying.

Katie: "He wants to be with her"—**is that true?** Who's stopping him? He's free.

Marisa: And I have made that clear, too.

Katie: So **how do you react when you think the thought** that he wants to be with her?

Marisa: Oh, I hurt.

Katie: And he's living with you?

Marisa: I guess I'm not fully in the present. I'm not *living* the fact that he loves me and he's with me.

Katie: He's living with you, and in your mind you have him living with her. So *no one's* living with the guy! *[Marisa and the audience* *laugh.]* Here's this beautiful man, and no one's living with him! *[Marisa laughs even harder.]* "I want him to live with me, I want him to live with me!" Well, when are you going to begin? How do you treat him when you believe that he wants to be with her and the truth is that he's living with you?

Marisa: I don't treat him well. I push him away.

Katie: And then you wonder why he likes to be with her.

Marisa: Yes. Yes.

Katie: Give me a stress-free reason to believe the thought that he wants to be with her when the fact is that he's with you.

Marisa: A stress-free reason?

Katie: You can't *make* him come home. He comes home because he wants to. **Who would you be if you didn't believe this thought?**

Marisa: Oh! . . . *[With a big smile]* I would have no problem.

Katie: "He wants to be with her"—**turn it around.**

Marisa: He wants to be with me.

Katie: Yes. That could be as true or truer.

Marisa: Yes. Yes.

Katie: I heard you say he looked happy.

Marisa: Yes.

Katie: Isn't that what you want?

Marisa: Oh, I definitely want his happiness. I've told him so. At whatever price.

Katie: "I want his happiness"—**turn it around.**

Marisa: I want my happiness.

Katie: Yes.

Marisa: Very badly.

Katie: Isn't that the truth?

Marisa: Yeah.

Katie: You want him to be happy because that makes you happy. I say, skip the middleman and be happy now. He'll follow. He has to, because he's your projection.

Marisa *[laughing]*: Yes.

Katie: His happiness is his responsibility.

Marisa: Definitely.

Katie: And yours is your responsibility.

Marisa: Yes. I understand.

Katie: No one can make you happy but you.

Marisa: I don't know why that is so difficult.

Katie: Maybe because you think it's *his* job to love you and make you happy when you don't know how to yourself. "I can't do it—you do it."

Marisa: It's easier to give it to somebody else.

Katie: Is that true? How could he prove that he loves you? What could he do?

Marisa: I have no idea.

Katie: Isn't that interesting! Maybe he doesn't, either. *[Marisa and the audience laugh.]* Except maybe he can just come home and be your husband.

Marisa: Yesterday I would have told you, "He can prove it by not seeing her again." That would have made me happy. Now I can't say that.

Katie: You're seeing reality a bit more clearly. Let's look at the next statement.

Marisa: What do I think of him? I don't know what to say. I love him.

Katie: Turn it around.

Marisa: I love myself. That has taken me a while.

Katie: Don't you just love yourself when you love him?

Marisa: I never saw it like that. Yeah.

Katie: Let's look at the next one, angel.

Marisa: *I don't ever want to feel that my happiness depends on somebody loving me.*

Katie: "I am willing . . ." and read it again.

Marisa: I am willing to feel that my happiness depends on somebody loving me.

Katie: Yes, because it's going to hurt to believe that thought. And then judge him again, or whoever it is, ask four questions, turn it around, and bring yourself back to sanity, back to peace. The pain shows you what's left to investigate. It shows you what's blocking you from the awareness of love. That's what pain is for. "I look forward to . . ."

Marisa: I look forward to feeling that my happiness depends on somebody loving me?

Katie: Yes. Some of us are returning to sanity, because we're tired of the pain. We're in a hurry. No time to mess around. It's good that you think, "Oh, I'd be happier if he were different." Write it down. Put it up against inquiry.

Elise Is Ignoring Me

The following dialogue, which occurred in Paris in 2018, is a wonderful example of how jealousy and insecurity can ruin a relationship. But Bernard came with an open mind and a trust in inquiry, so he could see that it wasn't his girlfriend but his own thoughts that were causing his anger and feelings of abandonment. And when he questioned those thoughts, he found not only a renewed love and appreciation for her but a renewed love and appreciation for himself.

Bernard: *I'm angry with Elise because she's ignoring me and she's passionately interested in another man.*

Katie: You know how she is. *[Laughter from the audience.]* So, sweetheart, what's the situation?

Bernard: We're in a dance hall in the countryside.

Katie: Okay. She's ignoring you. So what is that situation? What is she doing in that moment when you have the thought "She's ignoring me"?

Bernard: I'm sitting down. Two people come in. And she starts talking to that man—about dancing. And her eyes light up.

Katie *[emphasizing every word]*: Her eyes light up! *[Laughter from the audience.]*

Bernard *[laughing]*: And she speaks passionately with that man. They're the only two people left on Earth.

Katie: Even though you're there, too. *[Laughter from the audience.]*

Bernard: And two other people as well.

Katie: Okay. So she's ignoring you. Close your eyes. See her talking to him. And see yourself and the other two. She's ignoring you—**is it true?** *[Bernard scowls.]* So your answer is yes? *[Laughter from the audience.]*

Bernard: Yes.

Katie: Okay. So she's ignoring you. Look again. Can you absolutely know that it's true she's ignoring you? Yes, she's looking at him. Yes, she's looking only at him. Yes, she's looking starry-eyed. And she's ignoring you—**can you absolutely know that it's true?**

Bernard: No.

Katie: What did you just understand?

Bernard: I felt included in the room, with them.

Katie: Does that work for you? What you saw—does that feel right?

In other words, does what you experienced just now seem authentic? *[Bernard slowly nods his head.]* I understand that. Now close your eyes. In that situation, in that moment in time, **how do you react, what happens, when you believe the thought** "She's ignoring me."

Bernard *[very slowly]*: As if I've been abandoned. Nervous. And angry.

Katie: You have to see images of past and future before you can feel annoyed or angry. *[To the audience]* And I love that you all understand how the mind works and how believing these stressful thoughts is the cause—the *only* cause—of your stressful emotions. *[To Bernard]* You see images of the future and past, and you're asleep to that. And as you witness that dream, it's like watching a movie, and that's what causes your anger. No matter how quickly your temper rises, images of past and future have to be in place for anger to happen, and these images can appear and disappear in less than a second, so you may not even be aware of them. So close your eyes. You're seeing her talking to him with her eyes all lit up. You think the thought "She's ignoring me." What pictures of past and future do you see in your mind's eye as you sit there watching her now? Notice how you see images of how she used to look at *you* that way. Yes? *[Bernard nods.]* And you look at him, and then you have an image of *[her voice droops]* you. And your mind is comparing *[her voice perks up]* him with *[her voice droops again]* you, and you're sure she'll *never* look at you that way again. She'll always be thinking of him. *[Bernard smiles broadly.]* I understand why you're finding this so funny. This is what happened in that moment when you believed she was ignoring you. You witnessed these images of past and future, and you didn't even know what was going on. Eventually you will, because if inquiry becomes your practice, you'll become more aware of your thoughts the moment they're happening. And as you sit in that movie, you can be awake to the cause of the anger and confusion you're experiencing in that moment. So now drop the images. Close your eyes. Look at him. Look at her. And take that story off them. Get intimate. Get connected. **Who would you be without that thought,** without putting that story onto those two people, without comparing images in your head to real people—in other words, without comparing nothing to something?

Bernard: I would be happy for her. I'd be happy that she's able to talk about her passion for dancing.

Katie: Isn't that what you want for her? That's what I want for everyone I love. I want them to be happy. Why do *I* have to be the one who's making them happy? *[Play-acting as the ego]* But *no*, I want only *me* to give her that! *[In a normal voice]* That kind of love is so limited. It's conditional love. You got to see her happy. Now look again at yourself in that situation. Drop your story and look at yourself without the thought that she's ignoring you.

Bernard *[after a long pause]*: I'm at peace. It doesn't bother me.

Katie: Look again until you love it. I mean, that's your girlfriend. He's doing all the work. *[Laughter from the audience.]* You brought her there for a good time. *[More laughter.]* *[To the audience]* I'm serious, you know. *[Louder laughter.]*

Bernard: I can accept it.

Katie: It's a practice. So "She is ignoring me"—**turn it around.**

Bernard: *I'm* ignoring *her.*

Katie: Tell me about that.

Bernard: I'm ignoring her passion. I'm ignoring her feelings.

Katie: And later, did you punish her? Did you ignore her?

Bernard: I can't remember now. Probably.

Katie: "Probably" won't help you a lot. *[Laughter from the audience.]* It's something to look at. Did you leave together? Did you go home together?

Bernard: She stayed there for the rest of her vacation, and I left.

Katie: Well, she didn't stay in that dance hall for the rest of her vacation. So it seems that you left without her. When you ask yourself how that turnaround—"I'm ignoring her"—might be true, witness it in your mind's eye. Did you ignore her or punish her in any way? And then later, did you hold on to any kind of resentment? Did you stop calling her for a while? Get as close as you can. First see how the turnaround might be true in the micro, whether you ignored her in the situation at the dance hall, and then go out into the macro to see whether you ignored her at any time, in any way. And if you have ignored her, contact her, admit it, and make it right where you can. You created it, and you're the one who needs to end your part in it. It's where you leave the breadcrumbs to mark your path, like Hansel and Gretel. You just go back along the path and pick them up and find your way back home. It's a practice. "She's ignoring me"—**can you find another turnaround?** "I am . . ."

Bernard: I'm ignoring myself.

Katie: Where were you ignoring yourself?

Bernard: Because I love her, and the way I acted wasn't so loving.

Katie: Ah.

Bernard: I hurt myself by the way I acted.

Katie: Yes, by comparing yourself with him. You see what he looks like and how romantic and attractive he is.

Bernard: He's just a dancer. *[The audience laughs and applauds.]* I'm a dancer, too.

Katie *[laughing]*: Yes. But in that situation, when you're comparing, look at him and look at yourself. As soon as you compare, you lose. Look at that image of yourself that you were seeing that evening. Is that you? *[Bernard shakes his head.]* No one has ever seen himself. Not one human being has ever seen himself or herself. You've never seen your own face. You look in the mirror and your mind says that's you. And you're too fat, too thin, too old, too young, your nose is too big, too small, yadda yadda. You see in the mirror what you *imagine* yourself to be. And if you look at the image you were seeing that night, it was not to your best advantage. You're always more than him or less than him. And you're not comparing yourself to *him*, really; you're comparing an *image* of you to an *image* of him. You're comparing nothing to the apparent something. You're lost in the dream. "She is passionately interested in him"—is it true? You don't have to guess. Let's test it. Let's take another look. "She's passionately interested in him"—is it true? The key phrase here is "in him." "She's passionately interested *in him*"—**is it true?**

Bernard *[smiling]*: No.

Katie: What do you see? What brought up your no?

Bernard: She's interested in the dancer and in the dance.

Katie: How do you react, what happens, when you believe the thought "She's passionately interested *in him*"?

Bernard: I feel like fighting, yelling, being violent.

Katie: I love that you noticed this. Anytime you feel violent, you're in the past or the future; you're not in reality. Who would you be without the thought?

Bernard: Peaceful. Friendly. Interested.

Katie: Yes, sweetheart. When we're in reality, there's no envy, no jealousy, no more, no less. There's sanity. "She's passionately interested in him"—**turn it around.**

Bernard: She's *not* passionately interested in him.

Katie: No. She's passionately interested in *dance*. And in his experience of dancing. Now look at him, and look at her. Let's go back to the fourth question. **Who would you be without the thought** "She's passionately interested in another man"? Take that story off both of them and witness.

Bernard *[after a pause]*: They're like brothers.

Katie: They love to dance. He's a good dancer. There's a lot to learn there. Can you imagine joining the two of them in that situation, with your passion for dance?

Bernard: Not yet. *[Laughter from the audience.]*

Katie: Okay, so let's try it. And you can only do that if you really believe her interest was in dance and this dancer. So take your passion in there, with the two of them, and say nothing. Just listen.

Bernard *[after a pause]*: It's okay.

Katie: Did you learn a lot?

Bernard: Yes. I'm able to appreciate that man, the other dancer.

Katie: You all three share something in common. In that situation, you ignored yourself. You didn't join the conversation enough to even listen. And dance is where your passion is. And your passion is in joining her. So "She's passionately interested in him"—**can you find another turnaround?** "I am . . ."

Bernard: I am passionately interested in her.

Katie: And "I am passionately interested in . . ."

Bernard: Dance.

Katie: And "I am passionately interested in . . ." There are three of you there. *[Laughter from the audience.]* I want to take you to a place where you haven't been yet. So there's him, there's you, and there's her. *[Pause. More laughter.]* **Another turnaround:** "I am passionately interested in . . ."

Bernard *[slowly, with a sheepish smile]*: In him. *[Loud laughter and applause.]*

Katie: Yes. Right? Can you see how that's true? He's a good dancer. He shares her passion for dance.

Bernard: Yes. I can see how that might be true.

Katie: Sweetheart, don't go to these places if it's not authentic for you. See if a turnaround feels true. Try it on like a new pair of shoes. Maybe it fits; maybe it doesn't. This one seems like it could be valuable for you, because when there's something you're interested in, what you're believing can take it away from you. What we're thinking and believing really can cost us something or someone who could be a great teacher for us. We can miss what's so valuable—a great opportunity for our own growth. Okay, let's take a look at statement number two.

Bernard: *I want Elise not to be interested in him in that way. I want her to look at me with loving eyes. I want her to put me first.*

Katie: Okay. So you want her not to be interested in him in that way. And what way is that? Romantic? But truthfully, when you look at it, was it romantic? Or was she passionately interested in him as a dancer? Which way were you thinking of when you wrote "that way"?

Bernard: That she would be in love with him.

Katie: So "I want Elise not to be interested in him in that way"—**is it true?** *[To the audience]* You all understand that he doesn't want her to look at this man with love and fascination. How many of you have been in a relationship where your partner chose someone else? *[Many hands go up in the air.]* So let's all do this Work. *[To Bernard]* Close your eyes. You have to be there. You have to witness it in your mind's eye for this question to be answered. You have to really look at her and at yourself in that situation. Anchor yourself there; meditate on that moment in time. See the look on her face. See the sparkle in her eyes. So you don't want her to be interested in him in that way—**is it true?**

Bernard *[after a long pause]:* Yes.

Katie: People kill people over this one. They kill, they fight, they maim, they make war over it. They hurt the ones they love. So it's not a little thing that I'm asking here. You don't want her to be interested in him in that way—**can you absolutely know that it's true?**

Bernard [*after another long pause*]: No.

Katie: How do you react, what happens, when you believe the thought "I want Elise not to be interested in him in that way"?

Bernard: I want to lock her up and keep her away from other men.

Katie: Lock her up. Keep her small. Keep her from what she loves. The look on your face shows me that this couldn't be further from your true nature. It's hell. And then the very thing that you love that person for, you kill. You kill her passion. So, sweetheart, look at him. Look at her. And take that story off her. **Who would you be without the thought** "I want her not to be interested in him in that way"?

Bernard: I would let her go free.

Katie: Without your story, she's free. She's this beautiful free spirit, which is what you fell in love with in the first place. So "I want Elise not to be interested in him in that way"—**turn it around.**

Bernard: I *want* her to be interested in him in that way.

Katie: Yes. That will save you from a life of suffering. And it could also be that when you're in that clear state of mind, she shows you whom you *don't* want to be with. You want her to be in love with him if she *is* in love with him. And she shows you that you don't want to be with a woman who falls in love with other men. It doesn't mean you won't be with her. But it shows you clearly what you don't want in your life.

Bernard: Yes, I can see that.

Katie: Your next statement: "I want her to look at me with loving eyes"—**is it true?** She's looking at him, in that moment in time, and do you really want her to look at you with loving eyes?

Bernard [*shaking his head*]: No.

Katie: I think you're growing up. You're becoming more mature in your thinking, so what you say and do will mature. "I want her to look at me with loving eyes"—**how do you react, what happens, when you believe that thought?**

Bernard: I get upset and angry. It's very frustrating. I feel disappointed.

Katie: Who would you be without the thought "I want her to look at me with loving eyes"?

Bernard: I'd be relaxed, comfortable, interested. I would be happy for her.

Katie: "I want her to look at me with loving eyes"—**turn it around.** "I want me . . ."

Bernard: I want me to look at myself with loving eyes.

Katie: Yes. So do that now. Close your eyes and look at yourself in that situation. See how tortured you are. Look at yourself—that innocent man—with loving eyes. Other than what you're believing, aren't you beautiful? Other than what you're believing, aren't you okay? So notice who you are when you're believing the thought. Now notice who you are without the thought. Has that other man caused your suffering, or has what you're believing caused your suffering?

Bernard: What I'm believing. That's so clear to me.

Katie: It's how you create your own suffering. And that's what stops you in your life: believing thoughts that can be questioned. "I want her to look at me with loving eyes"—**can you find another turnaround?**

Bernard: I want me to look at her with loving eyes.

Katie: Yes. So when you're at work or dancing or in a club or having breakfast and you think of her talking to that man with such passion, it could be that you experience that image as a loving, generous man. It could be that you see her with an open heart, happy for what she's experiencing. When you wake up to the dream, you're at peace with it the next time it appears. It goes well with breakfast. Otherwise, your resentment could cause of a lot of indigestion when you're having breakfast. The image may come when you're having breakfast or walking in the street or in bed at night, and the way you reacted to it that evening comes with it. But to question your thoughts is to break the spell, so when that situation appears again, you experience peace. And if you experience even the slightest bit of jealousy, there's still some Work to be done. Let's look at statement three now.

Bernard: *Elise should come back to reality. [Laughs.]* I feel a little bit ashamed now as I read what I wrote. *[Laughter from the audience.] She should stop throwing herself at others. She should respect her commitment to me and the fact that I'm there.*

Katie: Good. Let's skip the four questions for this one. You can answer them later, as homework. Let's just **turn the thought around** so that you can experience the opposite: "In that situation I should . . ."

Bernard: I should come back to reality.

Katie: Yes, because you're in the past and future and asleep to what's really happening. You're imagining her looking at you that way. You imagine a future of her running away with him. You imagine your life without her. So "I should come back to reality. And I . . ."

Bernard: I should stop throwing myself at others.

Katie: "I should stop throwing myself at her and at others."

Bernard: Ah. Yes, I see that.

Katie: "And I should . . ."

Bernard: And I should respect my commitment.

Katie: "To myself."

Bernard: To myself. And the fact that I am there.

Katie: Isn't that what you really want?

Bernard *[with great emotion]*: Yes! My God, Katie, it's so simple! Life becomes so simple!

Katie: It *is* simple. But trying to control another person's life to do that—it's not so simple. It's hopeless. What we really want is to do that ourselves. Other people are very hard to manipulate. It's easier just to work on ourselves. **Can you find another turnaround?** "Elise should . . ."

Bernard: Elise *should* throw herself at others. And she *shouldn't* respect her commitment to me and the fact that I'm there.

Katie: How does that feel?

Bernard: It's difficult to stop being a dictator. *[Laughter from the audience.]*

Katie: It's more difficult, though, to *be* one. *[Laughter from the audience.]* Especially with Elise. She doesn't do well with that. *[More laughter.]* She's got her own life, you know. And with Elise in that situation, your identity is at stake. "I'm the one she loves." Okay, let's look at statement four.

Bernard: *I need Elise to introduce me as an excellent dancer.* This one is going to make you laugh. *I need Elise to introduce me as a beautiful man involved in soul-searching. [Loud laughter and applause.] And to share that only with me.*

Katie: So you need Elise to introduce you as an excellent dancer—**is it true?**

Bernard: No.

Katie: And **how do you react** in that situation, **what happens, when you believe the thought** that that's what you need to make you happy?

Bernard: I feel superior.

Katie: And then when she does *not* introduce you as an excellent dancer, how does that feel?

Bernard: Well, I feel ignored.

Katie: Who would you be without that thought?

Bernard: Comfortable. I wouldn't need her to introduce me in any particular way. It would be perfectly fine if she just said, "This is Bernard."

Katie: Good. You'd be a comfortable, beautiful man involved in soul-searching, a great dancer, the lover of Elise. Now turn the whole thing around. They are mesmerized, looking into each other's eyes. So what would make you happy? Read this **turned around** to yourself: "I need me to . . ."

Bernard: I need me to introduce myself as an excellent dancer.

Katie: Yes. Imagine putting your arm around her and introducing yourself as an excellent dancer. And continue.

Bernard: I need me to introduce myself as a beautiful man involved in soul-searching. *[Laughter from the audience.]*

Katie: And for you to share that only with them. Or only with him, with your arm around her. So you were expecting a woman to do your job. *[Katie and Bernard laugh.]* Just imagine how this would improve that conversation.

Bernard: I can see that.

Katie: Okay, let's look at statement five.

Bernard: I can't believe I wrote this. *Elise is selfish, insensitive, hurtful, and disappointing.*

Katie: Yes, sweetheart, you're a different person from the one who wrote that. So "Elise is selfish, insensitive, hurtful, and disappointing"— **is it true?**

Bernard *[smiling]*: No.

Katie: How do you react, what happens, when you believe the thought "Elise is selfish, insensitive, hurtful, and disappointing"?

Bernard: I feel sad and angry. I pull away from her.

Katie: And **who would you be without the thought?**

Bernard: I would just love her. I would be supportive. I'd be her partner.

Katie: Yes, honey. Now let's **turn it all around** to yourself—just in that situation. Okay? "In that moment, I am . . ."

Bernard: I am selfish, insensitive, hurtful, and disappointing.

Katie: Does that fit? In that situation? In that moment, you're selfish. She's having a great time, and you react as if it's all about you. You're insensitive to her interests and passion. You're hurtful and disappointing, because you distance yourself from her. Now **turn it around** another way: "Elise is . . ." What's the opposite of selfish? Generous?

Bernard: She is generous, sensitive, welcoming, kind.

Katie: Yes. So other than what you're believing about her, is she okay? Is that the woman you love, other than what you're believing about her? She's beautiful and free and happy.

Bernard: Yes.

Katie: Let's look at statement six.

Bernard: *I don't ever want to feel ignored and pushed aside that way.*

Katie: The turnaround to number six is different from the other turnarounds. "I'm willing to . . ."

Bernard: I'm willing to feel ignored and pushed aside that way.

Katie: "I look forward to . . ."

Bernard: I look forward to feeling ignored and pushed aside that way.

Katie: That's very exciting, because it will let you know that it's time for another Worksheet. It's a wonderful way to know yourself and get closer to her. Thank you for giving us all the privilege to look so deeply into you. You really are a soul-searcher. *[Loud, sustained applause.]*

Bernard: Thank you so much, Katie.

My Father Was Horrible

This dialogue took place in 2018 before a large audience in a city on the West Coast. Marjorie thinks that she's "the toughest case," and indeed being abused as a child is a difficult kind of suffering to see through and overcome. You'll notice that in my facilitation I didn't use the four questions as thoroughly as I usually do. I wanted to be very gentle with her and let her find her enlightenment in her own time, in her own way. And she does. "You took the whole situation," she says, "and turned it upside down—what I've been believing my whole life!"

Marjorie *[from the audience]*: I'm really confused, Katie. I've read all of your books, I've watched most of your videos, and a lot of what you're saying is just really confusing me today. Am I supposed to look forward to what my father did to me?

Katie: Oh, no, honey.

Marjorie: My second question is, he's dead, and he keeps ruining my life from the grave, and I just came in here kind of understanding, and now I'm really confused. I don't understand a lot of what has happened here today. It seems like you keep giving a pass to people whose behavior is terrible.

Katie: All the more reason to question what you're believing about those terrible people and those terrible things, so that you can free yourself. That's what this is about.

Marjorie: Incest is incest is incest is incest.

Katie: Exactly so.

Marjorie: And leaving a child beside the road. I was called a blob of fat on the face of the earth. How do I look forward to that? I don't mean to come across as disrespectful, but I'm really, really confused.

Katie: Oh, honey, you have every right to be confused, and I don't find you disrespectful at all. There must be other people in this room who feel the same way.

Marjorie: Then can you help me understand? First, how do you do The Work with somebody who's dead? And second, how do I learn to look forward to the bad things he did to me?

Katie: Don't even put that on yourself. We're seeing examples here, like this last woman who did The Work with me and came to an understanding. But don't put that on yourself until you understand. It wouldn't be right. It wouldn't be honest. Fathers don't die; they live in here. *[Points to her head.]*

Marjorie: They live on forever.

Katie: They live on, and it's not done until it's done.

Marjorie: So how do I do The Work to get him out of my head? Because he's ruining my life right now.

Katie: Have you done a Worksheet on your father?

Marjorie: Oh, yeah.

Katie: Then let's take a look. Come into my parlor. *[Laughter from the audience.] [Marjorie walks up onto the stage.]* Do you really want to be free of it?

Marjorie: Oh, my God!

Katie: Okay, precious. Let's hear what you've written.

Marjorie: *I'm disgusted with my father because he was abusive, violent, hurtful, damaging, and a horrible father.*

Katie: Okay. So because you've written about him in a general way . . .

Marjorie: Mm-hmm.

Katie: When you go home, I invite you to find one specific situation where you were actually being incested.

Marjorie: Okay.

Katie: To be in that moment and to write the thoughts you were believing then, as you were being incested, and question those. But for now, let's walk our way through what you've written. So "he was a horrible father"—**is it true?**

Marjorie: Yes.

Katie: Okay. Good. A one-syllable answer. Now notice what just happened in your mind when you had the thought that he was a horrible father. Notice where your mind went when I asked you if it's true that he was a horrible father. Notice the images of the past that flash through your mind.

Marjorie: Mm-hmm.

Katie: That's huge. And when you see those images, notice the emotions that come up with them. Thoughts are the cause, and emotions are the effect. Cause and effect.

Marjorie: Mm-hmm.

Katie: "He was a horrible father"—**can you absolutely know that it's true?**

Marjorie: Yes.

Katie: "He was a horrible father"—**how do you react, what happens, when you believe that thought?**

Marjorie: I tense up. I feel sick. I feel furious at him. I resent the hell out of him. I get depressed. I feel self-pity. I feel that life is unfair.

Katie: Yes, honey. And **who would you be without the thought?** Who would you be if you didn't even have the ability to think that he's a horrible father?

Marjorie: If I didn't have that thought, I wouldn't be such an angry, upset, hyperalert, freaked-out person.

Katie: Okay. So when you're not thinking about him, you've got a balance going, whatever that is for you. But when something reminds you of your father, that image of your father and the horrible things he did come to your mind.

Marjorie: Right. Everything is a trigger.

Katie: So "He was a horrible father"—let's **turn it around.** What's the opposite of horrible?

Marjorie: Wonderful.

Katie: He was a wonderful father.

Marjorie [*after a long pause*]: I can't honestly say that.

Katie: Well, just try it on.

Marjorie: I can say it, but I'm going to throw up if I do.

Katie: Sweetheart, you're just trying it on, like a new pair of shoes. You can try on a pair of shoes. You don't know how they're going to fit. This doesn't mean that he was in fact a wonderful father. You're just trying it on.

Marjorie: It's like putting lipstick on a pig, though.

Katie: It is. So let's put the lipstick on the pig.

Marjorie: He's a pig.

Katie: Done. Let's just try.

Marjorie: He was a wonderful father. But it's not true.

Katie: You can see how difficult this is. We can all see it. But there's no way we're going to let him off the hook. He was a horrible father.

Marjorie: Yes, horrible.

Katie: But we're trying on a new pair of shoes. "He's a wonderful father." Just let it in for a few minutes and see if you can find any small way that that might be true. When I was doing this Work, I used to have a bucket by me, and there were times when I would have to vomit into it because of some of the things I had to look at.

Marjorie: I believe it.

Katie: Well, you're an expert. Okay, "He's a wonderful father." Let's try it on. Tell me one thing that was wonderful about him.

Marjorie: I don't think there was *anything* wonderful about him. But I can find something acceptable. He would give me little candies sometimes.

Katie: That's one.

Marjorie: Right.

Katie: What else was wonderful about him?

Marjorie: Well, if you take the sleaziness out of everything he taught me, I learned how to be a good businessperson and a negotiator with morals. I became somebody who works on behalf of troubled kids and turns all the misery into as positive stuff as I can. I try to make every ounce of suffering pay off, so to speak. He gave me that. But I'm not a happy person.

Katie: We're looking at where he was a wonderful father.

Marjorie: Okay.

Katie: Look at what he gave you. He gave you what you have of a very caring life. We heard your list. That's not a little thing. That's something that most of us would aspire to have.

Marjorie: Hmm. I never looked at it that way before. There was a lot of suffering to go through, though.

Katie: You know what I love about the past.

Marjorie: That it's over. Yes, I've heard you say that.

Katie: And who are you working with? Troubled children.

Marjorie: Right.

Katie: And so many other things.

Marjorie: Yes. I never saw it that way, really.

Katie: So just be with it.

Marjorie: I guess I wouldn't be who I was if he hadn't been so horrible-slash-wonderful.

Katie: Let's not guess. Let's really understand this. It's not easy. Just keep the bucket near you.

Marjorie: Okay.

Katie: The truth doesn't come easily to the ego. So now if people ask who your father was, you can tell them honestly that he was a horrible father *and* he was a wonderful father. And that you wouldn't be who you are today, you wouldn't be what you love most about yourself, without him.

Marjorie: But without him I would be a happier person.

Katie: Oh, well. You're guessing.

Marjorie: What would I be sad about?

Katie: Well, ask us. *[Pointing to the audience]* Most of us have or had fathers who didn't incest us or beat us or insult us, but we can find plenty of reasons to complain about them.

Marjorie: Are you saying that if I had a normal father, I wouldn't necessarily be a happy person? Is that what you're saying?

Katie: We don't need major reasons to be perfectly unhappy. I've known very rich people, people with loving parents, who were miserable.

Marjorie: Okay, I get that.

Katie: People with amazing fathers can be just as unhappy as you were. And even if they couldn't be *that* unhappy, suffering is suffering.

Marjorie: I never thought of it that way.

Katie: Suffering is suffering. We consider ourselves to be the special ones. But we aren't.

Marjorie: I do.

Katie: Mind is cause, and life is the effect. So your father was horrible, and what else?

Marjorie: What do you mean?

Katie: He was horrible, and . . . ?

Marjorie: I'm not sure what you're asking.

Katie: He was a horrible father, *and* he was a wonderful father.

Marjorie: I hear you.

Katie: Okay. And you understood it just a short time ago.

Marjorie: No, I still understand it.

Katie: All right. Your ego is going to want to drop the "wonderful" part, because there goes your identity.

Marjorie: But what if I said my father was a Nazi? Would you still be having the same conversation?

Katie: Yes.

Marjorie: Is there no line anywhere?

Katie: No.

Marjorie: There's no one you consider offensive, horrible, terrible, and disgusting?

Katie: And wonderful. And I'm not blind to people.

Marjorie: What if my father was like a Hitler?

Katie: I was once with a German woman in Berlin whose father was a Nazi official, and we were going through the Holocaust Museum together. They had old articles from a Berlin newspaper framed on the walls, and you could see where Nazism had just started, in the 1920s, and then where it progressed a little, and then here and then there, until it had taken over the whole country. It was extremely radical. The newspaper articles were talking about these horrific Nazis, and she was translating the German for me. And she was pointing to some of the photos with top-ranking Nazi officials and saying "Oh, So-and-so, we loved him, he was a friend of my father's. He came to dinner all the time, and he was such a charming and cultured man." And my jaw dropped. But she believed one set of thoughts onto him, and other people believed other things. It's from the position we sit in. There's no human being who doesn't have some good qualities. Even a Hitler. That doesn't mean that he wasn't a monster.

Marjorie: What good quality could you possibly find in Hitler?

Katie: Well, he loved dogs. He was a vegetarian.

Marjorie: Hmm. So are you saying that my seeing my father as horrible is—

Katie: No, seeing him as *just* horrible. As *only* horrible.

Marjorie: You're saying he's more than just horrible. There are some things about him that were acceptable, possibly.

Katie: More than that. He produced you.

Marjorie: He donated sperm.

Katie: He produced you, according to you. He produced the kind of caring person you are. But you keep taking it back.

Marjorie: Okay. I see.

Katie: And the ego is going to require that you keep taking it back. You've got to really want to be free to hold on to what you've understood.

Marjorie: Okay. I so want to not feel this way anymore.

Katie: It would be better to hold on to the thought that he's also wonderful, and then when you're breathless sometime in the middle of the night and you're just doubled up with suffering, you can remember that there's a tiny part of him that's wonderful. Not to con yourself out of your belief that he's horrible but to get a balance.

Marjorie: For myself.

Katie: Yes. Don't exaggerate. Don't pretend. No positive-thinking woo-woo here.

Marjorie: So you're not minimizing the horrible things that he did to me.

Katie: Of course not. I'm not crazy.

Marjorie: But what you're doing is trying to find a way to make—

Katie: I know the difference between what hurts and what doesn't hurt. Thinking of your father the way you've been thinking about him is terribly painful.

Marjorie: Okay. Okay. It felt like you were minimizing the bad things that people do, and to be on the receiving end of that bad stuff . . .

Katie: I have done enough hurtful things in my life that I understand why people do the things that they do. I look to myself. I look at what I was thinking and believing just prior to the hurtful things I said or did, and I see that there was no choice. I know how the mind works. No one is *only* horrible. Not if you're of right mind or open-minded enough to get to your right mind.

Marjorie: Because it hurts me to think he's horrible.

Katie: Exactly. To think that he's *only* horrible.

Marjorie: Okay. I think I finally understood. That was a hard place to get to.

Katie: It's a very hard place to get to, but you've just jumped a hurdle.

Marjorie: Yeah. I've been trying to jump that hurdle for a long time. Thank you.

Katie: Thank *you*. We're partners in this. I've done a little more inquiry than you have, but you can catch up with me.

Marjorie: I don't know. It doesn't—

Katie: You're smart. You know what suffering is. That's all you need to know.

Marjorie: I'm an expert on that.

Katie: Yes. Freedom is a little weird at first, too. At first, happiness can burn as badly as pain. It could be you're not even used to it. It just takes a little open-mindedness. He's abusive. What's the opposite of abusive?

Marjorie: Wow! Loving.

Katie: Yes.

Marjorie: That's foreign.

Katie: It's difficult, but it was there. Trust that.

Marjorie: I don't know if sociopaths can love or not. That's—

Katie: Well, as close as you can get to it. Here's how I started. Was there one moment when you thought he was coming after you and he didn't? Can you find that moment?

Marjorie: I don't know. He was pretty consistent.

Katie: Okay. That tells me there is at least one. You said, "*Pretty* consistent."

Marjorie: You want me to tell you a time when he could have done something bad and he didn't? He used to have the scissors on the table to cut my hair if it got in my eyes. He never actually cut it. The scissors were there, but he never actually used them. He just threatened to. Why is that important?

Katie: Because that is all there is.

Marjorie: You kind of lost me.

Katie: Okay. He was abusive. He had scissors right there, yet he wasn't abusive with those scissors when it came to cutting. That's one. If you can find one, you can find two.

Marjorie: Okay.

Katie: It has to be authentic. It has to be the real thing.

Marjorie: I'm looking for these things to—

Katie: To know the rest of who he is.

Marjorie: I just want him out of my head. I don't really want to know him. I want him to be in the grave, where he's supposed to be.

Katie: He is out of your head already, as the man you thought he was. He was only horrible. The thought that he was in any way wonderful—you couldn't even go there at first.

Marjorie: Right.

Katie: Now his identity has shifted. That's how you get him out of your head. He was abusive. He was also loving.

Marjorie: So if I can find some acceptable things and decent things—

Katie: You're shifting his identity. Every time that happens, your own identity shifts, because you realize that you've lived with a different father. With a real person, not the father in your mind.

Marjorie: Okay.

Katie: Before, he was only horrible. Now, he's horrible and also wonderful. And specifically, here, here, here. Your job is to continue to count, yet not erase the horrible.

Marjorie: Got it. But I'm only giving him this rebranding to save myself. Yes?

Katie: That's the road to save yourself, because otherwise you're in denial. These positive things were right under your nose, and you couldn't see them. Okay, he was abusive. What's the opposite?

Marjorie: Can I just go with "nonabusive"?

Katie: Yes.

Marjorie: That's more neutral.

Katie: Okay, but I sure like to take the high road, the difficult road.

Marjorie: I'd say "loving," but—

Katie: The scissors were there, but he didn't use them. You might find other small examples. And when you do, your ego may hate it. It may feel weird when your mind starts to open and there's some space there. Because you're open, you're allowing other things to come in. It's a big threat to your identity, which is "I am the woman with the abusive father."

Marjorie: I didn't understand that. It felt like you were taking his side, so to speak, but now I understand that you're just helping me see the good qualities. I'm choking on the words *good qualities* when it comes to him, but I can see that it's going to make me live in less pain. That was what I got really confused about in the previous Work sessions, the Black woman who talked about her White neighbors setting the dogs on her when she was a little girl or the woman with the alcoholic mother. It just seemed that—

Katie: That we're letting those terrible people off the hook.

Marjorie: Exactly.

Katie: But without inquiry we never let them off the hook. They're always with us, hanging from a hook in our minds. That's uncomfortable. It's living small. For someone as large as you are, with what you've got to do in this world, you don't need that.

Marjorie: Thank you. I've been dragging this stuff around from place to place to place, like extra baggage, for my entire life.

Katie: And everywhere you go, there it is.

Marjorie: It is.

Katie: He is . . . what's the opposite of abusive?

Marjorie: Nurturing. Caring.

Katie: Caring. I know how hard this is, sweetheart. It's like someone taking a lit cigarette and burning your skin.

Marjorie: He sold me out. Okay, nurturing and caring is what I *wished* he had been.

Katie: So open your mind to it. Where was he in reality nurturing and caring?

Marjorie: He took us to the coast. He took us to amusement parks. He took me to demolition derbies. I'm trying to think of some other good things but . . . *[Pauses to contemplate.]* He let us have a dog once, for a while. He didn't hit my mother. *[Shakes her head.]* Boy, this is really scraping the bottom of the barrel. He gave us shelter. He fed us. He gave us clothing.

Katie: The things that you're talking about—they don't sound so bottom of the barrel to me. There are many children in this world who pray that they had a father who could give them shelter and feed them and give them clothing. If you weren't so frightened, so traumatized, that list is a pretty amazing list. But because you were so traumatized, you didn't have a mind that could take advantage of the gifts.

Marjorie: That's true.

Katie: Nonetheless, appreciated or not, he was giving you those things that you just listed for us so easily.

Marjorie: This is really eye opening, *really* eye opening. Wow! It's like you took the whole situation and turned it upside down—what I've been believing my whole life! Because it started really, really young. Katie, you're living up to the hype. *[Laughter from the audience.]* I've listened to probably everything you've ever recorded, and I always waited for you to have somebody come up with my issue, or people to come up with parts of it, but nobody I've ever heard— Maybe I've missed some of your videos, but I always waited for somebody to come up and say he did this and this and this and now it follows me around, and I hope there are other people who have been waiting for you to have somebody like me up here.

Katie: When no one else would do it, I love that you volunteered.

Marjorie: I had nothing left to lose. I was in so much pain today listening to everybody. When I came here, I was fine, but in about half an hour I was a mess.

Katie: Yes, precious.

Marjorie: We've only questioned my first statement, and I really feel like I've gotten a lot already.

Katie: Good. You said that your father was damaging. Can you turn that around?

Marjorie: He was repairing. Yeah, he could fix anything. This is going to be a dated reference that millennials won't get, but he could always come up with the most ridiculous Rube Goldberg fix for anything. I went to college with a child's little stereo that he'd patched together to make it look like a teenager's stereo.

Katie: How playful!

Marjorie: When I drove across the country to go to college on the West Coast, he put a radio into my little VW bug and a little shelf. *[Pauses.]* I'd forgotten about those things.

Katie: So **turn the whole statement around** to yourself. "In some of those situations"—and this doesn't mean you don't have a right to be—but "In some of those situations, I was . . ." And read what you wrote about your father.

Marjorie: The first one?

Katie: Uh-huh.

Marjorie: In some of these situations I was abusive. I was violent. I was damaging.

Katie: I was abusive toward my father.

Marjorie: I was abusive toward my father.

Katie: Yes. So get still with it. If you're like me, you could be abusive with one little look.

Marjorie: I just disappeared. I didn't— Once I was old enough, I left, and leaving wasn't the solution I'd hoped for. When he died, I celebrated.

Katie: I can understand that.

Marjorie: I thought his death was going to set me free. It didn't.

Katie: No, you took him with you.

Marjorie: I was violent.

Katie: Were you violent toward him?

Marjorie: I wrote him a letter when I remembered all the bad stuff. I wrote him a letter and confronted him with it. I guess that was pretty violent.

Katie: I don't know. *Your* opinion is what matters.

Marjorie: I wouldn't want to receive a letter like that from my child.

Katie: That tells me you wouldn't want to send it, but that's what you did. So where were you a horrible daughter?

Marjorie: I'm sure he felt I was a horrible daughter.

Katie: What cause would you give him?

Marjorie: Meaning why was I horrible?

Katie: No. What things did you do that someone might see as horrible?

Marjorie: What horrible things did I do?

Katie: It could be just a tiny little nothing thing, but to you it was horrible. We're looking at how you hurt yourself.

Marjorie: I took all the gifts he ever gave me and destroyed them. I threw them away. I threw away everything he'd ever given me, so I wouldn't have the memories. I disappeared. I went into hiding.

Katie: He didn't do that. You did.

Marjorie: I understand. I was drowning. I drowned the best way I could.

Katie: Exactly. In his name.

Marjorie: That's a completely different way of looking at everything. I've never been able to make this leap on my own. I can see it now.

Katie: Where were you abusive toward him? Where did you make it known?

Marjorie: When I got to be a teenager, I just wouldn't take it anymore, and I would scream at him.

Katie: "I wouldn't take it anymore" puts the blame on him. It's a kind of justification. But there's no one to blame. You've had your time there, and it won't set you free. *How* were you abusive to him? Not why.

Marjorie: I would scream at him and tell him what a crummy father he was and confront him on some of his behaviors. Now that I'm a parent, I can see that that would not be great at all. It's just really hard to see things from his point of view. I've never, ever stopped long enough to do that.

Katie: Or to take a good look at yourself.

Marjorie: No, I am painfully aware of how flawed I am and the parts of him that are—

Katie: No, we're talking about *you*—specifically where *you* were abusive, damaging, violent, and so on.

Marjorie: I can see all those things in me.

Katie: And that's where self-hatred comes from.

Marjorie: I've got plenty of that.

Katie: Well, you'd have to.

Marjorie: Right. The only way you can survive is to have strong emotions one way or the other.

Katie: If you can call that survival.

Marjorie: Barely. Wow! This is just revolutionary for me!

Katie: So let's look very gently at statement two.

Marjorie: *I want my father to have been different or at least not abused me so badly. I want him to stop ruining the family from the grave, causing both my sisters to hate me and leaving me to have to deal with being excluded from the will, as he threatened he would do my entire childhood.* That's a lot.

Katie: So you want him to have been different. I'm inviting you now to go deeper, because the ego loves this kind of thing. It's a special I,

I, I. Go to your core. *[To the audience]* I invite you all to this. *[To Marjorie]* You want him to have been different.

Marjorie: Mm-hmm.

Katie: Consider that. **Is it true?**

Marjorie: Well, it's a done deal. He's dead. He's never going to be any different.

Katie: That's justification. It's using logic rather than going deep for your answer. Let's go back to the question. You want him to have been different—**is it true?**

Marjorie: No, it's impossible.

Katie: Okay, now go beyond that.

Marjorie: Am I missing something?

Katie: Yes, but I know you; you're going to go there. You want him to have been different—**is it true?** Look at your identity. If he had been different, what would happen to your identity?

Marjorie: Well, I would be somebody different.

Katie: You're left with "Who am I?"

Marjorie: Right.

Katie: And that's really scary.

Marjorie: Well, it's not like I'm so phenomenal the way I am.

Katie: I'm asking you for a depth that I think you can go to.

Marjorie: I'm not sure what you're asking me. I feel like everyone knows the answer but me.

Katie: I don't think you're alone. *[To the audience]* How many of you don't understand where I'm going? *[About a third of the audience raise their hands.]* There's a lot of experience sitting here. "I want my mother to be different"—when I questioned that one, I had an amazing experience, and I had to undo everything in my world. After that, every thought appeared to me as the beloved. I wanted to smell it, taste it, touch it, kiss it. So "I want my mother to have been different"—is it true? Oh, no. I had so much invested in that. My whole identity was tied up in it. If I prove myself wrong, she comes out the winner. You know that winning/losing thing.

Marjorie: "I want him to have been different." The only thing that comes to mind is that he's dead and it's me that needs to change because there's no one else in the equation but me. I've been trying since I was young.

Katie: So go back to when he was alive. Go back to the space you've written this Worksheet from.

Marjorie: Okay.

Katie: You want him to have been different—is it true?

Marjorie: It would never have happened. No, I get it. He was the way he was. He was born that way. He died that way.

Katie: So you're safe in all your misery.

Marjorie: I don't know what you're trying—

Katie: That's okay.

Marjorie: I'm so confused. I am trying really hard to understand what you're getting at, and it's going right over my head.

Katie: Well, it's probably not going over your head. It's probably that you haven't encountered it. So it's not yours to understand yet. Go to the place where he abused you.

Marjorie: Mm-hmm.

Katie: Are you up for describing that? A moment when you were at your most frightened?

Marjorie: He would chase me around the house, and I tried to get away from him, and the whole house would shake. My sister would be standing there eating a sandwich, and my mother would be standing there watching, and sometimes I would run out of the house, and then they'd lock me out. And sometimes I'd be in the snow barefoot, or they'd leave me beside the road in strange places. Those were probably the worst times. I could deal with the beatings.

Katie: They would leave you by the side of the road and drive away?

Marjorie: Right.

Katie: Okay. So be there now.

Marjorie: It's easy.

Katie: So, beautiful little girl, they've left you. You don't know where you are. You don't have any money. You're completely lost.

Marjorie: Yes.

Katie: What do you most fear?

Marjorie: Being left there indefinitely.

Katie: So they've abandoned you?

Marjorie: Yes.

Katie: Close your eyes. Be the little girl on the side of the road. I'm going to talk to her, okay?

Marjorie: Yes.

Katie: Little girl, is your fear that they're not coming back for you?

Marjorie: Right.

Katie: So they're never coming back for you. You'll never see them again—**is it true?**

Marjorie: It didn't turn out to be true, but it feels that way.

Katie: Remember, the answer to the first two questions consist of one syllable only. It sounds like your answer is yes.

Marjorie: Yes.

Katie: So, little girl, **can you absolutely know that it's true** they're never coming back for you?

Marjorie: No. I really get this one. The fear was worse than the actual event. That I get.

Katie: Good. So, little girl, close your eyes again. Notice what happens in your mind's eye, and notice what happens emotionally. **How do you react when you believe the thought** that they're never coming back for you?

Marjorie: I just fall apart.

Katie: Notice the images of past and future when you believe the thought that they're never coming back for you.

Marjorie: It just tears me up.

Katie: What do you see specifically?

Marjorie: What am I feeling?

Katie: No. What do you see in your mind's eye?

Marjorie: Oh, me just standing there endlessly having to figure out a way out of the situation.

Katie: And you see that there's no way.

Marjorie: Right.

Katie: That's your future. You see that there's no way.

Marjorie: Yes, that's how it feels. It feels like I just have no solution.

Katie: Now we're meditating on that moment. You believe that they're never coming back for you, and what do you imagine? Do you imagine that you'll die there on the side of the road? Do you imagine being alone forever? What do you see? You have to go back to her. You have to be there now, not here now.

Marjorie: I would kind of almost dissociate, I think. I would just so completely freak out that I would be panicky without clear thoughts. I think the fear would just be so extreme.

Katie: Terror.

Marjorie: Especially the first few times, because after a while I learned that they would always come back eventually.

Katie: But you didn't know that then.

Marjorie: I didn't know that then.

Katie: So they're never coming back for you. Okay. Little girl, drop your story.

Marjorie: I see that's not true now.

Katie: Drop your story *then*, little girl. We're meditating on then, not now.

Marjorie: Okay.

Katie: Be the little girl then, and as her drop the story.

Marjorie: Okay.

Katie: Little girl, **who would you be without the thought** that they're never coming back for you? Look at where you are. Notice. What do you see?

Marjorie: I would have been able to handle the situation a hundred times better.

Katie: Just tell me what you see. You see yourself standing there?

Marjorie: Maybe I would have sat down or tried to find some place to be.

Katie: Just look at where you are. Are you standing, or are you sitting?

Marjorie: I'm standing.

Katie: You're standing. Now look around you. See the sky.

Marjorie: Yes.

Katie: Are there clouds?

Marjorie: No.

Katie: Okay. Just a clear sky. Can you see the road?

Marjorie: Yes.

Katie: Can you see where you're standing?

Marjorie: I'm on the edge of the road.

Katie: On the edge of the road. Now, aside from what you're thinking and believing, are you safe? Are you okay?

Marjorie: In theory, I'm safe and okay.

Katie: No. No theory here. Other than what she's thinking and believing, look at that little girl. Is she okay?

Marjorie: Technically she's okay. *[Smiles at Katie.]* You're going to complain about the "technically." *[Laughter from the audience.]* She's okay.

Katie: Yes. She really is. This isn't about dropping your mind. It's not like that. We're just taking a clear look. The question is, **Who would you be** in that situation **without the thought** that they're never coming back for you?

Marjorie: I get it.

Katie: You'd be at home.

Marjorie: I get it. I actually do get it.

Katie: Then when you sit in that, you begin to experience the ground as home.

Marjorie: Okay.

Katie: Whether there are any flowers there or it's just gravel, it's home.

Marjorie: Okay.

Katie: It's home, and there's even more. You have clothes. You have the sky. Aside from what you're thinking and believing, can you find one time in your entire life when you weren't okay? It doesn't happen. You're always okay. But you believe yourself into terror and panic and other kinds of suffering. The life of a believer is hard. The illusion is like a contest between the imagined and the real, but the real doesn't compete.

Marjorie: But you're not minimizing his behavior. You're just saying that if I can find what was okay in the situation, then instead of its being so overwhelming and haunting, I can maybe find some peace in it. Is that what you're saying?

Katie: Aside from what you were thinking and believing, where was the problem?

Marjorie: Well, to be an eight-year-old on the side of the road by yourself is not optimal. I'm going to make that radical statement.

Katie: Unless she's awake to reality.

Marjorie: Okay. I guess I just have to keep telling myself that you're only pointing these things out because it will help bring me more peace.

Katie: If you keep pointing them out to yourself, they'll keep bringing you more peace.

Marjorie: Okay. I'm sort of getting parts of it.

Katie: You've held on to these beliefs like cement. So we start questioning them and finding opposites. We get a balance. Then we begin to understand that this Work, if you just stay with it, is like checkmate. Take it slow. You might take "'I want him to be different'—is it true?" and just sit in that for a week. Just that one question.

Marjorie: Okay.

Katie: And keep at it until your whole Worksheet is done. You've got the rest of your life to do it.

Marjorie: I hope I can live long enough.

Katie: It's exciting, isn't it?

Marjorie: I think I'm the toughest case.

Katie: So "They're never coming back for me"—**turn it around,** little girl.

Marjorie: They *are* coming back for me.

Katie: It could be just as true. One is not more valid than the other in that moment.

Marjorie: Okay.

Katie: It could be just as true. You don't know. In the meantime, you may as well make yourself at home.

Marjorie: Okay.

Katie: Find one moment when you were not okay in your life.

Marjorie: Me? There are so many to choose from.

Katie: Well, choose just one.

Marjorie: Okay. I'll just do the one I think about. Regularly when they'd kick me out of the house barefoot into the snow in the middle of the winter. That was tough.

Katie: Yes. That was really tough. And what about the incest?

Marjorie: I wouldn't wish it on anybody.

Katie: What was the most frightening time during your experience?

Marjorie: It was actually when I remembered it. I dissociated, which fifty to seventy percent of kids do. When I got recalls, it was . . . I thought I was going insane.

Katie: How old were you when you got these recalls?

Marjorie: I had just given birth to my daughter, so I would have been in my thirties.

Katie: Okay, in your thirties. So up till then you hadn't been incested?

Marjorie [*pausing for a while to contemplate*]: Yes.

Katie: Good.

Marjorie: Katie, that's amazing!

Katie: You got that one. No incest until you were thirty.

Marjorie: Correct.

Katie: And then it popped into your head, and in that moment you were incested.

Marjorie: Right.

Katie: So your father wasn't even there.

Marjorie: Well, he had done plenty of other things I remembered.

Katie: I'm talking about just the incest.

Marjorie: Yes. You're correct.

Katie: So really, he wasn't even there to incest you. It all happened when you were thirty.

Marjorie: Now that I understand why you say it, yes, I can agree with that.

Katie: Ah, sweetheart, you're amazing.

Marjorie: It's a tough, tough, tough leap, but now that I understand why you keep putting lipstick on the pig, I can make that leap. I'm pretty desperate not to live the rest of my life this way.

Katie: So did he incest you, or did you incest yourself at thirty? He wasn't in the room. There's the first clue.

Marjorie: No, I guess I've been doing it to myself.

Katie: I would drop the "I guess."

Marjorie: Yes, I've been the one hurting myself for the last decades. Yes.

Katie: Ah, you're amazing. Thank you.

Marjorie: Am I free?

Katie: I'll leave that answer to you.

Marjorie: Thank you.

Katie: One more thing. What did you write on statement number six?

Marjorie: *I don't ever want my father to ruin another moment of my life.*

Katie: **Turn it around:** "I'm willing . . ."

Marjorie: I'm willing to have my father ruin another moment of my life.

Katie: "I look forward . . ."

Marjorie: I look forward to my father ruining another moment of my life.

Katie: Yes, because you know a little more about what that is and how to deal with it.

Marjorie: I hope I can just hang on to that turnaround somehow.

Katie: Don't even hang on to it. Just do your Work. Have The Work for breakfast, and have a good day.

Marjorie: I thought you had met your match in me, but apparently not. Thank you so much, Katie.

Katie: You're very welcome.

Stanley Didn't Have to Die

I did The Work with Joyce at a 2018 fundraising event for Spirit Rock Meditation Center in Marin County, California. You may think that she is crazy, with her visions of a dead man. But many of us have strange thoughts that we fervently cling to. My job here was to enter her world and help her loosen the thoughts that were stressful, not the ones that seemed benign.

Joyce: *I'm angry with Stanley because he died and he didn't have to yet, and now we have no future.*

Katie: So Stanley died, and he didn't have to do that. Okay. Was it suicide? What was it?

Joyce: No, it was health issues. He couldn't breathe.

Katie: Okay. Stanley didn't have to die—**is it true?**

Joyce: He didn't have to get sick, he could have—

Katie: Sweetheart, the answer to the first two questions is either yes or no. We're meditating on Stanley's dying. He didn't have to die—**is it true?** So just contemplate that question. And wait to be shown.

See what you see when you look inside. That question is an invitation. It invites the creative mind, your own wisdom, to go beyond the answer you think you know.

Joyce: He did have to die, except when I argue with him.

Katie: Okay. Now just notice how many words were in your answer. He didn't have to die—**is it true?** Is your answer a yes or a no?

Joyce: Yes.

Katie: So is it true that Stanley didn't have to die? I'm hearing that your answer is yes.

Joyce: Yes, because he wasn't an old man, really.

Katie: Okay, so if you take this Work in as something you want to experience at home, as a practice, you might go inside and contemplate the question like this: "Stanley didn't have to die"—is it true? Look at all the yeses, all the reasons you think he didn't have to die, and continue to look for noes too, reasons why it wouldn't be true, in the interest of fair play and balance, in the interest of inquiry. And when you come up with a definite yes or a definite no, you're just going to feel that. You've been shown. But if you say, "Yes, because . . ." or "Yes, but . . . ," you don't have to feel the answer. If you say, "No, because . . ." or "No, but . . . ," you don't have to feel it. And even if you get a "Yes, because . . ." or a "No, because . . . ," it doesn't stop what's being shown to you. The questioning is allowed to continue in you, and you just sit in that. Give it time, without interrupting it, so that it has time to continue in a part of your consciousness. *[To the audience]* So for those of you who want to take this into your practice, notice how your mind wants to interrupt with defense or justification. *[To Joyce]* What's the specific situation with Stanley that you were anchored in? What were you thinking of when you filled in the Worksheet?

Joyce: Oh, I saw myself a few days ago sitting at the kitchen table, and I sensed his presence, and he was right there. He's often right there, but why does he have to be not in his body? So I argued with him.

Katie: How do you react, what happens, when you believe the thought "He didn't have to die"? You argue with life.

Joyce: Yes. I get really angry at him and very sad that he left me.

Katie: And you're not grateful that he appears to you in your mind. It's like, that's not enough, I want him to be real. Stanley can only give you so much. So close your eyes now. Stanley's there, at—what was it? At breakfast?

Joyce: Yes.

Katie: Okay. Sitting at the breakfast table. **Who would you be without the thought** "Stanley didn't have to die"? Just witness Stanley there, sitting at the table with you. Just drop your story and be with Stanley. There he is. **Who would you be without the story** that he died?

Joyce: I'd be happy.

Katie: Do you feel the intimacy?

Joyce: Katie, do we ever interact with people in the now?

Katie: And what now would that be?

Joyce: Now, now.

Katie: And where did that now go?

Joyce: Back there.

Katie: Where? So there's your answer. "Stanley didn't have to die"— **turn it around.**

Joyce: Stanley did have to die. He really did, and I wanted him to. I didn't want him to suffer.

Katie: Let's look at statement two now. One thing about Stanley at breakfast a few days ago, there were two of you, and only one of you was suffering.

Joyce: That's very true.

Katie: It wasn't Stanley. He's doing fine when you compare the two of you. He's good company. Okay, let's look at statement two.

Joyce: *I want Stanley to change the way life works and come back to me in his body, but in his current enlightened state.* I really think these things, Katie.

Katie: I'm going to skip the questions for this statement, but you shouldn't do that at home. You should put your statement up against all four questions before you do the turnarounds. But right now, in the interest of time, let's go straight to the turnaround. "I want Stanley to change"—**turn it around.** "I want me . . ." Read it that way.

Joyce: I want me to change the way life works and come back to me in my body, in my current enlightened state. That's truer.

Katie: Stanley doesn't need you to work on him anymore. Let's just work on you.

Joyce: True.

Katie: And when you question what you're believing about Stanley, that will wake you up. Let's look at statement three.

Joyce: *Stanley shouldn't be okay with having died. He should talk with the ascended masters and fix this situation.* Because he's there, and he's fine with it. I see that.

Katie: So he shouldn't be okay with having died—**is it true?** Look at him at the table.

Joyce: He's blissful.

Katie: He shouldn't be okay with having died—**is it true?**

Joyce: No. It's just not true. I wouldn't want any less for him.

Katie: Okay, so without discussion, because I want you to experience it: He shouldn't be okay with having died—**is it true?** Look at him at the table before you answer. What do you see?

Joyce: I wouldn't want him to have any less than what he has now. No, it's not true.

Katie: He shouldn't be okay with having died—**is it true?** Now give me your answer in just one syllable.

Joyce: No.

Katie: You get it? We're not guessing here. He looks okay to you. In reality. No matter what your mind is putting onto the him you see. And **how do you react, what happens, when you believe the thought** that he shouldn't be okay with having died? And there you are at the table with him and he looks fine, you think.

Joyce: I feel alone and abandoned and lost, with him right there in front of me.

Katie: Now **who would you be** at the table **without the thought** that he shouldn't be okay with having died?

Joyce: Joyous and blissful and in deep contact with him. I can feel it. It's only my mind that's driving me crazy.

Katie: Yes. It's certainly not affecting Stanley. *[Laughter from the audience.]*

Joyce: Not at all.

Katie: So he shouldn't be okay with having died—**turn it around.** What's the opposite of "He shouldn't"?

Joyce: He *should* be okay with having died. He *is* okay with having died.

Katie: Nice to catch up with him. If he's going to show up at your table, it's nice to be aware of who you're sitting with. We even try to change them, even though we see that they're perfectly happy the way they are. So Stanley should be okay with having died. There's another turnaround: to the self. "I should . . ."

Joyce: I should be okay with having died.

Katie: With Stanley having died.

Joyce: I should be okay with Stanley having died.

Katie: Yes. And he still shows up for breakfast. *[Joyce and the audience laugh.]*

Joyce: He's still a good husband.

Katie: "He should talk with the ascended masters and fix this situation"—**is it true?**

Joyce: There's nothing to fix.

Katie: Sweetheart, I want you to get used to one-syllable answers. "He should talk with the ascended masters and fix this situation"—**is it true?**

Joyce: No.

Katie: It's not a matter of doing it right or wrong; it's a matter of experiencing what you're shown. "He should talk with the ascended masters and fix this situation"—**how do you react, what happens, when you believe that thought?**

Joyce: Oh, I get anxious. I feel unsettled in my heart. I get angry at him for not fixing the situation.

Katie: For not fixing what doesn't need to be fixed. *[Laughter from the audience.]* Who would you be, sweetheart, at breakfast with Stanley apparently sitting in that chair . . . Look at him. **Who would you be without the thought** that he needs to talk to any masters and fix the situation?

Joyce: I'd be present with him.

Katie: Yes, not off in the future finding masters for Stanley. We nag them when they're alive, and we don't give up when they move on. *[Laughter from the audience.]* No one's safe from our advice. *[More laughter.]* So turn the statement around: "Stanley should talk with the ascended masters and fix this situation." **Turn it around.** What's an opposite?

Joyce: Stanley shouldn't talk with the ascended masters. Not to fix anything.

Katie: Yes. So continue just to try it on. Does he look like he needs to talk with an ascended master when he shows up for breakfast?

Joyce: Oh, God, no. He's fine.

Katie: It's so nice for you to catch up with Stanley.

Joyce: Yes, I wanted him to fix it so he would do what I want.

Katie: Turn it around to yourself: "*I* should talk . . ."

Joyce: I should talk with the ascended masters and fix this situation.

Katie: And an ascended master showed up for breakfast: it was Stanley. So talk with him. When he shows up, talk. He's ascended, and he seems to be okay. He's a master, as far as I'm concerned. A master is someone who's totally fine with what is.

Joyce: Yes, he is.

Katie: It doesn't matter what thoughts are in your head: do you love them yet? Is everything welcome there? Is your mind at home in itself? Are you loving what is? Who cares what arises? If you don't love it, if you're not totally comfortable with it, it could use a little questioning. That's why all thoughts have a right to live. It's not as though they're not living in your head anyway. And the more you argue with them, the more painful it is, the more identified as a victim you become. Let's look at statement four.

Joyce: *I need Stanley to figure out how to fix this terrible situation.*

Katie: I'm going to shorten your sentence for convenience' sake. Look at Stanley sitting there at the table. It's a terrible situation—**is it true?**

Joyce: No.

Katie: And **how do you react, what happens, when you believe the thought** "It's a terrible situation"? And he's just sitting there, looking fine.

Joyce: I get very sad.

Katie: Who would you be without the thought that it's a terrible situation?

Joyce: Enjoying so much just hanging out with him.

Katie: So **turn it around:** "It's not . . ."

Joyce: It's not a terrible situation.

Katie: Now switch the word *terrible* to its opposite.

Joyce: It's a— *[Hesitates.]*

Katie: Wonderful situation.

Joyce: It's a wonderful situation, and I don't need him to figure it out.

Katie: Yes, a nice little breakfast visit. I'm just curious, does he eat? He's beyond that, right?

Joyce: I used to try to get him to eat when he was in a body, and he didn't then, either. *[Loud laughter from the audience.]*

Katie: In or out of the body, Stanley knew his own mind. *[More laughter.]* "I need him to figure out how to fix this terrible situation"— **turn it around.** "I need me . . ."

Joyce: I need me to figure out how to fix this terrible situation, where I have this wonderful experience and turn it into not wonderful.

Katie: That's so exciting! Doesn't that give you an amazing life? And you find those ascended masters. They don't die or leave us until we're ready. It's just like that. There's no one who's not a master, but what we believe onto the people in our life is what demotes them to our awareness. Though it doesn't change reality, it doesn't change our nature, it doesn't change what love is. Let's move to statement five now.

Joyce: *Stanley is unkind. Stanley doesn't love me enough, or he would have already figured out a way to fix this.*

Katie: Is this starting to sound a little whacked to you?

Joyce: I have no other arguments left.

Katie: You finally met Stanley. So **turn it around.** "Stanley is . . ."

Joyce: Stanley is kind. Stanley does loves me enough, and he *has* figured out a way to fix this. He has figured out a way to be at my table visiting with me.

Katie: He fixed it.

Joyce: He's here all the time. So I never have to miss him, unless I go crazy.

Katie: And when you go crazy, you know what to do with it: identify the crazy thought, write it down, question it, and see what's there. In other words, see what's true.

Joyce: Yes.

Katie: Okay. Read statement six now.

Joyce: *I don't ever want to miss somebody I care about so deeply.*

Katie: Turn it around. "I'm willing . . ."

Joyce: I'm willing to miss somebody I care about so deeply.

Katie: Yes, because if you're really in that kind of grief, and then just remember, you have a way out of it. You can fill in another Work-sheet. "I look forward to . . ."

Joyce *[sighing]:* Oh, man! I look forward to missing somebody I care about so deeply.

Katie: That's really exciting! It shows you your unfinished business.

Joyce: And then I feel more love.

Katie: Yes, if you take care of it. Taking care of it, for me, means identifying what I believe about that person or situation, and getting very still, and questioning what I'm believing. It really is the truth that sets us free.

Joyce: I'm willing to do that.

Katie: And that somebody you care about so deeply is always going to be yourself. What you were thinking and believing kept you from this self that could even see your beloved. That's the self you miss. So this Work can catch you up with Stanley until you no longer need that old self and you no longer need Stanley. You're just fine with what is. A term for that, in your language, would be that you've ascended. You're an ascended master. We're ascending from these beliefs that keep us stuck in time.

Joyce: Or I'm nowhere, which is the same. There's one last statement on my Worksheet: *I don't ever want to have people I love leave their physical bodies before I do.*

Katie: Turn it around. "I'm willing . . ."

Joyce: I'm willing to have people I love leave their physical bodies before I do.

Katie: Because if you have a problem with it, it's time for another Worksheet. "I look forward to . . ."

Joyce: I look forward to having people I love leave their physical bodies before I do.

Katie: Yes. Otherwise you're living in a tantrum. "No one can die till I say so!" And every time someone you love dies, you go to war. You go to war with reality, and it's very painful. You know how to end that now, precious. Thank you. Nice Work.

I Need My Family's Approval

When Justin sat down to do The Work with me, he seemed like a misunderstood, idealistic teenager. It's not easy to find your own way when you believe that you need love, approval, appreciation, or *anything else* from your family. It's particularly hard when you want them to see things your way (for their own good, of course). As our inquiry progresses, Justin internally rejoins his family while at the same time honoring his own path.

Justin *[reading from his Worksheet]: I'm angry and confused and sad-dened by my family because they judge me. I'm angry that there is a mold that is placed before me. I'm angry at my family and acquaintances for thinking that their path is the only way. It saddens me that I receive the most love when I assume the predestined pattern and I follow the way they think things should be.*

Katie: Good. And the next statement?

Justin: *I want my family to be who they are and not limit their love and attention according to their perception and idea of my progress. I want them to accept me as I learn my own truth in this life and love me for having found parts of my own truth and foundation.*

Katie: Good. Read the first one again.

Justin: *I'm angry and confused and saddened by my family because they judge me.*

Katie: Okay. And not only is it the job of a parent, but it's the job of everyone in this world to judge. That's our job. What else is there? Everything's a judgment. Give me a thought that's not a judgment. "It's a sky"—that's a judgment. That's what we do. So parents shouldn't judge their children—**is that true?** What's the reality of it? Do they?

Justin: Yes.

Katie: Yes, honey. That's their job. **How do you react when you be-lieve the thought** "My parents aren't supposed to judge me"?

Justin: Well, it weakens me, because I feel that I need to— I don't know, I disagree with some of the things that I've been taught.

Katie: Let's stay in inquiry. Watch as your mind wants to move into its proof that it's right. When you notice this happening, gently move back to the question. **How do you react when you think that thought?** It weakens you. What else?

Justin: It stops me in my tracks, and I feel terrified.

Katie: How do you treat your parents when you believe the thought "I want you to stop judging me," and they keep judging you?

Justin: I rebel, and I become distant. And that's been my past so far.

Katie: Yes. So can you see a reason to drop this philosophy—which would argue with the reality of the ages—that parents shouldn't judge their children?

Justin: Yes.

Katie: Okay. Now what I want you to do after all these years is to give me a reason that is not stressful, just give me one sane or stress-free reason inside you to keep such a ridiculous lie.

Justin: Well, it's a foundation for your life. It's like a religious belief.

Katie: Does that reason feel peaceful?

Justin: No. *[Pauses.]* There isn't a peaceful reason.

Katie: This is an insane belief. People should stop judging people? What planet do you think you're on? Make yourself at home here: when you come to planet Earth, you judge us and we judge you. That's it. It's a nice planet to live on, once you get the ground rules straight. But this theory of yours is in direct opposition to what's really happening. It's crazy! **Who would you be without the thought?** Who would you be if you didn't have the ability to think such a crazy thought, "I want my parents to stop judging me"?

Justin: I would have inner peace.

Katie: Yes. It's called playing with a full deck. This is the end of the war inside you. I'm a lover of reality. How do I know I'm better off with what is? It's what is. Parents judge, that's it. You've had a lifetime of proof to know that this is true. So, honey, **turn it around.** Let's see what's possible. Let's see what does work.

Justin: I'm confused and saddened by me because I judge myself.

Katie: Yes. And there's another one: "I'm confused . . ."

Justin: I'm confused and saddened by me because I judge my parents and my family.

Katie: Yes. So I'll strike a deal with you: when *you* stop judging *them* for judging you, then go talk to them about judgment.

Justin: That's so true.

Katie: When you stop doing what you want them to stop doing, then you can talk to them. It may take a while.

Justin: I don't know if I'm ready now.

Katie: Yes, sweetheart. Now read number two on your Worksheet again.

Justin: *I want my family to be who they are and not limit their love and attention—*

Katie: They already *are* who they are. They're people who limit their love and attention and who judge, according to you.

Justin *[laughing]*: Okay.

Katie: That's who they are, it seems, until they aren't. That's their job, honey. A dog barks, a cat meows, and your parents judge. And they—what else did you say they do?

Justin: Well, they limit their love and attention according to—

Katie: Yes. That's their job, too.

Justin: But they're my family!

Katie: Yes, they are. And they limit and they judge. Sweetheart, this philosophy of yours is very stressful. Give me one stress-free reason to keep this philosophy that is so off the wall. I mean, we're talking "nuts."

Justin: I did feel nuts for quite some time.

Katie: Well, you would *have* to feel nuts for quite some time. You haven't asked yourself what's true and what's not. So **who would you be** in the presence of your family **without this thought?** Who would you be without the ability to think this thought that opposes reality?

Justin: I'd be fabulous! I'd be so happy!

Katie: Yes. I would go with that. It's also my experience.

Justin: But I want—

Katie: You can say "but" all you want, they're still going to do their job.

Justin: Yes.

Katie: Reality doesn't wait for your opinion, vote, or permission, sweetheart. It just keeps being what it is and doing what it does. "No. Wait for my approval." I don't think so! You lose, always. **Turn it around,** let's look at the possibilities. "I want me . . ."

Justin: I want me to be who I am—

Katie: Yes.

Justin: —and not limit my love and attention for myself according to my perception of the idea of my progress. That's hard to eat.

Katie: Oh, well! I like the part where you thought your parents should eat the same thing all these years. *[Laughter from the audience.]* So just sit with it a moment. I realize that I'm coming on strong, but these are great revelations. Without a story, revelations have room to surface from where they have always lived, inside you. There's another turnaround. Be gentle. "I want me . . ."

Justin *[after a pause]:* I'm not seeing it.

Katie: Read it the way you wrote it.

Justin: *I want my family to be who they are . . .*

Katie: "I want me . . ."

Justin: I want me to be who I am and not limit my love and attention according to—

Katie: Their.

Justin: —their perception and idea of my progress. Wow! I like that one.

Katie: Yes, it's living what you wanted them to live.

Justin: I just don't want to let it go; it just brings up this turmoil inside me.

Katie: It's supposed to, honey. Tell me more about the turmoil. What are your thoughts?

Justin: There are eleven children in my family, and they're all just going "You're not doing the right thing."

Katie: Well, they could be right. And you need to live what you need to live. Obviously, you need eleven, twelve, you need thirteen people coming at you so that you can know what's true for yourself. Your path is yours. Theirs is theirs. Let's look at the next statement.

Justin: *I want them to accept me as I learn my own truth in this life.*

Katie: They're going to accept what they accept. Have they made you accept the way they live? Can they do that? Have thirteen people convinced you to follow their path?

Justin: Well, that's my work, right? Because the foundation of their life—

Katie: Yes or no. Have they convinced you to walk their path?

Justin: No.

Katie: So if you can't accept theirs, what makes you think that they can accept yours?

Justin: That's true.

Katie: Put it in perspective. Thirteen people can't convince you, and you think you're going to convince all thirteen of them? If this is war, you're outnumbered.

Justin: I know.

Katie: **How do you react when you believe the thought** "I want them to accept my way" and they don't?

Justin: It's painful.

Katie: Yes. Lonely?

Justin: Oh, yeah.

Katie: Can you see a reason to drop this theory that anyone in this world needs to accept you at any time?

Justin: I need to drop that.

Katie: I'm not asking you to drop it. I'm just asking if you can see a good reason to. You can't drop concepts; you can only shine a little flashlight on them as you do inquiry and you see that what you thought was true wasn't. And when the truth is seen, there's nothing you can do to make the lie true for you again. An example we can work on is what you've written: "I want my family to accept my way." It's hopeless. How do you treat them when you believe that thought?

Justin: I get distant.

Katie: Who would you be in your family **without the thought** "I want them to accept my way"?

Justin: Outgoing, loving.

Katie: Turn it around.

Justin: I want me to accept myself as I learn my own truth in this life.

Katie: There! If they're not doing it, who does that leave? You. So, sweetheart, can you find another turnaround? "I want me . . ."

Justin: I want me to accept them as they learn their own truth in this life.

Katie: Yes. That's all they're doing. They're just doing what you're doing. We're all doing the best we can. Let's look at the next statement.

Justin: *I want them to love me for having found parts of my own truth.*

Katie: Whose business is it who you love?

Justin: My own.

Katie: Whose business is it who they love?

Justin: Theirs.

Katie: How does it feel when you're mentally over there running their lives, dictating who they should love and why?

Justin: It's not where I should be.

Katie: Is it lonely?

Justin: Yes, very.

Katie: So let's **turn it around.**

Justin: I want me to love them for having found parts of their own truth.

Katie: Bingo! Their truth, not yours. They have a way that is so fabulous that all thirteen of them agree! Give me an example of what they say that is so painful. What's the most painful thing they could say to or about you?

Justin: That I'm lost.

Katie: Can you find the place where you've been lost a while?

Justin: Oh hell, yeah!

Katie: Okay, so they're right. The next time they say, "You're lost," you can say, "You know, I noticed that, too, one day." Yes?

Justin: Yes.

Katie: So what other terrible thing did they say that might be true? I'll tell you that for me, when someone used to say something that was true, one way I knew it was true was that I immediately felt defensive. I blocked it off, and I went to war with them in my mind and suffered all that goes with it. And they were only saying what was true. As a lover of truth, don't you really want to know what that is? Often it's the very thing that you've been looking for. What else do they say that's painful?

Justin: I feel like they interrupt me when I try to describe what I'm going through. So that's painful.

Katie: Of course it is. You think we're supposed to listen?

Justin: But doesn't a child deserve that?

Katie: No. It's not a matter of deserving. They just don't listen. "There are twelve kids here; give us a break!" **How do you react when you believe the thought** "They should listen to me" and they don't?

Justin: Lonely.

Katie: And how do you treat them when you believe that thought?

Justin: I distance myself from them.

Katie: Pretty hard to listen when you're way over there!

Justin: Yes.

Katie: "I want them to listen, so I think I'll go away."

Justin: Yes. I see your point.

Katie: Is it starting to add up a little? **Who would you be** in that amazing family **without that thought?** Who would you be if you didn't have the ability to think the thought "I want them to listen to me"?

Justin: Content and peaceful.

Katie: A listener?

Justin: A listener.

Katie: Let's **turn it around.** Let's hear how *you* should live, sweetheart, not your family.

Justin: I want me to love myself for having found parts of my own truth and foundation. Yes, I do.

Katie: So just be with it a minute . . . And the other turnaround?

Justin: I want me to love them for having found parts of their own truth and foundation. Yes. I totally love them for their happiness, but— Okay, okay. *[Justin and the audience laugh.]*

Katie: You caught it! That's big. I love how you realized what's more true for you and the judgment stopped. You laughed and stayed real. Okay, the next statement.

Justin: I already know the answer to this one.

Katie: Ah, you are good! Once we get the hang of reality, honey—ah!

Justin: *I yearn for them to respect my music that I make and—*

Katie: Hopeless.

Justin: Yes, it is.

Katie: Turn it around.

Justin: I yearn for me to respect my music.

Katie: There's another one. "I yearn for me . . ."

Justin: I yearn for me to respect their music?

Katie: Here's what their music is: "We don't want to listen, we don't want to understand. Come on our path, it works for us, we know it will work for you." That's their music. We all have our music, honey. If someone says, "Come walk on my path, it's beautiful," all I hear is that they love me with all their heart and want to give me what they see as beautiful. It just doesn't always happen to be my way. It's certainly equal to mine, though. And I love it that their way works for them and brings them happiness. All these ways! There's no path that's higher than another. Sooner or later, we begin to notice. The communication for that is "I love it that your way makes you happy. Thank you for wanting to share it with me."

Justin: I can handle that when I settle down with everything else. It would be simple to say "I'm happy for you, and I'm happy for me."

Katie: "Leave yourself out of it; we don't care! We like to hear the part where you're happy for us. Get over it!" Painful stuff. No one wants to hear about you, certainly not at the level that we want you to hear about us. That's how it is for now. Knowing that can be the end of the war in you, and there's such strength in that, and I tell you truly that the truth of what we're speaking of today will flow through your music. Isn't that what you want?

Justin: Yes. I can't believe I never saw this before.

Katie: Oh, honey. I didn't see it for forty years, until I woke up to reality, the way you're doing today. It's always just a beginning. You might go home and ask your mom to sit with you for a while. And if she says, "No, I don't have time," good! Look forward to it. There's always another way to be with her. If she's changing diapers, you might say, "Can I help you?" Or you might sit with her and just listen to what she's saying, just watch what she's doing. Invite her to tell you about her path and listen to her life, watch her light up as she speaks of her God and her way, without letting your story interfere. There are many ways to be with your mother. It might be a whole new world for you. It opens an untapped world when you are clear about what you really want. No one can deprive me of my family—no one but me. I love it that you noticed today. There's no family to save. No family to convert. There's only one, as it turns out—you.

Justin: I like that.

Katie: Let's look at the last statement on your Worksheet.

Justin: *I refuse to be left unheard.*

Katie: "I'm willing . . ."

Justin: I'm willing to be left unheard.

Katie: "I look forward to . . ."

Justin: I look forward to . . . no, I don't . . . well . . .

Katie: If they don't hear you and it hurts, do The Work again. "They're supposed to hear me"—**is that true?**

Justin: No.

Katie: How do you react when you believe the thought "They should hear me" and they don't?

Justin: Terrible.

Katie: So **who would you be without this thought,** without this lie, "They should hear me"?

Justin: Whoa . . . It's such a simple question, but there's— Wow! I'd be happy. Peaceful.

Katie: "They should hear me"—**turn it around.**

Justin: I should hear me.

Katie: There's another one.

Justin: They shouldn't hear me.

Katie: Yes. Not unless they do. And there's still another one.

Justin: I should hear them.

Katie: Yes. Hear their song. If I want my children to hear me, I'm insane. They're only going to hear what they hear, not what I say. Let me see, maybe I'll filter their hearing: "Don't hear anything but what I say." Does that sound a little crazy to you? "Don't hear anything else, don't hear your own thoughts, hear what I want you to hear, hear me." Insane. And it just doesn't work.

Justin: You waste so much energy trying to—yeah—

Katie: Direct their hearing. Hopeless. I want them to hear what they hear. I'm not crazy anymore. I'm a lover of what is. I invite you to go somewhere and be still with yourself this evening. Just be with it. And then you may want to go home and tell your family what you've discovered about yourself. Tell them so that you can hear it. And notice the thought "I want them to hear me." Notice who you are with the thought and who you are without it. Don't expect them to listen. Just say it so *you* can hear it.

Peter Broke His Word to Me

This dialogue took place in Amsterdam in 2017. Barbara was dealing with one of the most painful situations a human can be in, one of the hardest lessons in Earth School: a spouse leaving the marriage without any warning. In a situation like this, the feelings of rage and betrayal can be overwhelming. Notice how convinced she is, at the beginning, of the righteousness of her position. The first crack in her armor comes when she answers the question "Who would you be without the thought?" From that point on, she keeps opening her mind to truths that she couldn't have imagined before, until she discovers that the man who apparently betrayed her is actually the man who has pointed her toward freedom.

Katie: Okay, sweetheart. Please read the first statement on your Worksheet.

Barbara: *I'm furious with Peter because he broke his word to me.*

Katie: What's the situation?

Barbara: This was the moment, after thirty years of being together and having raised the family, when he told me he was leaving me and the children. No explanation, nothing. Just a bomb. I came home with my son on Father's Day two years ago, and we had been having a brilliant three days' entrepreneurship weekend training, and we came home, this was like twenty past ten in the evening, and he said, "There's something I need to tell you and the children."

Katie: And where were you standing or sitting?

Barbara: Sort of in the entrance hall.

Katie: So you had just walked in the door.

Barbara: Together with my son. And my son was just out of reach, and then Peter said to me, "There's something I need to tell you." And I could sense something was up.

Katie: Yes.

Barbara: So I said, "Let's sit down, shut the door and not have the children hear this." And then he said, "Three weeks ago I met another woman, and I want to share the rest of my life with her, and I'm leaving you and the children."

Katie: Okay. So were you still standing in the hall, or did you go to another place?

Barbara: No, we sat down in the lounge, on the settee in the lounge.

Katie: He broke his word to you—**is that true?**

Barbara: Yes!

Katie: He broke his word to you—**can you absolutely know that it's true?**

Barbara [closing her eyes and pausing]: Yes.

Katie: Good. So close your eyes again, and see yourself in that situation with Peter and look at his face. Notice his body language. Look at yourself. Notice your body language and your emotions. He broke his word to you. **How do you react, what happens, when you believe that thought?**

Barbara: I just freeze. I'm in shock. I just can't believe it, and I don't accept it. Or I don't accept him. I don't accept him having the guts to put it to me like that.

Katie: Look at him now without the thought "He broke his word to you." Look at his face. Look into his eyes. Get really present. **Who would you be without the thought?**

Barbara: Who would I be without the thought?

Katie: Just drop your story. Look at Peter.

Barbara: Honestly? I'd be relieved. Wow! I never thought of this before.

Katie: Relieved. And how would you turn the thought around? Sometimes I find a turnaround that's a little weird. Do you want to hear it?

Barbara: Yes.

Katie [speaking slowly, in a depressed tone]: "He broke his word to me." And here's the turnaround. [Speaking in an energized, happy tone] "He broke his word to me!" Relief. And it's quite a jump from relief to happiness, but you could be going there.

Barbara: Yes, but the fear is still there. I'm relieved that he made the choice, because I realized I would never have made that choice myself. Never.

Katie: You may end up sending him a thank-you note. *[Laughter from the audience.]*

Barbara: Oh, I *have* written him a thank-you note.

Katie: Good.

Barbara: Not sent it, but I've written it. *[More laughter.]*

Katie: Can you find another turnaround?

Barbara: I broke my word to me.

Katie: What does that mean to you? Where in that situation did you break your word to him?

Barbara: That fear, the violence, kept me from speaking the real truth.

Katie: Yes.

Barbara: That's still the case.

Katie: Yes. We're just noticing. I have another turnaround. Would you like to hear it?

Barbara: Yes.

Katie: "He kept his word to me." In that situation, when you try that on, what do you see?

Barbara: He didn't keep his word to me the way I thought it then, but he was being honest with me. He was speaking truthfully. It was his truth.

Katie: All right, let's look at statement two.

Barbara: *I want him to acknowledge his breaking his word to me and explain to me why he chose what he chose to do. And I want him to take responsibility for his choices and his behavior.* Behavior—that's the fear part.

Katie: You want him to acknowledge his breaking his word to you—**is it true?**

Barbara: No.

Katie: And **how do you react, what happens, when you believe the thought** "I want him to acknowledge his breaking his word to me"?

Barbara: I put myself in a place of being dependent on his actions or his words. And I don't want that. I don't need that.

Katie: Yes. Now close your eyes and look at him without the thought that you want him to do this, that you want him to acknowledge breaking his word to you. **Who would you be without the thought** "I want him to acknowledge that he broke his word to me"?

Barbara: Who would I be? I would be . . . I would be more comfortable. And I would be able to focus on me and my life and not be so busy with what I think *he* ought to do or say.

Katie: Yes.

Barbara: I would be free.

Katie: So now close your eyes and look at him again in that situation. And just stay there and, without the thought "I want him to acknowledge" anything, just listen to him. Get connected. Take yourself out of there and listen to him. He's saying he's leaving. He wants to live with someone else.

Barbara: He has made up his mind. He wants to share the rest of his life with someone else.

Katie: Yes.

Barbara: Period. Hearing him without that thought is much less stressful.

Katie: Now **turn the thought around:** "I want me . . ."

Barbara: I want me to acknowledge—

Katie: "That I broke my word to myself."

Barbara: That I broke my word to myself.

Katie: Yes. And also "I want me to acknowledge that I broke my word to him."

Barbara: I want me to acknowledge that I broke my word to him.

Katie: So when you try that on, what do you see? Where is it that you broke your word to him?

Barbara: I never— There's a way of breaking your word by not saying the words, and that's what I've done. Not saying things I ought to have said.

Katie: Beautiful.

Barbara: At least . . . I have voiced rather than telling something.

Katie: Yes. I want him to take responsibility for doing what he did—**is that true?**

Barbara: Yes. *[Laughter from the audience.]* It's true that I think that. I realize that it doesn't help me.

Katie: No. So let's test it. **How do you react, what happens, when you believe the thought** that you want him to take responsibility for doing what he did?

Barbara: It's stressful, because I know it's not going to happen. And I have a really, really hard time owning up to myself that I don't need that.

Katie: Yes. Now notice your world without the thought "I want him to take responsibility for doing what he did." **Who would you be without that thought?** What would your world look like without it? What would that conversation look like without that thought? This really takes focus. Just look at him in that situation without this thought.

Barbara: What would it look like? Yes, I'm trying to find the words. I think it would look like— He can breathe freely, not having to explain anything. And I can let go of fearing what I don't want to hear. Or, rather—

Katie: Without that thought, you really don't care if he takes responsibility for doing what he did.

Barbara: Well, I think it's more that he doesn't owe me that. If he wants to, he can, but I shouldn't be thinking he owes me that.

Katie: It's just not something you insist on or even want him to do. Let's look at statement three.

Barbara: *Peter should make time to talk to me, show me that he cares about the children and me as a valuable person, and apologize for scaring me.*

Katie: So Peter scared you—**is it true?**

Barbara: Well, yes. Maybe not by what he said, but—

Katie: Well, let's meditate on that for a moment. You're in the discussion. The two of you are there. Peter scared you—**is it true?**

Barbara: No. I was scared, but he didn't scare me in that moment.

Katie: Peter said what he said. That's one thing. But you believed your thoughts about what he said, and that's what scared you. Peter scared you—**how do you react, what happens, when you believe the thought** "Peter scared me"?

Barbara: I break my word. When I believe that, I don't really hear what's going on. I hear what I *think* is going on.

Katie: Peter scared you. **How do you react, what happens, when you believe the thought** that he's the one who is scaring you?

Barbara: I don't know what happens. I just freeze.

Katie: So listen to what he says. Drop your story. Look at him without the thought "He's scaring me." Just take it in. Listen. Notice the images of past and future. What do you see? You see a life without him. What do those images of the future look like when you think the thought "He's scaring me"?

Barbara: That he will hit me again. And blame me.

Katie: Yes. **Who would you be without the thought** "He's scaring me"?

Barbara: I would trust myself.

Katie: So tell me who is scaring you? Is it Peter? Or the images in your head?

Barbara: My mind. My thoughts.

Katie: You see an image in your head of him hitting you. You see an image of the past when he hit you. You see an image of the future when he'll hit you. And you can't hear him in the present. You're frightened. And it's interfering with your listening.

Barbara: Yes. My thoughts are causing that.

Katie: Very few human beings can get still enough to see how powerful the mind is and what really frightens us. You can't be frightened if your mind stays in the present. The remembering is where the fear is. The anticipation is where the fear is. Our lives are either remembered or anticipated, and when it comes to what you have been through, it's so good to know who is frightening you. I love you have that all the days of your life. "Peter scared me"—**turn it around.** "Peter didn't . . ."

Barbara: Peter didn't scare me.

Katie: In that situation, it's was your own thoughts of past and future that scared you. And then you look at Peter with this fear. It seems as though he's doing it, but—

Barbara [*pointing to her head*]: It happens in here.

Katie [*making a kissing noise*]: Mmmwa! Let's look at the next statement on number three now.

Barbara: Peter should *show me that he cares about the children.* He should show me that he cares about the consequences his choice will have on the children. I didn't write that, but that's what it was. I didn't mean to say that he doesn't care about them. But the consequences of his choice.

Katie: So it would be "Peter should understand how this is going to affect the children"?

Barbara: Not necessarily the effects, but that it will have a profound effect on them. Yes.

Katie: "This will have a profound effect on our children."

Barbara: Yes. That's what I needed.

Katie: Is it true? Peter's leaving will have a profound effect on your children. So you're in that conversation with Peter, and you have the thought "Peter should understand that this will have a profound effect on the children." **Is it true** that he should understand that?

Barbara: Ah. Is it true that he should understand that? No. No.

Katie: Good one, huh?

Barbara: Yes. Thank you.

Katie *[to the audience]*: Are you all doing your Work? On those people who "should understand"?

Barbara: That's ridiculous, really. *[Laughter and applause from the audience.] [To the audience]* Thank you.

Katie: "Peter should understand that this will have a profound effect on the children"—**how do you react, what happens, when you believe that thought?**

Barbara: Incredibly angry. Self-righteous.

Katie: Close your eyes and look at Peter in that conversation, without the thought that he should understand. Without that, as you just said, ridiculous thought.

Barbara: Yes, that's just me lecturing. It has nothing to do with him. Yes, without the thought, I feel much lighter, freer. And more compassionate toward him.

Katie: Good stuff. Now **turn it around:** "I should . . ."

Barbara: I should understand that this has a profound effect on the children.

Katie: Yes. This advice is for you. He's going off to be happy. *[Laughter from the audience.]*

Barbara: Ah.

Katie: And you're going to be left with what? Whatever you're believing. And that's as bad as it's ever going to get.

Barbara: That's bad sometimes. What I'm thinking can be really bad.

Katie: It's like "Whew! That was a good one. That was depressing. That one really scared me." Once we understand them, these difficult emotions show us what we're believing, and we know how to question the thoughts behind them. This mind is so beautiful when you understand how to deal with it. It will bring you joy all the days of your life.

Barbara: I believe that. I've done The Work on my own with your book and your Worksheets before, also on this issue, and I got nowhere with that. But I've had wonderful results with other thoughts. So I know it can work. I never could figure out why. Yes, I think I know the why, but what I can do or how I can do that Work differently. Is that the question? So maybe I've given my own answer.

Katie: I think so.

Barbara: If I don't dare to speak my truth, then I can't do The Work. Yes. Okay. *[Laughter and applause from the audience.]* Yes. I got that. Thank you.

Katie: So the turnaround: "Peter shouldn't understand."

Barbara: No. He doesn't need to understand anything.

Katie: He should show you that he cares about the children—**is it true?**

Barbara: Yes, I think so. But no, he shouldn't. I do think it would help them. So I have convictions there.

Katie: So close your eyes. You see him? You're in the conversation. He should show you that he cares about the children—**is it true?**

Barbara: No. No. He doesn't have to show me. That's it. Okay.

Katie: Good. Trust your words. The ones you wrote on paper. It's really important. The ego's going to want to change them. Notice those images of past and future involving your children when you believe the thought "Peter should show me that he cares about the children."

Barbara: Yes. I don't want that thought anymore.

Katie: There's you. There's Peter. And then there is your imagination running into the past and future. And you see those poor children, whose father doesn't show that he cares.

Barbara: The poor children. "The father doesn't show *me* that he cares."

Katie: Very good. "Peter should show me that he cares about the children."

Barbara: Yes, exactly. And he should show his girlfriend. Yes, no. *[Laughter from the audience.]*

Katie: Well, you know, here's the way it works. What Peter was believing onto you, he has to believe onto this new relationship. He's going to take his beliefs with him. So let's just deal with your life.

Barbara: That's the good news.

Katie: Unless you're her. *[Laughter from the audience.]*

Barbara: In more ways than one. I don't mean that sarcastically. Yes. But I should let him go, too.

Katie: Well, whether you let him go or not, he's gone.

Barbara: Okay, yes.

Katie *[pointing to her head]*: You're talking about in here.

Barbara: It would help me if I can get him out of my—

Katie: No, keep him here. He's your teacher. He's the one who will enlighten you. That's what every human being is for. They bring you enlightenment. You look at what you're thinking and believing about them, and you wake up to reality like that. You become a better mother, a better friend, a better—an amazing life. Peter should show you that he cares about the children—**turn it around.**

Barbara: Um, Peter shouldn't show me that he cares about the children. And I should show—

Katie: Me.

Barbara: Me that I care about the children.

Katie: Yes. And if he's ever around, you can show him that you care about the children.

Barbara: Surely.

Katie: That one doesn't fit very well for me. I'll leave that one to you. You know what I mean? If I want to show anyone that I care, then I'm not really caring.

Barbara: No, I should live caring for the children.

Katie: Yes.

Barbara: Not by demonstrating but just by caring.

Katie: Yes. That's it. Okay, let's look at the next statement.

Barbara: Five. This is not very nice. *[Laughter from the audience.]*

Katie: Well, it says a lot for you that you wrote it. I've got to take seriously what I was believing in a situation, or I'm going to take it with me all the days of my life. I've got to question these beliefs. I see thoughts as unloved children. They scream for attention, and they come back and back and back and back. But if we just identify and take one dear child, one thought, no matter how vile, and we just write it down and sit with it the way you would sit patiently with your own child and just have this talk with it like: "Sweetheart, is it true?" You know, we're questioning thoughts. These are not people. It's what we're thinking and believing about people and about ourselves. So eventually the mind finds a home in itself. It ends the war with itself. And that's the enlightened mind. The kind mind. The one we're waking up to here. So read what you've written that you consider as unkind. And the ego is not kind. The ego is doing its best to stay and to identify as an object. And that's hard work. Because it can never be.

Barbara: Okay, I'll read it. *[Laughter from the audience.]* Peter is selfish, cowardly, untrustworthy, violent, weak, irresponsible, cruel, forceful, and intimidating.

Katie: Okay.

Barbara: It's not kind.

Katie: Well, you know, it's what you were thinking at that moment. In the interest of time, let's skip inquiry and **turn it around.** You can investigate it with the four questions when you go home. "In that moment with Peter, I was . . ." "In that moment with Peter, I am selfish . . ." And go down your list.

Barbara: I was selfish?

Katie: Uh-huh. So in that situation, where were you selfish? In that situation. Just that one. Where were you selfish?

Barbara: Demanding an explanation. Wanting him to live up to promises that he clearly wasn't able any longer to keep. And wanting to make him feel responsible for making me happy.

Katie: Good, sweetheart. I have another one. Where was I selfish? I wasn't celebrating his new life. Where was I selfish? I didn't take time out to say "What is she like?" *[Laughter from the audience.]* I could have asked him, "Where are you going to live? What are your plans? Does she love you?" Can you imagine that? Or are you not quite there yet?

Barbara: Well, yes, I am now.

Katie: Yay!

Barbara: But I wasn't in that moment.

Katie: That will give you a conversation the next time you're with him.

Barbara: Really?

Katie: Potentially, sooner or later. You know, it's all about me, me, me, me, me, and that is asleepness. That's why it's so painful. So where were you selfish in that situation? When you're doing this Work, it does take stillness, and it takes an open mind, and it takes courage. Because we're talking about the death of an ego. The death of false self. If it's all about me, that's false self. So it's a process. Now where were you cowardly?

Barbara: I was cowardly in not speaking my full truth.

Katie: And if you live with someone who hits you, that can also be very wise and you can thank yourself. But just to know the difference. One thing I love about The Work is that what we discover gives us a communication that is indisputably safe. It's wise, as opposed to defensive or coming from a place of want or need. So we learn a language in this Work through our turnarounds. "Peter is untrustworthy." In that situation, where were you untrustworthy? And we're just looking at a moment in time, one situation in time. So where is it that you were untrustworthy?

Barbara: I'm not sure.

Katie: Well, we look at the thoughts that we have questioned so far.

Barbara: Yes. Okay. I was untrustworthy in that moment by seeing but not wanting to acknowledge where he was, that he couldn't help himself. This was the only thing he could do and say. And I was really aware of that—acutely aware. And I just didn't want to know.

Katie: Yes.

Barbara: From my husband.

Katie: He was violent. In that situation, where were you violent?

Barbara: Telling him I didn't accept it. I didn't accept what he said.

Katie: Yes. Where were you irresponsible in that situation?

Barbara: I was irresponsible—

Katie: Notice the images of past and future that you were believing, as opposed to just hearing and seeing Peter in reality.

Barbara: I was irresponsible in the sense that I kept asking why. I kept asking for an explanation why and what's going to happen. I kept asking questions knowing there weren't going to be any answers.

Katie: Oh, that's beautiful to be in touch with. That can serve you your entire life.

Barbara: Yes. What worries me is that I realized that at the time I couldn't help myself.

Katie: Yes. But this Work can really help you. We can't change what we're not awake to. But once we're out of denial, once we wake up to reality, it changes on its own. We make clearer decisions because we're not so crazy. Where were you intimidating in that situation?

Barbara: I just kept asking the questions. And my tone of voice.

Katie: Yes.

Barbara: Damn.

Katie: And forceful.

Barbara: For two hours I asked questions. I think I found myself intimidating.

Katie: So, precious friend, let's look at number six.

Barbara: Okay. I don't ever—

Katie: Wait just a moment. *[To the audience]* How many of you are experiencing a very close connection with this woman right now? Would you raise your hands? *[Many people raise their hands.]* *[To Barbara]* Look. Just keep looking at their hands. *[To the audience]* How many of you see yourselves as you're listening to her Work? *[Most people keep their hands up in the air.]*

Barbara: Wow!

Katie: Let's look at number six.

Barbara: *I don't ever want to feel inferior, scared, dependent, or powerless again.*

Katie: Turn it around: "I'm willing to . . ."

Barbara: But I'm not!

Katie: Would you agree that it could happen again?

Barbara: Well, all of these things that were said and done could happen again, but I don't ever want to take it on board like that again. I don't need to take it as me being inferior. That's what I mean.

Katie: It's true. And you *could* take it that way again.

Barbara: Oh, yes. That's true. *[Laughter from the audience.]*

Katie: "I'm willing to . . ."

Barbara: I'm willing to feel inferior or scared or dependent or powerless again.

Katie: The moment you do, it's just another Worksheet. If you notice that you're feeling inferior, you begin to write down what you're thinking and believing, and don't trust your mind. If you don't write it down, your ego will take over the inquiry. This is a practice. It's a practice in stillness. And to just sit with it, just like twenty or thirty minutes every morning, it's so powerful.

Barbara: I just realized something. I want a quick fix every time. I don't spend twenty minutes on a question. So—

Katie: Oh, twenty or thirty minutes on a Worksheet every morning. What happens is all the choices in your life, what you eat, when you go to bed, what you do. The clearer your mind gets, the more sane your choices, until you can send her a thank-you note. Until then, your Work's just not done. And it would be a thank-you note where you really mean it. *[Laughter from the audience.]* So "I look forward to . . ."

Barbara: All of them? *[Laughter from the audience.]* I look forward to feeling inferior and scared and dependent and powerless again.

Katie: Yes. It's like a prayer. It's like "Keep bringing it on, so I can become enlightened to it every time." It's not done until it's done. And more people than I could possibly count are getting free of this. And you know it works because you've experienced it on your own. So twenty or thirty minutes every morning, and it's just like you're saying "Bring it on. Bring it on." Open your arms to the world and say, "Just take me." I live that way. I can honestly say that. It's like I'm living a life of "I'm willing to, I look forward to." And everything is welcome here. The worst that can happen is what I'm believing about me, about you, and the world. And that can be questioned. And again, it is a practice. I have enjoyed so thoroughly sitting with someone as beautiful as you. Thank you for this privilege.

Barbara: Thank you, too, Katie.

My Son and Daughter-in-Law Are Being Reckless

This dialogue took place in July 2020, in the midst of the coronavirus pandemic, on my webcast, *At Home with BK.* Gloria began the dialogue feeling what most parents feel: a desire for her children to be safe in dangerous times. But once she realized that this desire is a subtle form of selfishness, she was able to step back and take responsibility for her own fears. This will make her a saner human being and a better parent.

Gloria: *I'm upset with my son and daughter-in-law because they're being reckless.*

Katie: What's the situation?

Gloria: I saw on Facebook that they have a weeklong trip planned for September, when the second wave of the pandemic is supposed to be coming.

Katie: Yes, if we ever hit the end of this first wave.

Gloria: Yeah. I'm in Canada on a small island, and on the island where we are, there's only one case.

Katie: Oh, my goodness! Good job.

Gloria: Yes. We've got a good doctor here. But they're going to a Canadian hot spot. So I see that they're planning this airplane trip and the airplanes have just announced that they're going to pack their customers again. They're not having social distancing on the airplane anymore, so my son and daughter-in-law are going to be on a packed airplane in September going to a Canadian hot spot, and they're putting out feelers for friends and relatives to pick them up, and they're planning the hugs that they're going to have with them. And I'm having a heart attack.

Katie: Exciting! So now close your eyes. Where were you when you were looking at that Facebook page? Imagine yourself right there. In your mind's eye, you're opening the Facebook page, you're looking at it, and you have the thought "They're being reckless." So "They're being reckless"—**is it true?**

Gloria: Yes.

Katie: Can you absolutely know that it's true that they're being restless? *[To the Internet audience]* So all of you: join in this and answer the question for yourselves. Don't let the word *absolutely* fool you. That's just to support you to go more deeply than the first question if your mind says, "Yes" to "Is it true?" Go under that, and see if you missed anything. *[To Gloria]* The answer is always one word only. It's either yes or no. In that meditative state, just allow what is shown to you to live. Yes and no are equal; one answer isn't better than the other. We're just looking for the truth here—not the world's truth, not other people's truth, but your own. "They're being reckless"—**can you absolutely know that it's true?**

Gloria: No.

Katie: Just feel that.

Gloria: It's scary to feel it.

Katie: It *is* scary. The ego doesn't want to let go of its beliefs. That's dangerous to its existence. **How do you react, what happens, when you believe the thought** that they're being reckless?

Gloria: I'm scared. I want to protect them. I want them to listen to their mom.

Katie: That's how you react when you believe the thought as a mother. You believe that it's your job to enlighten them, to save their lives. If you don't, their death is your fault.

Gloria: Yeah.

Katie: It's not a little thing, this ego. This isn't about right or wrong, it's about waking up to a reality within you that you can't even imagine, it runs so deeply in you. It takes courage to question the thoughts that you believe. Okay, close your eyes. Let's look at that third question again. **How do you react, what happens** emotionally and physically, **when you believe the thought** "They're being reckless"? Get in touch with your emotions. And as you become aware of them, describe these emotions to us with your eyes closed.

Gloria: I'm afraid. I feel powerless.

Katie: Okay. Now, what are the physical reactions that happen when you believe the thought "They're being reckless."

Gloria: There's a tightening in my chest, a tightening in my throat, my stomach sinks, my hands sweat. My breathing is shallow.

Katie: Keep your eyes closed, and just experience how that may affect your immune system. The breath is shallow; the body is not flowing.

Gloria: It affects my ability to parent properly, too. It affects my ability to be present with myself and enjoy what's happening.

Katie: Stay in touch with your body. The question is **How do you react, what happens, when you believe the thought?** These emotions raise blood pressure, I've heard. They affect diabetes, blood sugar.

Gloria: My muscles get tight.

Katie: We're meditating in that moment as you're looking at the Facebook page. **How do you react when you believe the thought**

"They're being reckless"? There's only one way you can believe that thought. It's the ego's job to keep you in the not-now. So what movie images of past/future do you see in your mind when you go back and witness yourself in that situation, looking at the Facebook page?

Gloria: I see an image of trying to prevent my son from taking a trip I thought was dangerous a couple of years ago. I see a future of them getting sick. I see trips to the emergency room with my son when he was little because he had respiratory difficulties.

Katie: So you see those moments of a mother's terror for the life of her son in the past, and you see a future where you can't even get to him, the hospital's full or they won't let you in, and he dies alone. We've seen that on television where people can't get to their loved ones. Now, as you witness those images of past/future, those images of not-now, as you experience the movie of not-now, notice yourself looking at the Facebook entry without the thought "They're being reckless." Look at the Facebook page again. Catch up with your children's joy.

Gloria: They have a lot of really exciting plans. They're going to visit where my daughter-in-law is from, and they love traveling, and they've worked hard to make this happen, and they need to go.

Katie: And what was the cause of your suffering as you experienced reading the Facebook entry?

Gloria: Thinking that I know. Thinking that I know what's best.

Katie: Look at the movie.

Gloria: Ugh.

Katie: Have you ever been to a movie where it's frightened you and you wanted to run out of the theater?

Gloria: Uh-huh.

Katie: Well, this one you can't run out of because that's the life of a believer. The only way to escape the dream of suffering is to be awake to the dream, which means to look at who you are without the dream. Are you okay in that situation, other than what you're think-ing and believing?

Gloria: I'm okay.

Katie: Check it out. Don't take it for granted. Is your breath flowing?

Gloria: Yes.

Katie: There's a little smile on your face. You're waking up from the dream.

Gloria: It's really hard to separate the dream from the parenting.

Katie: Well, that's a dream as well. You have your children sick in the past and dead in the future, and you're missing the trip. Your thoughts are separating you from them. You can't call your son and say, "I read your Facebook page, sweetheart, and I see how excited you are!"

Gloria: I called them, and I didn't admit that I had seen the Face-book page. I just talked about how dangerous it is to travel.

Katie: Yes. So one of the ways you react to that thought is that you become deceptive.

Gloria: Yes. I think it's for their own good.

Katie: And she doesn't get to meet her mother-in-law, and he doesn't get to meet his mother. They meet deception. And as the ego would have it, just as you said, it's only for their own good. That's how we rationalize it. It's asleepness.

Gloria: It doesn't feel good.

Katie: No. One of my sons might say, "Mom, I'm jumping off a cliff. Save me." And I might say, knowing me, "Sweetheart, do you really think that's a good idea?" And if he says "Yes" and jumps, I respect that he's doing the best that he can. And if he says, "Mom, what do you think?" I can tell him the truth. "I don't want you to jump off the cliff, because I want you in my life."

Gloria: But they haven't asked.

Katie: No, I'm just saying "if." And that's a beautiful thing. They don't ask if they don't trust us, and we teach them deception. I think that's the difference. As far as I know, my sons have no hesitation in talking with me about very intimate matters. They bring these things to me because they trust me. It's amazing that they trust me so deeply when I realize what a crazed, desperately unhappy mother I was, the mother who raised them. I'm continually amazed and grateful when I look at the difference. Okay. **Who would you be without the thought** "They're being reckless"?

Gloria: I'd be calmer. I wouldn't worry so much.

Katie: "They're being reckless"—**turn it around.**

Gloria: They're not being reckless.

Katie: Good. **Can you find another turnaround?**

Gloria: Hmm. *[Pauses.]*

Katie: What's the opposite of reckless?

Gloria: Safe.

Katie: Well, try that one on. How are they being safe? What's an example?

Gloria: Well, they have access to all the information I have, and they've made their considered decision about how to conduct themselves in it, and they're adults, they can do that. They have their priorities.

Katie: Now look more closely. Where exactly is it that they're being safe? Why skim over the top when this is a meditative process? You have days to sit in this turnaround. "They're being safe." As you consider the turnaround, you might even call them and say, "I read your Facebook page, and I wondered how safe you're being. What plan do you have in place? I'm fascinated that you're taking the trip, and as your mother I really want to know. I stay informed about the pandemic, and if you ever need help, I'm here to support you in that. I can do research, or whatever it takes." Do you see what kind of conversation you can have?

Gloria: Uh-huh.

Katie: Your openness would just open up the conversation. It's a way of joining. It's the opposite of fear and deception. It's an innocent, fearless state of mind. We mature as we sit in inquiry and begin to know ourselves and what we're believing about our children. Our children are great teachers in that. But I don't really know my children until I question what I believe about them.

Gloria: Maybe they're being safe, even if their trip includes catching the virus and whatever consequences come of that.

Katie: I don't know. But to ponder it the way you're doing is to open your mind. An open mind flows directly into love. The ego's job, on the other hand, is to nail in the thought it believes, to solidify it into the opposite of love.

Gloria: That's not safe.

Katie: No, it's not safe. It's reckless to your health. It's reckless to the relationship you have with your son and his wife.

Gloria: That's not proper treasuring of my son.

Katie: No, it goes against the heart. We would do it differently if we knew how. And this Work is how. So "They're being reckless"—**can you find another turnaround?**

Gloria: I'm being reckless by solidifying my thoughts about them, not allowing things to flow, living out of fear.

Katie: And by not recognizing the *cause* of your fear. It's not your son and his trip. It's happening with you, in your mind, as you sit in your chair at home, and nothing terrible has happened. It's reckless to be lost in a dream that torments you. Okay, let's move to statement number two on your Judge-Your-Neighbor Worksheet.

Gloria: *I want them to avoid unnecessary travel during the pandemic.*

Katie: Is that true? *[To the audience]* And all of you, ponder that question. See how the statement applies to your own life, and then really consider if it's true. *[To Gloria]* **Is it true** that you want them to avoid unnecessary travel during the pandemic?

Gloria: I want them to do what they do.

Katie: Remember that the answer to the first and second questions consists of one syllable only. It's yes or no, period. When you say more than that, when you try to justify or defend or explain, you're no longer doing The Work. And remember that you're answering out of your state of mind in the situation—when you were looking at their Facebook page.

Gloria: Okay.

Katie: "I want them to do what they do" sounds rational and mature, but was that what you were thinking when you were in that situation?

Gloria: No, certainly not.

Katie: "I want them to avoid unnecessary travel during the pandemic"—**is it true?**

Gloria: Yes.

Katie: Good. Now get still. Drop under what you think you know, then drop under that, until the answer finds you. This is meditation. It takes a lot of stillness. "I want them to avoid unnecessary travel during the pandemic"—**can you absolutely know that it's true?**

Gloria: No.

Katie: Okay. *[To the audience]* Now, some of you are still a "yes." We all come to our own answers. This work is so powerful, and it doesn't matter whether your answer here is a yes or a no, because the point is to find your own truth, whatever is true for you as you sit in the question with an open mind. *[To Gloria]* So now let's move on to question three: **How do you react, what happens, when you believe the thought** "I want them to avoid unnecessary travel during the pandemic"? Close your eyes and witness the images that arise. We're looking at the cause of suffering. You believe the thought, and the effect is your suffering. That's what we're meditating in; that's what we're inviting. **How do you react, what happens, when you believe that thought?**

Gloria: There's a constriction in my chest. My breathing is shallow. My head is confused, scrambled. I see images of him in crowded airports and crowded airplanes and crowded buses.

Katie: Yes, so now you've left your own safety. You've already seen that right here, right now, you have everything you need. You're okay in reality. But you imagine yourself into airports and buses, and you imagine yourself into the past with your son and his compromised health. He gets the virus, with his compromised health, as you sit here in this given space—some people would say this God-given space or this friendly universe. The ego can say, "Yeah, but . . . Yeah, but . . . Yeah, but that's not being responsible." But other than what you're thinking and believing, you're okay. You're living in a state of grace, and you trade it for hell. It affects your body, it affects everything we go to doctors for, and then we take pills to shut down what? The mind. But what if we didn't try to shut it down? What if we met it with understanding, with the realization that we're only suffering because of our stressful thoughts? Without the thoughts, there's no suffering. Life is heaven. "I want them to avoid unnecessary travel during the pandemic"—**who would you be without that thought?**

Gloria: I would be relaxed. I wouldn't be trying, in my mind, to manipulate them into not going.

Katie: "I want them to avoid unnecessary travel during the pandemic"—**turn it around.** "I want me . . ."

Gloria: I want me to avoid unnecessary travel during the pandemic.

Katie: And what is that unnecessary travel?

Gloria: I'm sitting at my kitchen table, but in my mind I'm in a crowded airplane full of covid-19.

Katie: Yes. That's unnecessary travel. You don't have to go there. It's not necessary, and it's not helpful. It's causing you a lot of stress.

Gloria: I see that.

Katie: Yes. And we don't do it on purpose.

Gloria: Ah.

Katie: The stress arises to get your attention. How else can the mind identify as object, as an I? But when we question it, we begin to wake up from the dream.

Gloria: Okay.

Katie: There's no harm, no foul. I can breathe again.

Gloria: Aha.

Katie: I can brush my teeth without saying "Oh, I should do it later." This crazy dream affects everything, right down to brushing our teeth. You're just looking at the war within and how we get hooked on suffering and the stressful emotions that you're showing us so beautifully and how these emotions are caused by believing a thought. So anytime you experience the emotions, just know their cause. When you wake up from the dream, you say, "I'm such a silly goose. Ego, you got me again." It's not something bad we're doing. We're innocent. There's no harm. This is Earth School, it's why we're here, to wake up to who we really are.

Gloria: Thoughts about the children's safety are very good hooks.

Katie: Yes, they are. That's why we have children in our life. This Earth School is set up for the people we worry about. They're our teachers. The things we don't like—those are our teachers. We come to be very grateful for them, because they wake us up. *[To the audience]* I hope you're all getting a lot from this. In the States, we need good teachers. Some of us think that it's just marvelous not to wear a mask at the height of the pandemic. What a wild and wonderful world! Some of you might think, "That's crazy, how can they do that?" But what am I believing that's just as crazy? I look to myself. In what ways am I not wearing a mask? In what ways am I not protecting others, especially my children? I think I know what they should do. That's reckless. It's putting my children at risk.

Gloria: I certainly do that with my kids.

Katie: Yes. And if I believed what those antimask people believe, I wouldn't wear a mask, either. I'd have no choice. My job is to wake up, and when I think of those people, who endanger themselves and others, I experience compassion for them and for the people they love. I want to say it again: if I believed what they believed, I'd be in the same place. Ignorance is another term for asleepness. Okay, "I want them to avoid unnecessary travel during the pandemic"—**can you find another turnaround?** Let's look at the 180-degree opposite.

Gloria: I *don't* want them to avoid unnecessary travel during the pandemic. Hmm. I can find that in my intellect, I guess. But I really think that avoiding unnecessary travel is a good idea in a pandemic.

Katie: Well, that's what you may think, but your job here is to try on the turnaround. We're not exchanging one belief for another. We're just trying on the opposite, as if we're trying on a pair of new shoes, to see if they fit. "I *don't* want them to avoid unnecessary travel." How might this one fit?

Gloria: Well, I guess I want them to do what they need to do, what they want to do.

Katie: Don't guess. Really try this one on. Could it be just as true as your original statement?

Gloria *[after a pause]*: Yes. I don't want them to avoid unnecessary travel. I don't want them to avoid it if they really think that's what they need to do. To them it feels *necessary* to take this trip. There's been a death in her family, and they want to go. They think it's necessary. Their definition of necessary is their own. It's different from my definition.

Katie: Exactly. And there's a compassion in that. There's an understanding within you that wasn't there before. This changes the conversation. It doesn't mean that they won't catch the virus.

Gloria: They might. They're setting themselves up for it.

Katie: Not a lot a mother can do. They just make those trips and keep them from us.

Gloria: They have, in effect, kept it from me. I only happened to see it on Facebook.

Katie: "We don't want to bother Mom. We don't want to upset Mom."

Gloria: They think they're responsible for my happiness.

Katie: And I love that you're catching up with them, to be as kind to yourself as they have been to you, as sensitive to yourself as they've been.

Gloria: How do you see that?

Katie: They haven't told you about their trip. They're trying to spare your feelings. They don't want you to worry. That's kind.

Gloria: Oh, yeah. I hadn't looked at it that way. I just saw them as trying to avoid my involvement or—

Katie: No, that was you toward them.

Gloria: Ah. Okay.

Katie: Let's look at statement three, the shoulds.

Gloria: *They should stay home, they shouldn't go on packed airplanes, they should remember that my son has a history of respiratory trouble.*

Katie: So does any of that seem true to you, as you consider it? "They should stay home"—**is it true?**

Gloria: That's what the medical experts are urging us to do.

Katie: Okay. And I'm going to remind you about the answers to questions one and two: one syllable only. Yes or no. "They should stay home"—**is it true?**

Gloria: Yes.

Katie: Good. So during the covid-19 pandemic, they should stay home—**can you absolutely know that it's true?**

Gloria: No, I can't absolutely know that.

Katie: Sweetheart, see how it feels to answer with a simple no and nothing else. Just sit with it. Let it drop in.

Gloria: No. *[Long pause.]*

Katie: Even if they die, can you absolutely know that it's true that they should stay home? As I often say, "Who needs God when you have *your* opinion?"

Gloria: Yeah.

Katie: "This is my world. I'm the great leader who knows everything and decides everything, and I know that they should stay home, and I'm just going to be upset until they agree with me."

Gloria: That's my role as Mom: do whatever it takes to get them to do what's safe and best for them.

Katie: And we wonder why, with that attitude, we have poor family relations sometimes. Okay, what do you get if they said, "Oh, you're right, Mom," and they cancel their trip?

Gloria: I get to feel that they're safe, safer than they would have been. I get to know that they're not exposing themselves to unnecessary travel.

Katie: And what do *you* get for yourself? You get to feel secure.

Gloria: Yes. They've made my life easier.

Katie: So it's really all about you.

Gloria: Yes, I see that. It's all about me.

Katie: And if they don't die, what do you get? You get not to suffer.

Gloria: Yes. They could spare me a lot of suffering.

Katie: If they don't go, you're happy. If they do go, you're not happy. You, you, you. And then there's you, and then there's you. Just all about you. Nothing there for your son. But if you were thinking of what *he* wants, you could say, "Sweetheart, I saw on Facebook that you've planned this trip, and if you caught the virus and died, I just don't know how I'd manage, but I would."

Gloria: Yes. That's true. That's honest.

Katie: "And I prefer that you're in my life. I love you. And yes, I'm going to worry, and that's for me to take care of."

Gloria: I do have a preference for him being alive and healthy.

Katie: It's so that you can have a happy life.

Gloria: It's not about him having a happy life?

Katie: Well, the ego would tell you so, but it assumes that he doesn't. He wants to take this trip.

Gloria: But if he places himself in harm's way—

Katie: The question is, how dependent am I on my children?

Gloria: So I have to give him his freedom.

Katie: *You* have to give him his freedom? It's not yours to give. He *has* his freedom.

Gloria: I have to give myself my freedom from thinking that his . . .

Katie: I would just realize that I want them to stay home because *I'm* better off that way. "They shouldn't go on a packed airplane because they could die and then that would affect *my* life. I'd be heartbroken. My son should remember that he has respiratory trouble because that will keep him from going and it will make me feel better. I would be so relieved if they don't go." This isn't right or wrong. It's just about acknowledging that you don't leave a lot of room for your children. You don't respect their choices. **How do you react, what happens, when you believe the thought** that they should stay home and they don't?

Gloria: I feel anxious. Sometimes I'm terrified. I have a bad feeling in the pit of my stomach. I imagine that they're going to die, and that breaks my heart.

Katie: And what's causing these feelings—your son or your thoughts about your son?

Gloria: My thoughts about him, for sure.

Katie: Who would you be without the thought?

Gloria: I'd certainly be more peaceful. They could come or go, and it would be okay with me.

Katie: "They should stay home"—let's turn it around and see what you can give yourself that your children can't give you.

Gloria: Okay. *I* should stay home.

Katie: Yes. Stop traveling into your son's life.

Gloria: Stay in my own business.

Katie: Yes. Your business is to be at peace wherever you are. When we believe that our children are responsible for our peace, we suffer.

Gloria: It's giving them responsibility for something; it's inviting them into my business and taking them away from theirs, which isn't kind.

Katie: So "*I* should stay home." I should stay home in myself, awakened from the dream of hell. Hell in the future and the escape from hell in the past.

Gloria: I can take care of my breathing and my heart. It's much better for my breathing when he challenges me like this and I notice what's going on, and then I can stay home inside myself and take care of it.

Katie: And you can give yourself an internal life that you understand, as opposed to being lost in the dream. So let's continue with your statement on number three. "They shouldn't go on packed airplanes." **Turn that around.**

Gloria: *I* shouldn't go on packed airplanes. Well, okay, I won't go on packed airplanes in real life or in my imagination.

Katie: Yes, because your son hasn't bought a ticket for you. Just stay home.

Gloria: I've been going along uninvited on their trip.

Katie: "They should remember that my son has a history of respiratory trouble." **Turn it around.**

Gloria: I should remember that my son has a history of respiratory trouble.

Katie: Just remember that he's heard that story. He knows it. It's not as though he's going to forget. How many times has it been brought up in his lifetime?

Gloria: Oh, many times.

Katie: So he remembers.

Gloria: And he's doing what he feels is best with that.

Katie: Yes. He's busy in Earth School. Let's look at statement four.

Gloria: *I need them to think that it's best to be careful now. I need them to be home with me. I need them to say they won't go. I need them to cancel the trip.*

Katie: "For me to be happy, I need them to think it's best to be careful now." *[To the audience]* For those of you new to The Work, statement number four on the Judge-Your-Neighbor Worksheet is about happiness. Number three, which we just did, is about advice, so when we turn it around, we find advice to the self: "I should stay home. I shouldn't go on packed airplanes with my children. I should remember that my son has a history of respiratory trouble." That's for me to take care of. He survived.

Gloria: Yes.

Katie: Statement number four is about your happiness in that situation, sitting with Facebook. Okay, let's skip inquiry on this one and go right to the turnarounds. "I need them to think that it's best to be careful now"—**turn it around.** "To be happy, I need me . . ."

Gloria: I need me to think that it's best to be careful now. I need me to be home with me. I need me to say they won't go. I need me to cancel the trip.

Katie: Okay. So the first one. "For me to be happy, I need me . . ."

Gloria: To think that it is best to be careful now.

Katie: Be careful, now. Don't take your mind into a world you weren't invited to. They haven't even told you about the trip.

Gloria: Nope.

Katie: You're not invited. "To be happy, I need me to be . . ."

Gloria: Home with me.

Katie: Yes, stay home with you. Don't travel into your son's business. When you notice you're doing that, just thank yourself for sharing and come back home. It's not safe when you go there in your mind. It attacks your physical system, and rightfully so. But those emotions are a temple bell; its ring reminds you to look to cause. Cause is what you're thinking and believing, and emotions are there to wake you up. When you notice the stress, write those thoughts down and question them and turn them around. Okay, the next one: "To be happy, I need me to say . . ."

Gloria: To say they won't go.

Katie: Yes, I need me to say that they'll always be with me, inside me, and that they can't ever leave. Even if they go, they won't go. Do you understand?

Gloria: Yes.

Katie: There's another turnaround: "To be happy in that situation, reading the Facebook page, I need me . . ."

Gloria: I need me to say *I* won't go.

Katie: I need me to come back to myself. I need me to be content.

Gloria: I need me to feel content with staying home.

Katie: Yes. Staying home in yourself, with all the love and gratitude in your heart.

Gloria: It's a much friendlier place.

Katie: And it's respectful.

Gloria: Yes, respectful of us both.

Katie: Our children are on their path, and we know from experience there's not a lot we can do about it, except to alienate ourselves and our relationship with them. "To be happy, I need me . . ."

Gloria: To cancel the trip. I get a full refund.

Katie: I need me to cancel the trip anytime I go outside my own business. I need me to come back to this friendly universe that never stops loving us as a part of itself. We are nature itself, so we're really waking up to our true nature. Let's look at statement five.

Gloria: *They're foolish, reckless, inconsiderate, selfish, and ignorant.*

Katie: Okay. In the interest of time, let's skip inquiry on this one, too. I'll give that to you as homework. When you have time, question statements four and five. Be thorough. You can spend an hour on these questions, or a week. **So turn your statement around.** What's the opposite of *foolish*? "They are . . ."

Gloria: Wise.

Katie: To their minds, they are. Can you see that?

Gloria: Yeah.

Katie: I don't know if it's true, but they're making what they consider an informed decision. It's not the decision you'd make for yourself or for them, but it's theirs. What's the opposite of *reckless*?

Gloria: Mindful. They're being mindful about their decision.

Katie: Sweetheart, this is a great conversation you can have with them. "What are your plans? I know you've considered the pros and cons of taking this trip. Tell me how you made your decision. I really want to know." What's the opposite of inconsiderate?

Gloria: Considerate. They were considerate not to tell me, because they knew it would hurt me and make me worry.

Katie: "Be careful with Mom."

Gloria: Yes. That was very nice.

Katie: Yes, it was. The next one: selfish. What's the opposite of *selfish*?

Gloria: Giving, generous.

Katie: And the last one: What's the opposite of *ignorant*?

Gloria: Knowledgeable. Wise.

Katie: So consider these. We moved through them quickly, but you can sit in each one of them for an hour, a whole day, and take the trip that really matters, the trip into the self. There's suffering in the world, and there's a cause for this suffering, and the cause is what we're thinking and believing, the unquestioned mind. An unquestioned life is not worth living, as Socrates said. So **let's turn all this around** to the self: "In that situation, reading the Facebook page, in the state of grace, I am . . ."

Gloria: In that situation, I am foolish, reckless, inconsiderate, selfish, and ignorant. Wow! It's all true. I was foolish to love the dream more than my children.

Katie: Yes, and to use your children to keep you safe.

Gloria: Yeah, yeah. That's inconsiderate and selfish.

Katie: And ignorant. We really think that if they do what we want, we wouldn't be just as worried about something else.

Gloria: Yeah, yeah. Using my thoughts to avoid my own Work.

Katie: Good. Now read number six, the last one.

Gloria: *I don't ever want to see my son and daughter-in-law willingly endanger their own and others' health again.*

Katie: This could be a recurring dream with you, and as you're dreaming it again, as you're being dreamed it again, then stress and anxiety will let you know. So **turn it around:** "I'm willing to . . ."

Gloria: I'm willing to see my son and daughter-in-law willfully endanger their own and others' health again.

Katie: "I look forward to . . ."

Gloria: I look forward to seeing my son and daughter-in-law willfully endanger their own and others' health again.

Katie: In my mind's eye. That's like saying "I look forward to falling asleep again in the hypnotic trance of what isn't—what isn't real. I look forward to that because it shows me that my Work isn't done yet, until those things can occur to me and I'm awake to the fact that the image of my son in my head isn't my son, that my image of her isn't my daughter-in-law, that my image of an airplane isn't a real airplane, that it's all a dream." Until I'm awake to the dream, my Work's not done. So stress and worry will let you know you still have some Work to do. This is personal work. No one can do it for us. There's an invitation out there for us, and we can question what we're believing, or we can suffer, and in my experience I haven't found another choice. It's just me with me, and you're in me, and I see you as wise, as an awake, enlightened being catching up with your beautiful self. It's a privilege to do The Work with you. Thank you for being our teacher today.

Gloria: Thank you, Katie.

Katie: Sweetheart, you are so welcome.

Reality is
always kinder
than the stories
we tell about it.

5

Deepening Inquiry

Now we'll go deeper into the inquiry process and explore each of the questions and turnarounds in greater detail. My intention here is to support you as you begin to travel into the infinite mind and begin to realize that there's nothing to fear. There is nowhere you can travel where inquiry won't safely hold you.

The Work always brings us back to who we really are. Each belief investigated to the point of understanding allows the next belief to surface. You undo that one. Then you undo the next and the next. And then you find that you are actually looking forward to the next belief. At some point, you may notice that you're meeting every thought, feeling, person, and situation as a friend. Until eventually you are looking for a problem. Until, finally, you notice that you haven't had one in years.

Question 1: Is it true?

Sometimes it's immediately obvious that the statement you have written is simply not true. If the answer that comes to you is a clear no, then move on to question 3. Otherwise, let's look at some ways to examine question 1 further.

What's the reality of it?

If your answer to question 1 is yes, ask yourself: What's the reality of this situation?

Let's investigate the statement "Paul shouldn't watch so much television." What's the reality of it? In your experience, *does* he watch a lot of television? Yes: the reality is that Paul watches between six and ten hours of television on most days. How do we know that Paul should watch so much television? He does. That's the reality of it; that's what is true. A dog barks, a cat meows, and Paul watches television. That's his job. It may not always be that way, but for now, that's the way it is. Your thought that Paul shouldn't watch so much television is just your way of mentally arguing with what is. It doesn't do you any good, and it doesn't change Paul; its only effect is to cause you stress. Once you clearly see the reality that he watches so much television, who knows what changes can develop in your life?

Reality, for me, is what is true. The truth is whatever is in front of you, whatever is really happening. Whether you like it or not, it's raining now. "It shouldn't be raining" is just a thought. In reality, there is no such thing as a "should" or a "shouldn't." These are only thoughts that we superimpose onto reality. The mind is like a carpenter's level: when the bubble is off to one side—"It shouldn't be raining"—we can know that the mind is caught in its thinking; when the bubble is right in the middle—"It's raining"—we can know that the surface is level and the mind is accepting reality as it is. Without the "should" and "shouldn't," we can see reality as it is, and this leaves us free to act efficiently, clearly, and sanely. Asking "What's the reality of it?" can help bring the mind out of the story, back into the real world.

Whose business is it?

As I said earlier, I can find only three kinds of business in the universe: mine, yours, and God's (and for me, reality is God). Whose business are you in when you're thinking the thought that you've written? When you think that someone or something other than yourself needs to change, you're mentally out of your business. Of *course* you feel separate, lonely, and stressed! Paul's over there living his life in front of the television, you're mentally over there living his life, and there's no one here for you. Then you blame your loneliness and frustration on him. Ask yourself, "Whose business is it how much television I watch? Whose business is it how much television Paul watches? And can I really know what's best for Paul in the long run?" "Paul should watch less television"—is it true? Whose business is it?

Question 2: Can you absolutely know that it's true?

If your answer to question 1 is yes, ask yourself, "Can I absolutely know that it's true?" In many cases, the statement *appears* to be true. That's because your concepts are based on a lifetime of uninvestigated beliefs.

After I woke up to reality in 1986, I noticed many times how people —in conversations, the media, and books—made statements such as "There isn't enough understanding in the world," "There's too much violence," "We should love one another more." These were stories I used to believe, too. They seemed sensitive, kind, and caring, but as I heard them, I noticed that believing them caused stress and that they didn't feel peaceful inside me.

For instance, when I heard someone say, "People should be more loving," the question would arise in me "Can I absolutely know that that's true? Can I really know for myself, within myself, that people should be more loving? Even if the whole world tells me so, is it really true?" To my amazement, when I listened within myself, I saw that the world is what it is in this moment and that in this moment people can't possibly be more loving than they are. Where reality is concerned, there *is* no "what should be." There is only what is, just the way it is, right now. The truth is prior to every story. And every story, prior to investigation, prevents us from seeing what's true.

Now I could finally inquire of every potentially uncomfortable story, "Can I absolutely know that it's true?" And the answer, like the question, was an experience: no. I would stand rooted in that answer—solitary, peaceful, free.

How could no be the right answer? Everyone I knew, and all the books, said that the answer should be yes. But I came to see that the truth is itself and will not be dictated to by anyone. In the presence of that inner no, I came to see that the world is always as it should be, whether I oppose it or not. And I came to embrace reality with all my heart. I love the world, without any conditions.

Let's play with the statement "I feel hurt because Paul is angry at me." You may have answered, "Yes, it's true. Paul *is* angry at me. His face is red, his neck is throbbing, and he is shouting at me." So there's the proof. But go inside again. Can you really know that it's you Paul is angry at? Can you really know what's going on inside someone else's mind? Can you know by someone's facial expression or body language what he is really thinking or feeling? Have you felt fear or anger, for example, and observed yourself point the finger of blame at the person nearest you? Can you absolutely know what another person is feeling, even when he tells you? Can you be certain that he is clear about his own thoughts and emotions? Have you ever been confused about who or what you were angry at? Can you really know that it's true that Paul is angry at you?

To take it a step further, can you really know that you feel hurt because Paul is angry? Is Paul's anger actually *causing* your hurt? Might it be possible for you, in another frame of mind, to stand there in the full blast of Paul's anger and not experience it personally at all? What if you could simply listen, calmly and lovingly receiving whatever he says? After inquiry, that was my experience.

Suppose your statement is "Paul should stop smoking." Of *course* he should! Everyone knows that smoking causes lung cancer. Now go in deeper with the question. Can you really know that it's true that Paul should stop smoking? Can you know that his life would be better or that he would live longer if he stopped smoking? Can you really know what is best for Paul on his life's path? Can you know that if Paul stopped smoking, it would be best for him or you in the long run? I'm not saying that it wouldn't be. I'm just asking. "Paul should stop smoking"—can you absolutely know that it's true?

If your answer is still yes, good. If you think that you can absolutely know that that's true, that's as it should be, and it's fine to move on to question 3. Or if you feel a little stuck, you may want to try one or more of the following exercises.

When You Think That It's True

Sometimes you may not feel comfortable with your yeses to questions 1 and 2; they may make you feel that you're grinding to a halt in your inquiry. You want to go deeper, but the statement you've written or the thought that's torturing you appears to be an irrefutable fact. Here are some ways to coax your thoughts out into the open, to prompt new statements that can allow inquiry to go deeper.

"And it means that ____"

A powerful way of prompting yourself is to add "and it means that ____" to your original statement. Your suffering may be caused by a thought that interprets what happened, rather than the thought you wrote down. This additional phrase prompts you to reveal your interpretation of the fact.

Let's say you wrote, "I am angry at my father because he hit me."

Is it true? Yes, you *are* angry, and yes, he *did* hit you many times when you were a child. Try writing the statement with your added interpretation: "I am angry at my father because he hit me, and it means that _____." Maybe you would finish this statement with "and it means that he doesn't love me."

Now that you know what your interpretation is, you can take it to inquiry. Write down the new statement and apply all four questions and the turnarounds. His hitting you means that he didn't love you—can you really know that that's true? You may come to realize that it's your interpretation of the fact that is causing you stress.

What do you think you would have?

Another way of prompting yourself is to read your original statement and ask yourself what you think you would have if reality were (in your opinion) fully cooperating with you. Suppose you wrote, "Paul should tell me that he loves me." Your answer to "What do you think you would have?" might be that if Paul told you that he loves you, you would feel more secure. Write down this new statement—"I would feel more secure if Paul told me that he loves me"—and put it up against inquiry.

What's the worst that could happen?

When your statement is about something you think you don't want, read it and imagine the worst outcome that reality could hand you. Imagine your worst fears lived out on paper. Be thorough. Take it to the limit.

Your statement might be, for example, "I'm heartbroken because my wife left me." Now ask yourself, "What's the worst that could happen?" Make a list of all the terrible events that you think might happen as a result of your present situation. After each frightening scenario that comes to mind, imagine what could happen next. And then what could happen? And then what? Be a frightened child. Don't hold back.

When you've finished writing, start at the top of your list and apply the four questions and the turnarounds to each statement.

What's the "should"?

A fourth useful prompt is to look for a "should" or "shouldn't" version of your original statement. If your anger arises from the belief that reality should have been different, you might rewrite the statement "I am angry at my father because he hit me" as, "My father shouldn't have hit me." This statement may be easier to investigate. With the first form of this statement—"My father hit me"—we know the answer, or we think we know it. "Is it true? Definitely yes." We would stake our lives on it. With the rewritten form—"My father shouldn't have hit me"—we're not so sure, and we're more open to discovering another, deeper truth.

Where's your proof?

Sometimes you're convinced that your written statement is true and you believe that you can absolutely know that it's true, but you haven't looked at your "proof." If you really want to know the truth, bring all your evidence into the open and put it to the test of inquiry. Here's an example:

Original statement: *I am saddened by Paul because he doesn't love me.*

The proof that Paul doesn't love me:

1. Sometimes he walks by me without speaking.
2. When I enter the room, he doesn't look up.

3. He doesn't acknowledge me. He continues to do what he is interested in.
4. He doesn't call me by name.
5. I ask him to take out the trash, and he pretends not to hear me.
6. I tell him what time dinner is, and sometimes he doesn't show up.
7. When we do talk, he seems distant, as though he has more important things to do.

Investigate each of your "proof of truth" statements, using all
four questions and the turnarounds, as in the following example.

1. He sometimes walks by me without speaking. *That proves* that
   he doesn't love me. Is it true? Can I absolutely know that it's
   true? Is it possible that he is mentally absorbed in something
   else? Continue with all four questions and the turnarounds.
2. When I enter the room, he doesn't look up. *That proves* that he
   doesn't love me. Is it true? Can I absolutely know that it means
   he doesn't love me? Continue to test your proof with all four
   questions and the turnarounds.

Test your whole list in this manner, and then return to your original statement: "I'm saddened by Paul because he doesn't love
me"—is it true?

Finding your "proof of truth"

Think of a person in your life (past or present) who you think doesn't
love you. Then make a list of your proof that it's true.

Now investigate each "proof of truth" statement you have written
down, using all four questions and the turnarounds.

Question 3: How do you react, what happens, when you believe that thought?

With this question, we begin to notice internal cause and effect. You can see that when you believe the thought, there is an uneasy feeling, a disturbance that can range from mild discomfort to fear or panic. Since you may have realized from question 1 that the thought isn't even true for you, you're looking at the power of a lie. Your nature is truth, and when you oppose it, you don't feel like yourself. Stress never feels as natural as peace does.

After the four questions found me, I would notice thoughts like "People should be more loving," and I would see that thoughts like these caused a feeling of uneasiness in me. I noticed that prior to the thought, there was peace. My mind was quiet and serene. There was no stress, no disturbing physical reaction. This is who I am without my story. Then, in the stillness of awareness, I began to notice the feelings that came from believing or attaching to the thought. And in the stillness, I could see that if I were to believe the thought, the result would be a feeling of unease and sadness. From there it would go to "I should do something about this." From there it would shift to guilt; I didn't have the slightest idea of how to make people be more loving, because I myself couldn't be any more loving than I in fact was. When I asked, "How do I react, what happens, when I believe the thought that people should be more loving?" I saw that not only did I have an uncomfortable feeling (this was obvious), but I also reacted with mental images—of the wrongs I had once thought I'd suffered, of the terrible things I had once thought people had done to me, of my first husband's unkindness to our children and me—to prove that the thought was true. I flew off into a world that didn't exist. There I was, sitting in a chair with a cup of tea, and mentally I was living in the pictures of an illusory past. I became a character in the pages of a myth of suffering: the heroine of suffering, trapped in a world filled with injustice. I reacted by living in a stressed-out body and mind, seeing everything through fearful eyes, a sleepwalker, someone in an endless nightmare. The remedy was simply to inquire.

I love question 3. Once you answer it for yourself, once you see the effects of a thought, all suffering begins to unravel. You may not even realize it at first. You may not even know that you're making progress. But progress is none of your business. Just keep doing The Work. It will continue to take you deeper. The next time the problem you worked on appears, you may laugh in astonishment. You may not feel any stress; you may not even notice the thought at all.

Can you see a reason to drop the thought? (And please don't try to drop it.)

This is an additional question that I sometimes ask as a follow-up to question 3, because it can bring radical shifts in awareness. Along with the next additional question, it goes deeper into an awareness of internal cause and effect. "Can I see a reason to drop the thought?" "Yes, I can: I was at peace before the thought appeared, and after it appeared I felt contraction and stress."

It's important to realize that inquiry is about noticing, not about dropping the thought. That is not possible. If you think that I'm asking you to drop the thought, hear this: I am not! Inquiry is not about getting rid of thoughts; it's about realizing what's true for you through awareness and unconditional self-love. Once you see the truth, the thought lets go of *you*, not the other way around.

Can you find one stress-free reason to keep the thought?

Another question I sometimes ask is "Can you find one stress-free reason to keep the thought?" You may see lots of reasons, but they all cause stress, they all hurt. None of them is peaceful or valid, not if you're interested in putting an end to your suffering. If you find one that seems valid, ask yourself, "Is this reason peaceful, or is it stressful? Does thinking that thought bring peace or stress into my life? And do I operate more efficiently, lovingly, and clearly when I am stressed or when I am free of stress?" (In my experience, all stress is inefficient.)

Question 4: Who or what would you be without the thought?

This is a very powerful question. Who or what would you be without the thought? *How* would you be without the thought? Picture yourself standing in the presence of the person you have written about when he or she is doing what you think he or she shouldn't be doing. Now, just for a minute or two, close your eyes, take a deep breath, and imagine who you would be if you didn't have the ability to think this thought. How would your life be different in the same situation without the thought? Keep your eyes closed and watch the person without your story. What do you see? How do you feel about him or her without the story? Which do you prefer—with or without your story? Which feels kinder? Which feels more peaceful?

Many people answer this question by saying "I'd be free," "I'd be peaceful," "I'd be a more loving person." You could also say, "I'd be clear enough to understand the situation and act in an appropriate, intelligent way." Without our stories, we are not only able to act clearly and fearlessly; we are also friends, listeners. We are people living happy lives. We are appreciation and gratitude that have become as natural as breath itself. Happiness is the natural state for someone who knows that there's nothing to know and that we already have everything we need, right here, right now.

The answer to question 4 may leave us without an identity. This is very exciting. You're left *with* nothing and *as* nothing other than the reality of the moment: woman sitting in a chair, writing. This can be a little scary, since it leaves no illusion of a past or future. You

might ask, "How do I live now? What do I do? Nothing is meaningful." And I would say, "'With no past or future, you won't know how
to live'—can you really know that that's true? 'You don't know what
to do, and nothing is meaningful'—can you really know that that's
true?" Write down your fears, and walk yourself through inquiry
again on these subtle, intricate concepts. The goal of inquiry is to
bring us back to our right mind, so we can realize for ourselves that
we live in paradise and haven't even noticed.

"Who would you be without the thought?" is the form of question 4 that I suggest if you're new to The Work. Sit with it. Let any
thoughts or pictures come and go as you contemplate this form of
the question. It can be an extremely rich experience. You may also
want to play with the original form of question 4: "What would you
be without the thought?" "Peace" is the answer that people often
come to. And again I ask, "What would you be without even that
thought?"

The Turnarounds

Finding turnarounds is a very powerful part of The Work. It's the
part where you take what you have written about others and see if it
is as true or truer when it applies to you. As long as you think that
the cause of your problem is "out there"—as long as you think that
anyone or anything else is responsible for your suffering—the situation is hopeless. It means that you are forever in the role of the victim. So bring the truth home to yourself and begin to set yourself
free. Inquiry combined with the turnarounds is the fast track to self-
realization.

For example, the statement "Paul is unkind" turns around to "I
am unkind." Go inside and find the situations in your life where this
seems true for you. How were you unkind to Paul in the situation
you're writing about? (Look at your answers to the questions "How
do you react when you think the thought 'Paul is unkind'? How do

you treat him?") Aren't you being unkind in the moment when you are seeing Paul as unkind? Experience what it feels like when you believe that Paul is unkind. Your body may tense, your heart may speed up, you may feel flushed—is that kind to yourself? You may become judgmental and defensive—how does that feel inside you? Those reactions are the results of your uninvestigated thinking.

When Paul insults you, for example, how many times do you replay that scene in your mind? Who is more unkind: Paul (who insulted you once today) or you (who multiplied his insult over and over again in your mind)? Consider this: Were your feelings the result of Paul's action itself or your own judgments about it? If Paul insulted you and you didn't know about it, would you suffer? Be still for a moment. Go deep. Stay vigilantly in your own mental business as you sit with this.

The Three Kinds of Turnarounds

There are three kinds of turnarounds. A judgment can be turned around to yourself, to the other, and to the opposite. There are many possible combinations of these three to play with. The point is not to find the most turnarounds but to find the ones that set you free from the nightmare you're innocently attached to. Turn the original statement around any way you want to until you find the turnarounds that penetrate the deepest.

Let's play with the statement "Paul should appreciate me."

First, turn it around to yourself:

"I should appreciate myself." (It's my job, not his.)

Next, turn it around to the other:

"I should appreciate Paul." (If I believe it's so easy for Paul to appreciate me, can I appreciate Paul? Can *I* live it?)

Then turn it around to the opposite:

"Paul shouldn't appreciate me." (That's reality; sometimes.
Paul *shouldn't* appreciate me, unless he does).

Be willing to go inside with each turnaround and ask if it's as
true as or truer than the original statement. Find authentic examples
of how it is true in your life. Own it. If that seems difficult for you,
add the word "sometimes" to the turnaround. Can you own that it's
true *sometimes*, even if only in the moment that you're thinking that
it's true about the other?

You might want to make a list of the many ways and situations
where you haven't appreciated Paul. Make a list of the ways you don't
appreciate other people and situations in your life. Make a list of
things that you do for yourself and for others, and discover how you
don't always appreciate yourself.

**I suggest that you always use the four questions before applying
the turnarounds.** You may be tempted to take a shortcut and skip to
the turnarounds without putting your statement up against inquiry
first. This is not an effective way of using the turnarounds. If you
don't ask and answer the questions first, the turnarounds can feel
harsh and shameful; the feeling of judgment turned back onto yourself can be brutal if it occurs prior to thorough self-education, and
the four questions give you this education. They end the ignorance
of what you believe to be true, and the turnarounds in the last position feel gentle and make sense. By asking the four questions first
and going inside for the answers, you will make it possible to experience the turnarounds as revelations rather than mental gymnastics.

The Work is not about shame and blame. It's not about proving
that you are the one in the wrong or forcing yourself to believe that
someone else is in the right. The power of the turnaround lies in the
discovery that everything you think you see on the outside is really a

projection of your own mind. Everything is a mirror image of your own thinking. Once you have learned to go inside for your own answers and open yourself up to the turnarounds, you'll experience this for yourself. In discovering the innocence of the person you judged, you'll come to recognize your own innocence.

Sometimes you may not find the turnaround in your behavior or actions. If that's the case, look for it in your thinking. For example, the turnaround for "Paul should stop smoking" is "I should stop smoking." Perhaps you have never smoked a cigarette in your life. It may be that where you are smoking is in your mind. Over and over, you smoke with anger and frustration as you picture Paul smelling up your house with cigarette smoke. Do you mentally smoke more times in a day than Paul does? Your prescription for peace, then, is for you to stop smoking in your mind and to stop being so smoking angry about Paul's smoking. Another suggestion is to substitute something else for the word *smoking*. Maybe you've never smoked, but is there something that you use in the same way that you think Paul uses cigarettes: food, drugs, credit cards, or sex? Your turnaround could be "I should stop using credit cards to make myself feel better." Be willing to take the advice that you're giving him, the advice that shows you how to live in your own business.

The Turnarounds in Action

Self-realization is not complete until it lives as action. Live the turnarounds. When you see how you have been preaching to others, go back and make amends, and let them know how difficult it is for you to do what you wanted them to do. Let them know the ways you manipulated and conned them, how you got angry, used sex, used money, and used guilt to get what you wanted.

I wasn't always able to live the advice that I so generously held out for others to live. When I realized this, I found myself on equal ground with the people I had judged. I saw that my philosophy wasn't so easy for any of us to live. I saw that we're all doing the best we can. This is how a lifetime of humility begins.

Reporting is another powerful way I found to manifest self-realization. In the first year after I woke up to reality, I often went to the people I had been judging and shared my turnarounds and realizations. I reported only what I had discovered about my part in whatever difficulty I was experiencing. (Under no circumstances did I talk about *their* part.) I did this so that I could hear it in the presence of at least two witnesses: the other person and myself. I gave it, and I received it. If, for example, your statement was "He lied to me," one turnaround would be "I lied to him." Now you list as many of your lies as you can remember and report them to that person, never in any way mentioning his lies to you. His lies are his business. You are doing this for your own freedom. Humility is the true resting place.

When I wanted to move even faster and more freely, I found that apologizing and making heartfelt amends was a wonderful shortcut. "To make amends" means to right the perceived wrong. What I call "living amends" is farther reaching; it applies not only to one particular incident but to all future incidents of that kind. When I realized through inquiry that I had hurt someone in my past, I stopped hurting anyone. If even after this I hurt someone, I told them immediately why I had done it, what I had been afraid of losing, or what I had wanted to get from them; and I began again, always with a clean slate. This is a powerful way to live freely.

A heartfelt apology is a way to undo an error and begin again on an equal and guiltless basis. Apologize and make amends for your own sake. It's all about your own peace. What good is it to be a talking saint? We've got an earth full of them. Peace is who you already are, without a story. Can you just live it?

Go through your list of examples of how the turnarounds are true for you, and underline each statement where you feel that you

harmed someone in any way. (Your list of answers to question 3—
"How do you react, what happens, when you believe that thought?"—
could keep you very busy with reporting and apologizing.) Make
amends to yourself by making amends to others. Give back in equal
measure what you believe you took at their expense.

Honest, nonmanipulative reporting, coupled with living amends,
brings real intimacy to otherwise impossible relationships. If any
people on your Worksheet are dead, make living amends through
the rest of us. Give us what you would have given them, for your own
sake.

I knew a man who was very serious about his freedom. He had
been a junkie and a thief, had broken into many houses, and had
been very good at what he did. After he had been doing The Work
for a while, he made a list of everyone he had ever stolen from and
what he had taken, as exactly as he could remember. When he finished the list, there were dozens of people and houses on it. Then he
began to turn it around. He knew he would end up in jail, yet he had
to do what was right for him. He went house by house and knocked
on each door. He was African American, and some of the places he
returned to were not very comfortable for him, because he had beliefs about prejudice. But he just kept working with these beliefs and
knocking on the doors. When people answered, he would tell them
who he was and what he had stolen; then he would apologize and
say, "How can I make this right? I'll do whatever it takes." And no
one ever called the police. They would say things like "Okay, fix my
car" or "Paint my house." And he would do the job with pleasure and
then put a check mark by their name on his list. And every stroke of
the paintbrush, he said, was God, God, God.

I have a son, Ross, who has been doing The Work for a long
time. Eight or nine years ago, I noticed that, as we shopped, he would
sometimes say, "Wait for me, Mom, I'll be right back," and leave me
for ten minutes or so. On one occasion, I watched him through the
store window choose a shirt, take it to the cashier, and pay for it.

Then he went back to the shelf, looked around to make sure that no one was watching, put the shirt back, and walked out of the store. I asked him what he was doing. He said, "A while ago, I stole things from five or six stores. It was horrible, Mom. Now when I see a store where I stole something, I walk in, find an item like the one I stole, pay for it, and put it back. I tried turning myself in. I'd say, 'Here's the money for what I stole, and if you want to prosecute, it's okay with me.' And they'd get confused, they'd call in the manager, and the manager wouldn't know what to do with the money, he'd tell me that it was too complicated for the computers. And if they called the police, the police would say that you have to be caught in the act. So they'd end up telling me that there was nothing they could do. But I really needed to turn it around. So I found this way. It works for me."

Ross also likes to play with an exercise that I recommend, which is to do a kind act and not get found out; if you're found out, the act doesn't count, and you start over. I have seen him at amusement parks watch children who don't seem to have enough money. He'll pull out a bill from his wallet, stoop down in front of the child, pretend to pick it up from the ground, and hand it to him, saying "You dropped this, dude," then quickly walk away without ever looking back. He's an amazing teacher of how to practice the turnaround through living amends.

It's generous to yourself to bring this practice into everyday life. And the results are nothing short of miraculous.

The Turnaround for Statement 6

The turnaround for statement 6 on the Judge-Your-Neighbor Worksheet is a little different from the other turnarounds. "I don't ever want to . . ." turns around to "I am willing to . . ." and "I look forward to . . ." For example, "I don't ever want Paul to lie to me again" turns around to "I am willing to have Paul lie to me again" and "I look forward to having Paul lie to me again."

These turnarounds are about embracing all of life, just as it is. Saying—and meaning—"I am willing to . . ." creates open-mindedness, creativity, and flexibility. Any resistance you may have is softened, and that allows you to open up to the situation in your life rather than keep hopelessly applying willpower to eradicate it or push it away. Saying and meaning "I look forward to . . ." actively opens you to life as it unfolds. Some of us have learned to accept what is, and I invite you to go further, to actually *love* what is. This is our natural state. Freedom is our birthright.

For example, "I don't ever want to live with Paul if he doesn't change" turns around to "I am willing to live with Paul if he doesn't change" and "I look forward to living with Paul if he doesn't change." You may as well look forward to it; you could find yourself living with him, if only in your mind. (I have worked with people who are still bitter even though their mate has been dead for twenty years.) Whether you live with him or not, you will probably have this thought again, and you may feel the resulting stress and depression. Look forward to these feelings; they're reminders that it's time to wake yourself up. Uncomfortable feelings will bring you right back to The Work. This doesn't mean that you have to live with Paul. It just means that you're no longer closing yourself off from reality. Willingness opens the door to all of life's possibilities.

Here are two more examples from our sample Worksheet.

Original statement 6: *I refuse to watch Paul ruin his health.*
Turnarounds: "I am willing to watch Paul ruin his health."
"I look forward to watching Paul ruin his health."

Original statement 6: *I don't ever want to be ignored by Paul again.*
Turnarounds: "I am willing to be ignored by Paul again."
"I look forward to being ignored by Paul again."

It's good to acknowledge that the same feelings or situation may happen again, if only in your thoughts. When you realize that suffering and discomfort are the call to inquiry and to the freedom that follows, you may actually begin to look forward to uncomfortable feelings. You may even experience them as friends coming to show you what you have not yet investigated thoroughly enough. It's no longer necessary to wait for people or situations to change in order to experience peace and harmony. The Work is the direct way to orchestrate your own happiness.

No one can hurt me;
that's my job.

6

**Doing The Work
on Work and Money**

For some of us, life is controlled by our thoughts about work and money. But if our thinking is clear, how can work or money be the problem? Our thinking is all we need to change. It's all we *can* change. This is very good news.

Many of us are motivated by a desire for success. But what is success? What do we want to achieve? We do only three things in life: we stand, we sit, we lie horizontal. Once we've found success, we'll still be sitting somewhere until we stand, and we'll stand until we lie down or sit again. Success is a concept, an illusion. Do you want the $3,900 chair instead of the $39 one? Well, sitting is sitting. Without a story, we're successful wherever we are.

Doing The Work on job-related issues can have far-reaching consequences. When I work with corporations, I sometimes invite all the employees to judge one another. This is what employees and bosses have always wanted: to know how they look from each other's point of view. Then, after the judgments, they all do The Work and turn it around. The result can be a startling increase in clarity, honesty, and responsibility, and this in turn inevitably leads to a happier, more productive, and more efficient workforce.

I once did The Work with an executive who said, "My assistant has been with me for ten years. I know she doesn't do the job well, but she has five children." I said, "Good. Keep her here so she can teach the rest of your employees that if they have enough children, they can work for you, whether they do their job well or not." And he said, "Well, I just can't fire her." I said, "I understand that. So put someone qualified in her position, send her home to her five children who need her, and send her a paycheck every month. That's more honest than what you're doing now. Guilt is expensive."

When the executive read his Worksheet to the woman, she agreed with everything he had written about her job performance, because it was clear and true. And I asked her, "What do you suggest? What would you do if you were *your* employee?" People usually fire themselves when they realize what's going on, and that's just what she did. She found a similar job in another company, closer to her home, where she was able to be both a good assistant and a good mother. The executive realized that he had never investigated the thoughts that had led him to be "loyal" to an assistant who in reality had been just as uncomfortable with the situation as he was.

I've never seen a work or money problem that didn't turn out to be a thinking problem. I used to believe that I needed money to be happy. Even when I had a lot, I was often sick with the fear that something terrible would happen and I would lose it. I realize now that no amount of money is worth that kind of stress.

If you live with the uninvestigated thought "I need my money to be safe and secure," you're living in a hopeless state of mind. Banks fail. Stock markets crash. Currencies deflate. People lie, bend contracts, and break their promises. In this confused state of mind, you can make millions of dollars and still be insecure and unhappy.

Some people believe that fear and stress are what motivate them to make money. But can you really know that that's true? Can you be absolutely certain that without fear or stress as a motivator, you wouldn't have made the same amount of money or even more? "I need fear and stress to motivate me"—who would you be if you never believed that story again?

After I found The Work inside myself—after it found me—I began to notice that I always had the perfect amount of money for me right now, even when I had little or none. Happiness is a clear mind. A clear, sane mind knows how to live, how to work, what emails to send, what phone calls to make, and what to do to create what it wants without fear. Who would you be without the thought "I need my money to be safe"? You might be a lot easier to be with. You might even begin to notice the laws of generosity, the laws of letting money go out fearlessly and come back fearlessly. You don't ever need more money than you have. When you understand this, you begin to realize that you already have all the security you wanted money to give you in the first place. It's a lot easier to make money from this position.

Just as we use stress and fear to motivate ourselves to make money, we often rely on anger and frustration to move us to social activism. If I want to act sanely and effectively while I clean up the earth's environment, let me begin by cleaning up my own environment. All the trash and pollution in my thinking—let me clean that up by meeting it with love and understanding. Then my action can become truly effective. It takes just one person to help the planet. That one is you.

When I work in a prison, there are maybe two hundred men from a cell block sitting there, looking down at the floor, their arms folded across their chests. I do The Work with them, and then the guards bring in another two hundred. These are all hardcore violent men—many of them are in prison with life sentences for rape and murder—and I'm the only woman in the room. I don't say a word until they make eye contact with me. This is not easy for them to do. There is some kind of unspoken code that they have, to keep people like me out of their culture. But I just stand in front of them, waiting for eye contact. I may walk into the rows and pace slowly up and down as I wait for just one man to look me in the eyes. The moment it happens, the moment one man does that, he always looks down really fast, but it's too late. There was contact. No one but me has seen his glance; it happens so fast that there's no way the others would have been able to see that it happened. Yet immediately, the code begins to break down all over the room. Two or three others look me in the eyes, then another eight, then another dozen, and then everyone is looking at me, laughing, turning red, and saying things to one another like "Sheeeeeeit!" or "Man, she crazy." And it's done. Now I can speak to them and give them The Work, and all because one man dared to look me in the eyes.

I love thanking those men for sacrificing their entire lives to teach our children how not to live—and therefore how to live—if they want to be free. I tell them that they are the greatest teachers and that their lives are good and needed. Before I leave I ask them, "Would you spend the rest of your life in prison if you knew that it would keep one child from having to live what you're living?" Many of those violent men understand, and they just well up with tears like sweet little boys.

There is nothing we can do that doesn't help the planet. That's the way it really is.

He's So Incompetent!

Gary is annoyed by his incompetent employee. Is the person who annoys you someone you work with? Or is it your spouse or your children who didn't do the dishes thoroughly enough or who left toothpaste in the bathroom sink? See if you can find an example in your life, and go inside for your own answers as Gary goes inside for his.

Gary: *I'm angry at Frank because he is incompetent when he works for me.*

Katie: Okay. Frank should be competent—is it true?

Gary: I think so.

Katie: Can you absolutely know that it's true? Whoever told you that? His résumé said "competent." His recommendation said "competent." It's all over the place. You hire him, and he's supposed to be competent. What's the reality of it in your experience? Is he?

Gary: In my experience, he's not.

Katie: So that's the only place you can sanely come from: reality. Is it true that he should be competent? No. He's not. That's it. That's your reality. So we can keep going over this until we get the "Is it true?" thing, because when you understand this, you become a lover of reality and move into balance. How do you react when you believe the lie that he should be competent when he works for you and he's not?

Gary: It's frustrating and anxiety producing. I feel like I have to carry his work. I have to clean up behind him every time. I can't leave him alone to do his work.

Katie: Can you see a reason to drop the thought that he should be competent? And I'm not asking you to drop it.

Gary: It would make me feel better if I could drop it.

Katie: That's a very good reason. Can you find one stress-free reason to keep this thought that opposes reality?

Gary: Yes. Well, I don't see what you mean by "opposes reality."

Katie: The reality, as you see it, is that he's not competent. You're saying he should be. That theory is not working for you, because it opposes reality. I hear you say that it causes you frustration and anxiety.

Gary: Okay, I think I'm pulling this apart. The reality is that he's just not competent. What's making me crazy is thinking he's supposed to be competent rather than just accepting what he is.

Katie: He's incompetent whether you accept it or not. Reality doesn't wait for our agreement or approval. It is what it is. You can count on it.

Gary: Reality is what is.

Katie: Yes. Reality is always much kinder than the fantasy. You can have a lot of fun at home with what I refer to as the "proof of truth" exercise. He should be competent—where's your proof? Make a list and see if any of it really proves that he should be competent when you put it up against inquiry. It's all a lie. There *is* no proof. The truth is that he should *not* be competent, because he's just not. Not competent for that job.

Gary: The fact is that he's not competent, and I do what I have to do to make up for it. What I don't need to give myself is the extra baggage of "He *should be* yadda yadda yadda."

Katie: Very well said.

Gary: All my job-related angst was about thinking that Frank should be competent. The truth is that he's just not competent. The piece that I added, which made me nuts, was that he should be competent. The fact is that I'm going to do what I have to do. I'm going to back-fill until he's not my problem anymore. I'm just going to do it. By adding that he should be competent, I work myself up into a fucking emotional tizzy. Welcome to New York!

Katie: I didn't know you used the F-word in New York. *[Laughter from the audience.]*

Gary: Yeah, we do. Occasionally.

Katie: So who would you be without this insane story that argues with reality?

Gary: I would just be in the flow and do what I have to do in my job.

Katie: Who would you be, standing with this man at work, without the story?

Gary: I would be compassionate and effective.

Katie: Yes. "Frank should be competent"—turn it around.

Gary: Frank should not be competent.

Katie: You've got it. Not until he is. That's reality for now. There's another turnaround.

Gary: I should be competent. That is true.

Katie: Let's look at statement number two on your Worksheet.

Gary: *I want Frank to take responsibility for his part of the project.*

Katie: Turn it around.

Gary: I want me to take responsibility for my part of the project.

Katie: Yes, because until you stop focusing on his incompetence, you're not taking full responsibility for the project.

Gary: And I should take responsibility for his part of the project.

Katie: Yes, if you want the job done with competence and there's no other way. Okay, let's go on to the next statement.

Gary: *He should step up to the plate as an expert in his field and as a project leader.*

Katie: Is that true? I mean, where would the man even get the ability? "Hey, you—the one with no competence—you should step up to the plate!"

Gary: No. It's insanity. I'm with you. He just does what he does.

Katie: How do you treat Frank when you believe that fantasy?

Gary: I turn into a tough guy. I think he has to get it done quicker, and I'm all over him.

Katie: Not very effective. Can you see a reason to drop the thought?

Gary: Absolutely.

Katie: So let's turn it around.

Gary: *I* should step up to the plate as an expert in my field. I'll just step up. It's got to be done.

Katie: He's the expert who brings you to the highest level of competence in your life. No mistake.

Gary: Yes. He's my teacher. I can feel that.

Katie: Good. Let's move on to your fourth statement.

Gary: *I need him to carry his portion of the project.* And I see now that I don't really need that.

Katie: Hopeless?

Gary: Absolutely hopeless. I need me to carry his portion *and* my portion of the project if I want it done.

Katie: Let's look at the next statement.

Gary: *Frank is incompetent.*

Katie: Turn it around.

Gary: I am incompetent.

Katie: In the moment that you see him as incompetent, you're incompetent. He's perfectly competent for what he was supposed to bring you, and that was clarity. That's what he brought. And he may bring more—who knows?

Gary: I don't really feel that turnaround. I think I'm very competent.

Katie: Just not where *he's* concerned. You weren't competent enough to see that he's not supposed to be competent.

Gary: That I agree with. That's my incompetence. He needs to be watched even though he is very senior. I need to watch over myself. That's truer. I can be insane sometimes.

Katie: You've found the internal world. When you see that it's only your thinking that you need to work with, then every problem you experience in the world becomes a joy to bring to inquiry. For people who really want to know the truth, this Work is checkmate; it's the end of suffering.

Gary: I got stuck when I tried to do this myself earlier in the week. I thought I was right. Once I bring it all inside, then all the turnarounds start to make sense.

Katie: The guy walks in, you put your story onto him, and you call your suffering his fault. You believe your story and live in the stressful fantasy that he is the problem. Without the thought that this man should be more competent than he is, it might come to you to fire him. If you fired him, that would free him to get to a job where he *is* competent. Then he could be competent where he's needed. And now there's space for the man or woman who does belong in the position with you. Two weeks later, the guy may call you and say, "Thank you for firing me. I hated working with you. And I love my new job." Anything is possible. Or it could be that because you've done this inner Work and gotten clearer about your thinking, you may look at the guy on Monday morning and see a competence that you never noticed before. Okay, read the last statement of your Worksheet.

Gary: *I don't ever want to have him or a person like him on my team.*

Katie: Turn it around.

Gary: I am willing to have him or a person like him on my team. And I look forward to having him or a person like him on my team, because it brings me into my inner space to find the solution.

Katie: You do this very well. Welcome to The Work.

Uncle Ralph and His Stock Tips

The following dialogue demonstrates that even though someone is passionately attached to his own story and therefore to his own suffering, he may still break free if he's willing to go through the whole inquiry with patience. Even if, as Marty points out, the exercise seems "only mental" for a long time, it can suddenly make sense on a far deeper level.

I love not rushing the process. Mind doesn't shift until it does, and when it does shift, it's right on time, not one second too late or too soon. People are just like seeds waiting to sprout. We can't be pushed ahead of our own understanding.

To benefit from this dialogue, you don't need to understand the technical issues Marty is talking about; all you need to know is that the price of his stock went up and then way down and that his emotions went with it.

Marty: *I'm angry at my uncle Ralph for giving me some bum tips on the stock market that cost me all my money.* I got indebted to him when he bailed me out on some margin calls—some stocks I borrowed money to buy—and the stocks continued to tumble. And the other stock tip, his big tip, lost eighty-five percent of its value in two years. And my uncle is in an unconscious pissing contest with me.

Katie: Yes.

Marty: He's always trying to prove that he's better than everyone by the size of his bank account, and he happens to be a wealthy man, and so he didn't have to borrow anything. I had to borrow when the one stock was going down and the other stock was doing well to have any chance of being able to pay him back all the money that he lent me.

Katie: I hear it.

Marty: And so I kept building up a debt to him, and then recently—this has been going on for two and a half years, it just came to a head—I finally told him, when his other stock went way, way down, I said, "You know, Ralph, now that they've both tanked, I've lost all my money and some of your money." At which point he said, "Listen, you motherfucker, I *told* you to not borrow and you borrowed. You betrayed me; you went against me; you did this, you did that." And I only got in one word edgewise, which was "Ralph, I needed to buy your other stock, and I just didn't have the money." But I didn't say why I needed to buy it, which was to have some hope of paying him back. And I also wanted to make some money, I mean my own fear and greed went in there, too. But—

Katie: Sweetheart, just read what you wrote. It's important that you read what you wrote, not narrate a story.

Marty: Okay, okay. I'm sorry. *I want Uncle Ralph to bail me out, give me back the $60,000 I started with plus the other $35,000 that I'm due, to pay off my credit card debts and take responsibility for having incorrect information and for causing me and my family these financial losses.*

Katie: Good. Keep reading.

Marty: *Uncle Ralph should pay off my debts and give me a hundred grand. He shouldn't demand his money from me, because I can't pay. I need Uncle Ralph to bail my ass out from financial ruin. I need him to take responsibility and at least try to get along with me as responsible adults for what we both did. Ralph is a demanding, controlling, possibly vindictive person, who is not interested in the truth as much as he is in proving that he is always right and highly intelligent.* Okay, the last one?

Katie: Yes.

Marty: *I don't ever want to listen to his stock tips or owe him money again or take his petty, irate, childish shit.*

Katie: Yes. Good. Well done. Okay, sweetheart, would you read the first statement again, just the way you wrote it?

Marty: Okay. *I'm angry at my uncle Ralph for giving me some bum tips on the stock market that cost me all my money, some of his, and threatens me with*—Ah, I can't read my writing.

Katie: Okay, so let's stop there. He gave you the tip?

Marty: Uh-huh.

Katie: Okay. If I offer you this cup, you don't have to take it. It's up to you whether you take it or not. And there's no right or wrong here. Uncles should not give nephews tips on the stock market—is it true? What's the reality of it? Do they?

Marty: Well, he wanted me to make money, and that's why he gave me the tips.

Katie: So what's the reality of it? He gave them to you.

Marty: He gave them to me, and I took them, and I played them to the hilt. It got my ass in a sling.

Katie: We all know up front that stock tips are risky, but knowing that doesn't keep us from acting on them. And realizing what we've done is scary sometimes at two o'clock in the morning or at two o'clock in the afternoon. Some of us end up jumping out of buildings. So uncles shouldn't give nephews bum tips—is it true?

Marty: Yes, right. It's true!

Katie: And what's the reality of it? Do they?

Marty: Yes. My uncle gave me a bum tip, and he doesn't admit that it was a bum tip.

Katie: Okay. Uncles are supposed to admit their errors—is that true?

Marty: Yes, you're damn tootin'. Uncles are supposed to admit their errors.

Katie: And what's the reality of it? What's your experience with it?

Marty: He forced all the blame on me, and that—

Katie: So your experience is no, they don't admit their errors.

Marty: That's right.

Katie: So is it true that uncles should admit their errors?

Marty: I think it's true that *all* people should admit their errors.

Katie: Oh, well! And what's the reality of it? Do they always? Is it true that uncles should admit their errors?

Marty: Yes.

Katie: And what's the reality of it?

Marty: He's not doing it.

Katie: He's not doing it. So I ask you, on what planet is this supposed to happen? Is it true that people should admit their errors? No. Not until they do. I'm not asking for morality here. I'm just asking for the simple truth.

Marty: But just let me say that I really try to admit my own errors. And what's more, in the action that I'm taking, in sending him all my money and assets, I'm admitting my errors by my actions.

Katie: You are. I live the way you do.

Marty: I hope not.

Katie: I like myself when I take responsibility for my actions. But "People should admit their errors"—is it true? No. How do we know that people are not supposed to admit their errors?

Marty: Because they don't.

Katie: They don't. This is so simple, sweetheart, that we've been missing it for thousands of years. It's the truth that set me free. If you argue with it, you lose. I'm a lover of reality, not because I'm some sort of spiritual being but because when I argue with it, I lose inside myself. I lose the contact with the place inside that is home. How do you react when you believe the thought that he should admit his errors and he doesn't?

Marty: I feel victimized.

Katie: What else? How does it feel inside?

Marty: I feel pain, sadness, rage, fear—

Katie: Separation?

Marty: Yes, all the bad stuff.

Katie: The reason you feel all this turmoil is that you're stuck in the center of a lie. It's not true that he should admit his errors. That's the lie. The world has been teaching this lie for centuries, and if you're tired of the pain, it's time to notice what's true. It's not true that people should admit their errors, yet. This is a tough one for some of us, and I invite you to go there. This Work demands absolute, simple, pure integrity. That's all, and the willingness to hear the truth. It would be much better for you if he admitted his error and gave your money back; your highest spiritual path, your greatest freedom, would be if he admitted his error and gave your money back—can you absolutely know that that's true?

Marty: That that would be my highest spiritual path?

Katie: Yes.

Marty: Umm . . .

Katie: Just a yes or no. Can you absolutely know that it's true?

Marty: I don't know.

Katie: That was my experience, too. I can't know if that's true.

Marty: You know, well, let's put it this way: I could say yes, and then I'd feel a sense of justice, but I don't know that justice is necessarily the same thing as peace.

Katie: I agree; justice isn't the same as peace. I don't care about justice. I care about your freedom, the truth inside you that can set you free. This is the ultimate justice.

Marty: No, I know. I'm talking about divine justice. I'm saying that the truthful thing would be to really sit down as two grown men and look where—because I made mistakes, too.

Katie: He should sit down with you—is that true?

Marty: Yes, definitely true.

Katie: What's the reality of it?

Marty: He ain't.

Katie: He ain't. It's not happening.

Marty: Right.

Katie: So how do you react when you think the thought that he should sit down with you like a grown man and he doesn't?

Marty: Well, I feel that I've been wronged, and I feel righteous, and I feel like shit.

Katie: Yes, that's the result. So it's not that he's not sitting down with you that hurts; it's your believing the thought that he—

Marty: That he should.

Katie: That he should. So just be there a minute. See if you can locate that. Who would you be without the story that he should sit down with you like a grown man or that he should admit his error and apologize? Who would you be without that story? I'm not asking you to drop your story. I'm simply asking who you would be in your daily life today without that story.

Marty: I know I'd be free of any expectations from him.

Katie: Yes.

Marty: Which I guess would make me more whole within myself.

Katie: Yes.

Marty: But you know, I—

Katie: Notice how you're about to go into your story when you say "but." Just be still with it.

Marty [after a pause]: I really don't know how it would feel.

Katie: That's right, sweetheart. We're so used to holding on to the lie about what's really happening that we don't know how to live freely. And some of us are learning how, because the pain is just too great not to learn. In my experience, when I don't hold on to the story, I get up, brush my teeth, have breakfast, do what I do all day, come here, and do all the same things but without the stress—without the hell.

Marty: Sounds great. And you know, as fleeting as it may have been, I have had a taste of the free state, so I know that state, and I would certainly like to live that way. That's why I'm here.

Katie: So read that part again.

Marty: Okay, the first part. Now I'm able to read my writing. *I'm angry at my uncle Ralph for giving me some bum tips on the stock market that cost me all my money.*

Katie: So now we're going to do what we call a turnaround. The Work is: judge your neighbor, write it down, ask four questions, turn it around. That's it. Simple stuff. So now we're at the point where we're going to turn it around. "I'm angry at myself . . ."

Marty: I'm angry at myself . . .

Katie: "For taking . . ." He gave, you took.

Marty: For taking his stock tips and believing him.

Katie: Yes, that's close. Keep it very simple. Now read it again, and read it just the way you wrote it. "I'm angry at myself . . ."

Marty: I'm angry at myself for giving me—

Katie: Yes, honey.

Marty: Oh! I'm angry at myself for giving me some bum tips on the stock market that cost me all my money?

Katie: Yes. You gave them to yourself.

Marty: I see that. I gave the tips to myself by accepting them from him.

Katie: Exactly. He can't give them to you unless you take them. You've been believing your own mythology. I think you're starting to understand what we're doing here.

Marty: That's a hard pill to swallow.

Katie: Well, there's one thing harder to swallow, and that's what you've been living, and how you put yourself at the mercy of other people.

Marty: Yeah. It sure doesn't feel good.

Katie: Let's look at the next one.

Marty: *I want Uncle Ralph to bail me out.*

Katie: Okay. So you want Uncle Ralph to bail you out—is it true?

Marty: Yeah, if he were an honorable man. Yeah.

Katie: Why is that? Whose money did you invest?

Marty: Some of his, some of mine.

Katie: Okay, yours and his, but let's look at your money. You invested it in stock tips that you gave yourself after hearing them from your uncle.

Marty: Right.

Katie: And you want him to bail you out?

Marty: Well, if you put it like that . . . no.

Katie: Good. So what does he have to do with any of it, aside from sharing with you what he believed to be true at the time?

Marty: Nothing.

Katie: Correct. Nothing.

Marty: But the thing is, right at this moment it's very mental to me. It's all in my head. I still feel the anger.

Katie: Just stay with the process. If it seems mental right now, that's the way it's supposed to be. How do you react when you think the thought that you want him to bail you out? Or that it would even be for your highest spiritual good if he bailed you out?

Marty: I feel all this anxiety and terror and the bad stuff that I'd rather not have.

Katie: And you can focus on that, and you don't have to bail yourself out.

Marty: Right.

Katie: You just focus on the thought that he's supposed to do it, and you tell yourself why you're right, and you never win, because you *can't* win that. The truth is that he's not supposed to bail you out. He didn't invest your money. You did.

Marty: Right.

Katie: But putting the focus over there on him rather than on what's true keeps you from knowing and therefore living your integrity, which is to bail yourself out. You know, there's nothing sweeter than you bailing yourself out. Who got you into this? You did. Whose job is it to get you out when your uncle says that he won't? Yours. If Uncle Ralph does it, then you don't ever get to realize that you can do it.

Marty: That's true.

Katie: And then when Uncle Ralph says no, you resent him and continue to focus on him, and you don't bail yourself out, because you're not in a position to notice that you can do that. And you die yelling "It's not fair! What did I do to deserve such a heartless uncle?"

Marty: I agree with you. It's true.

Katie: So give me one good reason to hold on to the mythology that he's supposed to bail you out, when the truth is that he hasn't.

Marty: For him, it would be a little bit more than lunch money.

Katie: That's a good one! What I discovered right away was that there were only three kinds of business in the universe—mine, yours, and God's. And if you don't use the G-word, put the word *nature* there or *reality.* So this is a test of discernment. Whose business is his money?

Marty: His business.

Katie: That's it.

Marty: I'm making it my business. That's what hurts.

Katie: Yes. Now here's what I noticed: when I mentally go into your business, I start getting this stress inside me. Doctors call it names like ulcers, high blood pressure, cancer—all of it. And then the mind attaches to that, and it creates a whole system to hold up the first lie. Let your feelings tell you when the first lie begins. Then inquire.

Otherwise you get lost in the feelings and in the stories that lead to them, and all you know is that you hurt and that your mind won't stop racing. And if you inquire, you catch the first lie through noticing your feelings. And you can just stop the mind by putting the story you're attached to onto a Judge-Your-Neighbor Worksheet. There's a portion of your stressful mind stopped, even though it may still be screaming in your head. Now put the statements up against inquiry, ask the four questions, and turn your statements around. That's it. You're the one who sets yourself free, not your uncle. You bail yourself out, or you're not going to get bailed out—haven't you noticed?

Marty: I agree with everything you said. It's right on the beam. It's just that at this point in time, I'm not in touch with my own ability to bail myself out.

Katie: Well, in this country we have bankruptcy. If I put myself in it, I get myself out of it. And if I file for bankruptcy, I eventually pay every debt I owe, because living this way offers me the freedom I'm looking for. I don't care if it's a dime a month. I, too, act as an honorable person, not because I'm spiritual but because it hurts if I don't. Simple.

Marty: Yes, that's the reason, I agree.

Katie: People think, "When I make a whole lot of money, then I'll be happy." I say let's skip that part for now and be happy from here. You got yourself into it. Your uncle had nothing to do with it so far.

Marty: I'm with you on that. I'm realizing that he didn't do it. *I* did it, and in a certain way it's kind of thrilling to sit with, and it's also like "Oh, shit!"

Katie: Yes, welcome to reality. When we begin to live in reality and see it for what it is without our old stories, it's incredible. Look at this for a moment without a story. It's all reality: God. I call it God because it rules, it always is what it is. And the myth of an uncle's responsibility would keep me from the awareness of that. It's so simple. Okay, so whose business is your uncle's money?

Marty: His.

Katie: And whose business is it what he does with his money?

Marty: His.

Katie: I love it!

Marty: I'm clear on those two now. I wasn't before. I really thought it was my business.

Katie: And did you sign your inheritance over to him?

Marty: Yup.

Katie: Okay. Whose money is it now?

Marty: His.

Katie: And whose business is it what he does with his money?

Marty: His.

Katie: Don't you love it? Life is so simple when we move back into our own business.

Marty: I don't feel very good about it now.

Katie: Sweetheart, when we realize something this basic, sometimes we're like a newborn foal. At first our legs won't even work. We just get wobbly and have to sit down. What I suggest is that on the other side of this session, you go somewhere and sit with it for a while and just be still with what you're realizing. It's big. Let's look at the next statement.

Marty: Okay. *Uncle Ralph should pay off my debts and give me a hundred grand.*

Katie: Wonderful! I love it! Now turn it around.

Marty: I should pay my debts and give myself a hundred grand.

Katie: This is very exciting. And if your mind isn't in his business, you would be amazed at the space that opens up for you, the power that opens up to solve your own problems. It's—well, it can't be told. It just can't be told. But it's the truth that sets us free to act clearly and lovingly, and there's such excitement in it. Okay, let's do another turnaround. "I . . ."

Marty: I should pay my debts and give myself a hundred grand.

Katie: "And give my uncle a hundred grand." *[Marty and the audience laugh.]*

Marty: Oh, man!

Katie: Whatever it is that you owe him.

Marty: I should pay my debts. You know, I probably do owe him another hundred grand.

Katie: So there it is.

Marty: I should pay my debts and give my uncle a hundred grand. Wow!

Katie: Yes. For your own sake. Even if the man has billions and billions of dollars—it doesn't matter. It's for *your* sake.

Marty: I agree. I absolutely agree with that.

Katie: Yes. So he should give you a hundred grand—what for?

Marty: Well, that would make all of these two and a half years of activity a basic wash.

Katie: And then you'd be happy?

Marty: Well, no.

Katie: How do you react when you believe the thought that he's supposed to give you a hundred grand?

Marty: I'm sore.

Katie: Yes. Who or what would you be without that thought?

Marty: Free.

Katie: Let's look at the next statement.

Marty [*laughing*]: *I need Uncle Ralph to bail my ass out from financial ruin.* This is hysterical!

Katie: Okay, now turn it around.

Marty: I need myself to bail my ass out from financial ruin.

Katie: You see how you've begun to end your own suffering? People lie on their deathbed at the age of ninety saying "It's all my uncle's fault." We don't have to do that anymore. And that's the offering here: judge your uncle, write it down, ask four questions, turn it around. And then send him a thank-you note. How do we know it's for your highest good that your uncle hasn't bailed you out? He hasn't. You're being given a great gift, and when you step into the truth, that gift becomes visible and available. And you end up like a little boy—new.

Marty: I would like that.

Katie: I really appreciate your courage. It would be wonderful to call him and tell him the turnarounds in your own language. For example, you might say, "Uncle Ralph, every time I call you, I want something from you. And I want you to know that *I* know I do that. I'm clear about it. And in no way do I expect you to bail me out. I've come to see that your money is yours and that I owe you and that I'm working on it, and if you have any suggestions, I'm open. And I'm sincerely sorry for what I've done." And when he says he has some great stock tips, you can say thank you and make your own decisions and not blame him if you do use them and lose money. You gave yourself those stock tips.

Marty: Yes. In fact, I even asked him for them, because I had come into some money and I knew he had a lot, so I wanted to know what he thought I should do with it.

Katie: The greatest stock market you can invest in is yourself. Finding this truth is better than finding a gold mine.

Marty: That thing about calling my uncle with what you just said—as much of it as I can retain—feels incredibly threatening to me.

Katie: Of course. You get to be wrong, and he gets to be right.

Marty: And I don't even know that he'd sit still to listen to it.

Katie: No, you don't. Okay, let's look at the next statement.

Marty: *I don't ever want to listen to his stock tips or owe him money* again *or take his petty, childish, irate shit.*

Katie: You might do all this again, if only in your mind. There might also be some residue left in you. And I can tell you that when you let go of one thing, everything falls like dominoes, because concepts are what we are working with—theories that have never been investigated. These concepts may appear again, and this is good news when you know what to do with them. You may expect something from him again, and it's going to hurt if it's out of alignment with your integrity.

Marty: That's true. Yes, that's actually true. It's hard to admit, but it's true.

Katie: Yes, but it's easier to admit it than not to admit it.

Marty: Yes . . . I don't know . . . I don't know if I'm there yet, but—

Katie: You could play the scenario over again in your mind, and if there's something left that you're attached to, if something hurts, it will plunge you back into The Work. So read it just as you wrote it, but say, "I'm willing to . . ."

Marty: Okay. I'm willing to listen to his stock tips and owe him money? *[Pauses.]* I guess I am. I am willing to listen to his stock tips and owe him money, and I am willing to take his petty, irate shit.

Katie: Yes. Because if you feel pain around it, it will put you back into The Work, if you want some freedom. Now "I look forward to . . ."

Marty: I look forward to . . . wait a minute . . . I'm confused now.

Katie: Just do it. Just trust the process. "I look forward to . . ."

Marty: Okay. I look forward to listening to his stock tips and owing him money and taking his petty, irate shit?

Katie: Yes. Because it's possible that you'll play that scenario over again.

Marty: Not likely, because I don't think he'd ever give me a tip again, and I don't think I'll ever have any money to play the market again. Not that I want to, anyway.

Katie: You might play this scenario in the middle of the night when you wake up in a cold sweat.

Marty: Oh.

Katie: That's when these things are often done.

Marty: Right.

Katie: And you can just grab your pad and pencil or your smartphone and judge your uncle again and clean yourself up. Every concept that has ever existed is inside you. It's not personal. After all these thousands of years, the thoughts are still in each of us, waiting to be met with some friendship and a little understanding finally, rather than with pills and running and hiding and arguing and sexing because we don't know what else to do with them. When the thoughts arise, just meet them with some integrity. "He owes me"—is it true? Can you absolutely know that it's true? How do you react, what happens, when you believe that thought? Ask yourself. And who would you be without the thought? You would have an uncle you care about, and you would be responsible for yourself. Until you love him unconditionally, your Work's not done. Close your eyes now, and look at your uncle trying to help you. *Look* at the guy without your story.

Marty: Do you want to know what my experience was?

Katie: Yes.

Marty: I'm still feeling the pain of his verbal abuse.

Katie: Okay, verbal abuse—turn it around. "I'm feeling the pain . . ."

Marty: I still am feeling the pain of *my* verbal abuse.

Katie: Toward him in your mind.

Marty: I'm still feeling the pain of my verbal abuse toward him in my mind?

Katie: Yes.

Marty: Maybe everyone else here is getting this. I'm not.

Katie: What's an example of his verbal abuse?

Marty: "Marty, you don't know nothin'. I told you to do it this way, and you did it your own way."

Katie: Okay, let's stop right there. Could it be that he's right and that's what you don't want to hear? That's not verbal abuse. We call it "verbal abuse" when someone tells us the truth about ourselves and we don't want to hear it. That is, we *think* we don't want to hear it. Deep down inside us, we hunger for the truth.

Marty: Okay. I see that. That's true.

Katie: There's no such thing as verbal abuse. There's only someone telling me a truth that I don't want to hear. If I were really able to hear my accuser, I would find my freedom. The "you" you're identified with doesn't want to be discovered, because that is its death. When someone tells me that I lied, for example, I just go inside to see if they're right. If I can't find it in the situation they've mentioned, I can find it in some other situation, maybe twenty years ago. And then I can say, "Sweetheart, I *am* a liar. I see where you're right about me." In this we've found something in common. They know I'm a liar, and now I know it. We join and connect. We both agree. I can find those pieces of who I am from them. This is the beginning of self-love.

Marty: That's right. Oh, my God, I never saw that!

Katie: If your uncle says something that hurts, he's just revealed what you haven't wanted to look at yet. The man is a Buddha. *[Marty* *and the audience laugh.]* These people that we're close to will give us everything we need, so that we can realize ourselves and be free of the lie. Your uncle knows exactly what to say, because he's you, giving you back to yourself. But you say, "Go away, I don't want to hear it." And you say it mostly in your mind. Because you think that if you got honest with him about it, he might not give you money. Or affection or validation.

Marty: He's never given me any validation.

Katie: Good! I'm *loving* this guy. *[Marty and the audience laugh.]* He leaves that for you to do, and he just holds his truth.

Marty: If you met him, I don't know if you'd think he was an enlightened being.

Katie: What I know is that he knows the things about you that you haven't wanted to look at yet. And the truth is that he can guide you to the things you really do want to look at. If you go to a friend and say, "Oh, my uncle has treated me so badly," your friend will say, "You poor fellow, that's really a shame." What I say is, find an enemy. They won't give you that sympathy. You go to your friends for refuge, because you can count on them to agree with your stories. But when you go to your enemies, they'll tell you, straight up, anything you want to know, even though you may think you don't want to know it. Your uncle can give you material that's invaluable if you really want to know the truth. Until you do, you have to resent your uncle.

Marty: You mean that everything I'm defending against is the truth that I don't want to see? Holy shit! No wonder I've been seeing my uncle as an enemy! This is amazing!

Katie: Uncles have never been the problem, and they never will be. It's your uninvestigated thinking about your uncle that's the problem. And as you inquire, you set yourself free. Your uncle is really God in disguise as an uncle. He's giving you everything you need for your freedom.

Angry at Corporate America

A question I often hear is "If I do The Work and I'm no longer fearful for the planet's welfare, why would I get involved in social action? If I felt completely peaceful, why would I bother taking action at all?" My answer is "Because that's what love does."

The fear of not being fearful is one of the biggest stumbling blocks for people who are beginning inquiry. They believe that without stress, without anger, they wouldn't act, they would just sit around in bliss with drool running down their chins. Whoever created the impression that peace isn't active has never known peace the way I know it. I am entirely motivated without anger. The truth sets us free, and freedom acts.

When I take people to the desert, they may see a tin can lying under a cactus and ask, "How can anyone do that to this beautiful desert?" But that tin can *is* the desert. It's what is. How can it be out of place? The cactus, the snakes, the scorpions, the sand, the can, and us—all of it. That *is* nature, not a mental image of the desert without the can. Without any stress or judgment, I notice that I just pick up the can. Or I could tell the story that people are polluting the earth and that there is no end to human selfishness and greed and then pick up the can with all the sadness and anger I'd be feeling. Either way, when it's time for the can to move, I'm there, as nature, picking up the can. Who would I be without my uninvestigated story? Just happily picking up the can. And if someone notices me picking it up and my action seems right, that person may pick up another can. We're already acting as a community, beyond anything that we planned. Without a story, without an enemy, action is spontaneous, clear, and infinitely kind.

Margaret: *I'm angry at corporations because they think about money only.*

Katie: So they think about money only—can you really know that that's true? I'm not saying that it's not. I'm not here with a philosophy or the right or wrong of it. Just inquiry.

Margaret: Well, it seems like that.

Katie: Sweetheart, the answer to the first question is one syllable: yes or no.

Margaret: Oh. *[Pauses]* Yes.

Katie: Can you absolutely know that they think about money only?

Margaret: Hmm. *[Pauses]* No.

Katie: How do you react when you believe the thought that they only care about money?

Margaret: I get angry and frustrated, and I don't want to support them as people.

Katie: Yes, even though you do support them. You use the products they put out, their electricity, their oil and gas. You feel guilty as you do it, yet you continue, and maybe, just like them, you find a way to justify your action. So give me a stress-free reason to believe the thought that these people only care about money.

Margaret: Well, that way I make a difference. I at least do what I can do.

Katie: I hear from you that when you believe that thought, you experience anger and frustration. And how do you live when you think that you've made a difference and they're still cutting down trees? You think that only through further stress can the planet be saved. Now give me a stress-*free* reason to believe that thought.

Margaret: There is no stress-free reason.

Katie: No stress-free reason? So who would you be without this thought, this philosophy, that they only care about money?

Margaret: Peaceful. Happy. Maybe clearer.

Katie: Yes. And maybe more effective, energized, less confused, and in a position to make a real difference in ways that you haven't even imagined yet. In my experience, clarity moves much more efficiently than violence and stress. It doesn't make enemies along the way, and therefore it can sit comfortably at a peace table, face-to-face with anyone there.

Margaret: That's true.

Katie: When I come at a corporate official or a logger, pointing my finger and in any way blaming him or his company for destroying the atmosphere, however valid my information is, do you think that he'll be open to what I'm saying? I'm scaring him with my attitude, and the facts can get lost, because I'm coming from fear myself. All he'll hear is that I think he's doing it wrong, it's his fault, and he'll go into denial and resistance. But if I speak to him without any stress, in total confidence that everything is just the way it should be right now, I'm able to express myself kindly and with no fear about the future. "Here are the facts. How can the two of us make it better? Do you see another way? How do you suggest that we proceed?" And when he speaks, I'm able to listen.

Margaret: I understand.

Katie: Let's take a look at statement number two.

Margaret: *I want corporations to start taking responsibility, to start respecting life, care for the future, be in support of the environment and third-world countries, stop abusing animals, and stop thinking about money only.*

Katie: Sweetheart, let's turn it around and see what you would experience with that. Turn around statement number two. Say it again with you in all of it. "I . . ."

Margaret: I want to start taking responsibility, I want to start respecting life and care for the future. I want to be in support of the environment and third-world countries, and I want to stop abusing animals. I want to stop thinking about money only.

Katie: Does that ring a bell?

Margaret: Well, I really feel I'm— That's what I'm working on all the time.

Katie: And wouldn't you rather work on it without the frustration, stress, and anger? But when you come at us—the corporate people—self-righteously, all we see is the enemy coming. When you come at us clearly, we can hear from you what we already know in our hearts about the welfare of the planet, and we can listen to you and your solutions without feeling threatened and without having to be defensive. We can see you as a loving and attractive person, as someone easy to work with, someone to be trusted. That's my experience.

Margaret: Well, that's true.

Katie: War teaches only war. You clean up your mental environment, and we'll clean up our physical one much more quickly. That's how it works. Let's look at the next statement on your Worksheet.

Margaret: *Corporations should be caring and give back to the planet, use their money to support environmental groups, build habitats, support freedom of broadcasting, should wake up and start thinking about tomorrow.*

Katie: So they don't care—can you really know that that's true?

Margaret: Well, again, it seems like it, doesn't it?

Katie: That's a lot of words, sweetheart. Can you find a simple yes or no? Can you absolutely know that it's true that they don't care?

Margaret: No.

Katie: How do you react when you believe the thought "They don't care"?

Margaret: Sometimes I get really depressed. But it's good, because I also get very angry. I get very motivated and work very hard at making a difference.

Katie: How does the anger feel inside you?

Margaret: It hurts. I can't stand what they're doing to our planet.

Katie: Doesn't all that anger feel violent inside you?

Margaret: Yes.

Katie: Anger is violent. Feel it.

Margaret: But it motivates me to act, so it's good to have *some* stress. We need it to get things moving.

Katie: So what I hear from you is that violence works, violence is the way to a peaceful solution. That doesn't make sense to me. We humans have been trying to prove this point for eons. What you're saying is that violence is healthy for you but that corporations shouldn't use it against the planet. "Excuse me, corporations, you should stop your violence and treat the planet peacefully, and by the way, violence really works for me in my life." So you need violence to motivate you—is that true?

Margaret *[after a pause]*: No. Those bouts of anger leave me depressed and wiped out. Are you saying that without the violence, I would be just as motivated?

Katie: No, sweetheart, that was you. What I would say is that I don't need anger or violence to accomplish things or to motivate myself in any way. If I were to feel anger, I would do The Work on the thought behind it. This leaves love as the motivator. Is there anything more powerful than love? Think of your own experience. And what could be more motivating? I hear from you that fear and anger are depressing. Think of yourself when you love someone—how motivated you become. Who would you be without the thought that you need violence as a motivator?

Margaret: I don't know. That feels very strange.

Katie: So, sweetheart, let's turn it around: "I . . ."

Margaret: I don't care. Yes, that's true. I haven't cared about those people. And I should be caring and give back to the planet. I should use my money to support environmental groups, build habitats, support freedom of broadcasting. I should wake up and start thinking about tomorrow.

Katie: Yes. And if you do that genuinely, without violence in your heart, without anger, without pointing at corporations as the enemy, then people begin to notice. We begin to listen and notice that change through peace is possible. It has to begin with one person, you know. If you're not the one, who is?

Margaret: Well, that's true. That's very true.

Katie: Let's look at the next statement.

Margaret: *I need them to stop hurting and destroying, to start making a difference, and to respect life.*

Katie: So you need them to do that—is that true?

Margaret: Well, that would be a great start.

Katie: You *need* them to do that—is that true?

Margaret: Yeah.

Katie: Are you going inside yourself? Are you really asking? You need them to clean it up—is that true?

Margaret: Well, I don't need it for my everyday survival or anything like that, but yeah, that would be great.

Katie: I hear that. And that's what you need to be happy?

Margaret: That's what I want. I know what you mean, but it's so—

Katie: You know, this brings about incredible terror inside you. How do you react when you think the thought that this is what you need, and corporations are doing—oh, my—they're doing what they do? They're not listening to you. You're not even on their board of advisers. *[Laughter from the audience.]* They're not accepting your calls. You just get their answering machines. How do you react when you think the thought that you *need* them to clean it up and they don't?

Margaret: It feels frustrating. Painful. I become agitated and get very angry, very scared.

Katie: Yes. A lot of people won't even bring children into the world because that thought runs through them without investigation. They live in such fear when they're attached to this belief. Can you see a reason to drop the belief? And I'm not asking you to drop it.

Margaret: Yeah. I can see many reasons, but I'm really afraid that—

Katie: If you dropped the belief, what would happen?

Margaret: I wouldn't care anymore.

Katie: And I would ask you, if you didn't believe this, you wouldn't care, you would lose all caring about the environment—can you really know that that's true?

Margaret: No.

Katie: If we don't suffer, we won't care: what a thought! How do you react when you think the thought that stress is caring, that fear is caring? How do we react when we believe that thought? We become the champions of suffering. But only for a good cause. Only in the name of humanity. We sacrifice our lives to suffering. The story goes that Jesus suffered for hours on the cross. How many years have you lived with these nails through your body?

Margaret: I understand.

Katie: Let's turn it around, sweetheart.

Margaret: Okay. *I* should stop hurting and destroying.

Katie: Stop hurting and destroying yourself in the name of cleaning up the planet. "When the planet is cleaned up, then I'll be peaceful." Does that make sense? Your pain—is that how we're going to clean up the planet? Do you think that if you hurt enough, if you suffer enough, someone will hear you and do something about it?

Margaret: Okay. I see it. I need to start making a difference. And I need to start respecting my life.

Katie: Yes, yours. It's a beginning.

Margaret: So I need to start respecting my own life.

Katie: Yes. Take care of yourself, and when you find peace, when your mental environment is balanced, then be the expert who can go out to balance the planet— fearlessly, caringly, and effectively. And in the meantime, do the best you can, just like the rest of us, even us corporate people. How can an internally imbalanced, frustrated woman teach others how to clean up their act? We have to learn that ourselves first, and that begins from within. Violence teaches only violence. Stress teaches stress. And peace teaches peace. And for me, peace is entirely efficient. Well done, honey. Nice Work.

Would you rather
be right
or free?

7

Doing The Work
on Self-Judgments

～⌒～

One year for his birthday, I bought my grandson Race a plastic Darth Vader toy because he had asked for it. He had just turned three; he didn't have a clue about *Star Wars*, even though he wanted the Darth Vader toy. When you put a coin into Darth Vader, you hear the *Star Wars* music and Darth Vader's heavy breathing. Then his voice says, "Impressive, but you are not a Jedi yet," and he lifts his sword as if to emphasize the point. After Racey heard the voice, he said, "Grandma, I not a Jedi," and shook his little head. I said, "Honey, you can be Grandma's little Jedi." And he said, "I not," and shook his head again.

A week or so after I gave him the toy, I called him on the phone and asked him, "Sweetheart, are you a Jedi yet? Are you Grandma's little Jedi?" And he said, in a sad little voice, "I not." He didn't even know what a Jedi was, he wasn't even asking, yet he wanted to be one. So the little guy was taking orders from a plastic toy and was walking around disappointed at the ripe old age of three.

Shortly after that, I was invited by a friend to fly over the desert in his plane. I told my friend about the Jedi thing and asked if Racey could come with us. He said yes, smiling over an idea he had. He made arrangements with the ground crew, and as we landed, we heard a voice over the cabin speakers announcing, "Racey, you are a

Jedi! You are a Jedi now!" Racey rolled his little eyes in disbelief. I asked him if he was a Jedi yet. He wouldn't answer me. When we got home, he ran straight to Darth Vader. He dropped in his coin, the music began, with the heavy breathing, the sword rose, and the deep voice said, "Impressive, but you are not a Jedi yet." That seemed to be the way of it. I asked him one more time, and he told me, "Grandma, I not."

Many of us judge ourselves as relentlessly as that plastic toy played its recording, telling ourselves over and over what we are and what we're not. Once investigated, these self-judgments simply melt away. If you've been following the instructions and have done The Work by pointing the finger of blame outward, you will have noticed that your judgments of others always turn back toward you. When those turned-around judgments feel uncomfortable, you can be sure that you've hit a belief about yourself that you haven't investigated yet. For example, "He should love me" turns around to "I should love myself," and if you experience stress with that thought, you may want to take a look at it.

As you become fluid with the four questions and turnarounds, you'll begin to discover for yourself that The Work is equally powerful when the one you're judging is yourself. You'll see that the "you" you judge is no more personal than everyone else turned out to be. The Work deals with concepts, not people.

The four questions are used in exactly the same way when you apply them to self-judgments. For example, let's consider the self-judgment "I am a failure." First, go inside with questions 1 and 2: Is it true? Can I absolutely know that it's true that I'm a failure? My husband or wife may say so, my parents may say so, and I may say so, but can I absolutely know that it's true? Could it be that all along I have lived the life I should have lived and that everything I've done has been what I should have done? Then move on to question 3: Make a list of how you react, how you feel physically, and how you treat yourself and others when you believe the thought "I am a fail-

ure." What do you do specifically? What do you say specifically? Do
your shoulders slump? Do you snap at people? Do you go to the refrigerator? Continue with your list. Then go inside with question 4:
Experience what your life would be like if you never had this thought
again. Close your eyes and picture how you would be without the
thought "I am a failure." Be still as you watch. What do you see?

The turnarounds for self-judgments can be quite radical. When
you use the 180-degree turnaround, "I am a failure" becomes "I am
not a failure" or "I am a success." Go inside with this turnaround, and
let it reveal to you how it is as true as or truer than your original
statement. Make a list of the ways in which you are a success. Bring
those truths out of the darkness. Some of us find this extremely difficult at first and may be hard pressed to find even one example. Take
your time. If you really want to know the truth, allow the truth to
reveal itself to you. Find three successes each day. One could be "I
brushed my teeth." Two: "I did the dishes." Three: "I breathed." It's a
wonderful thing to be a success at being what you are, whether you
realize it or not.

Sometimes replacing the word "I" with "My thinking" will bring
a realization. "I am a failure" becomes "My thinking is a failure, especially about myself." You can understand this clearly when you go
inside to answer question 4. Without the thought "I am a failure,"
aren't you perfectly fine? It's the thought that is painful, not your life.

Don't get stuck in the turnarounds, as if there's a right or wrong
way of doing them. If a turnaround doesn't work for you, don't worry.
This is as it should be. Just move on to the next statement. Inquire
sincerely, and let the turnarounds find you.

When I argue with
reality, I lose—
but only 100 percent
of the time.

8

Doing The Work with Children

I am often asked if children and teenagers can do The Work. My answer is "Of course they can." In this process of inquiry, we're dealing with thoughts, and people of all ages—eight or eighty—have the same stressful thoughts and concepts: "I want my mother to love me," "I need my friend to listen to me," "People shouldn't be mean." Young or old, we believe concepts that through inquiry are seen to be nothing more than superstitions.

Even young children can find The Work life-changing. During one children's workshop, a six-year-old girl got so excited that she said, "This Work is amazing! Why didn't anyone ever tell me about it?" Another child, a seven-year-old boy, said to his mother, "The Work is the best thing in the whole wide world!" Curious, she asked, "What is it that you like so much about The Work, Daniel?" "When I'm scared and we do The Work," he said, "then afterward I'm not scared anymore."

When I do The Work with young children, the only difference I'm aware of is that I draw from a simpler vocabulary. If I use a word that I think might be beyond them, I ask them if they understand it. If I feel that they really don't understand, then I say what I mean in another way. But I never use baby talk. Children know when they are being talked down to.

The following excerpt is from a dialogue I had with a five-year-old girl.

Becky [*frightened, not looking at me*]: There's a monster under my bed.

Katie: There's a monster under your bed—sweetheart, is that true?

Becky: Yes.

Katie: Sweetheart, look at me. Can you absolutely know that that's true?

Becky: Yes.

Katie: Give me your proof. Have you ever seen the monster?

Becky [*beginning to smile*]: Yes.

Katie: Is that true?

Becky: Yes.

Now the child is beginning to laugh and warm up to the questions, to trust that I'm not going to force her to believe or not to believe, and we can have fun with this monster of hers. Eventually, the monster has a personality, and before the end of the session, I'll ask the child to close her eyes, talk to the monster face-to-face, and let the monster tell her what he's doing under the bed and what he really wants from her. I'll ask her just to let the monster talk and to tell me what the monster said. I've done this with a dozen children who were afraid of monsters or ghosts. They always reported something kind, such as "He says he's lonely" or "He just wants to play" or "He wants to be with me." At this point, I can ask them, "Sweetheart, there's a monster under your bed—is that true?" And they usually look at me with a kind of knowing amusement that I would believe such a ridiculous thing. There's a lot of laughter.

It's so simple to move to the next question at any point. For example: "How do you react at night in your room alone when you believe the thought that there's a monster under your bed? How does it feel when you believe that thought?" "Scary. I get scared." Here they often begin to squirm and fidget. "Sweetheart, who would you be, lying in bed at night, if you couldn't think the thought 'There's a monster under my bed'?" "I'd be okay" is what they usually answer. I love at this point to say to children, "What I learned from you is that without the thought you're not afraid and with the thought you are afraid. What I learned from you is that it's not the monster that you're afraid of, it's the *thought*. This is such good news. Whenever I'm frightened, I know that I'm just frightened of a thought."

Parents always report that after the session the nightmares stop occurring. I also hear that parents don't have to talk their children into coming back to see me. We share an understanding together as a result of inquiry. I once worked with a four-year-old boy, David, at his parents' request. They had been taking him to a psychiatrist because he seemed so intent on hurting his baby sister. They always had to keep track of him; whenever he had the chance, he would attack her, even in front of his parents. He would poke her, pull her, try to push her off surfaces, and he was old enough to know that she would fall. They saw him as seriously disturbed. He was getting angrier and angrier. The parents were at their wits' end.

In our session, I asked David some of the questions on the Judge-Your-Neighbor Worksheet, and the mother's therapist wrote down his answers. The parents did The Work in another room. When they returned, I had them read their Worksheets on each other in front of the child, so that he could understand that there would be no punishment for expressing his feelings honestly.

Mother: *I'm angry at the new baby because I have to change her diapers all day long and can't spend more time with my David. I'm angry at Dad because he works all day and can't help me change diapers for the new baby.*

Mother and Father continued to judge each other and the baby in front of the little boy. Then it was David's turn to hear his statements read out loud. *I'm angry at Mommy because she spends all her time with Kathy. I'm angry at Daddy because he's not home enough.* Finally, we heard his statements about his little sister.

David: *I'm angry at Kathy because she doesn't want to play games with me. I want her to play ball with me. She should play with me. She shouldn't just lie there all the time. She should want to get up and play with me. I need her to play with me.*

Katie: She should play with you—honey, is that true?

David: Yes.

Katie: David, sweetheart, how does it feel when you think that thought?

David: I'm mad. I want her to play with me.

Katie: How did you learn that babies should play ball with you?

David: My mommy and daddy.

As soon as his parents heard the answer, they knew what was happening. Throughout the entire pregnancy, they had told the little fellow that soon he would have a brother or sister who would play games with him and be there as his playmate. What they had failed to tell him was that the baby would have to grow before she could run or hold a ball. When they explained that to David and apologized to him, he of course understood. He left her alone after that. They later informed me that the troubling behavior had stopped, that they were all working on clear communication, and that he was beginning to trust them again.

I love working with children. They come to inquiry so easily, just as we all do when we really want to be free.

Abby and Zoë Don't Want Me to Play with Them

Here, from 2007, is an example of doing The Work with an older child, a remarkably tuned-in nine-year-old girl. Notice how honest she is in answering the questions. She even sees a turnaround's truth where I didn't. There's no defense or justification in her mind, and that allows her to go inside and loosen the beliefs that have been making her unhappy.

Katie: Okay, sweetheart, sit here. Let's get closer. What did you write?

Zeffi: *I am angry at Zoë because she took Abby from me.*

Katie: Zoë took Abby from you—is that true?

Zeffi: Yes.

Katie: Zoë took Abby from you—can you absolutely know that it's true that Zoë did that?

Zeffi: No, no.

Katie: Where did you get that no?

Zeffi: Well, I'm not *absolutely* sure that she did that.

Katie: Very good. How do you react, what happens, when you believe Zoë took Abby away from you?

Zeffi: Well, I get really stressed, and then I start blaming Abby for following Zoë and going with her . . . yeah.

Katie: And what happens when you believe that thought and you run into them, when you see them together?

Zeffi: Well, I ask, "Can I play with you?" And they're like "Well . . . we're not really playing, but . . . yeah, sure." And so it doesn't feel good, and I know they really don't want me there.

Katie: Wow! *[To the audience]* Would someone write down "They don't really want me there"? That's a sidebar we can do The Work on later. *[To Zeffi]* So when you're at home or doing your homework or doing the dishes or going to bed, how do you react when you believe the thought "Zoë took Abby away from me"?

Zeffi: Well, I can't go to sleep. And then when I wake up for school, I don't really want to go, and I start dreading recess. Yeah.

Katie: I invite you to close your eyes and look at yourself going to sleep and waking up and getting ready to go to school and at recess, without the thought "Zoë took Abby away from me." Who would you be without that thought?

Zeffi: Well, I think I would just see Abby and Zoë, and they're having fun. And I'm noticing they're like "Oh, yeah, well, yeah, yeah, I guess you can play with us," then I'm not wanted and I don't really feel good there, and so I could just go play with the boys, and they're playing great fun games, and they include anybody. *[Laughter from the audience.]*

Katie: That sounds very intelligent to me. So who would you be, waking up in the morning, dressing for school, without the thought "Zoë took Abby away from me"?

Zeffi: Well . . .

Katie: Just close your eyes and imagine yourself getting up without that thought.

Zeffi: I would just sort of know that I'm not going to try and bother them, and if they want to play with me, they can come and they can ask me, and I can play with Ian, another one of my friends. He's really nice. Or the first grade—they're fun.

Katie: A lot of options out there.

Zeffi: Yeah.

Katie: Who would you be, getting up without the story at all?

Zeffi: Happy!

Katie: So close your eyes again, and just trust that it's okay to keep them closed. Now imagine yourself getting up without a story. Just watch. Who would you be without your story?

Zeffi: I think I would be happy to get up and get dressed and eat breakfast and grab my lunch and my snow pants and hurry outside and get in my dad's car and then go to school, and you know, I only have two recesses. I could just hang out with the teachers or something.

Katie: Boy, do you have options! Abby and Zoë are looking like a very small world now.

Zeffi: Yeah.

Katie: So. "Zoë took Abby away from me"—turn it around. Find an opposite.

Zeffi: Zoë *didn't* take Abby away from me.

Katie: Now give me an example of how that could be true.

Zeffi: Well, Zoë just came along. She was in kindergarten, she couldn't help going to school, and Abby met her, and they became friends.

Katie: Wow! That doesn't have anything to do with you, does it?

Zeffi: No! And Abby still likes me.

Katie: Yes. So can you find another turnaround for "Zoë took Abby away from me"? Try "I . . ."

Zeffi: Okay. I took Abby away from Zoë.

Katie: That doesn't seem to work.

Zeffi: Well, it actually sort of does.

Katie: Tell me.

Zeffi: Well, because I tried to get Abby to play with me, by like asking her "Who do you like better?"

Katie: Wow, and leaving Zoë out!

Zeffi: Yeah.

Katie: It does work, doesn't it?

Zeffi: Uh-huh.

Katie: Oh, my goodness. So you think that Zoë is just like you.

Zeffi: Yes.

Katie: Because you do that, you think she would do that.

Zeffi: Yeah.

Katie: But we can't really know, can we? Can you find another turn-around?

Zeffi: Okay. *[Pauses.]* I took me away from me.

Katie: Tell me about that.

Zeffi: Well, when I'm thinking "Oh, it's so bad!" and "Zoë took Abby away from me," I start getting into Zoë's business. And there is nobody to live *my* life, because I'm over there living Zoë's life.

Katie: Wow! It sounds like you've been listening to some Katie tapes.

Zeffi *[laughing with the audience]:* Yes!

Katie: So you just take yourself out of your life. You'd rather be with them than with you.

Zeffi: Yes. But I wouldn't rather be with them. I'm just in their business.

Katie: It's more fun to be with you.

Zeffi: Yeah, and the boys and the first grade and Ian and Miss Watson, my teacher.

Katie: It really opens up a whole other world for you at school, doesn't it, without Abby?

Zeffi: Yeah.

Katie: So if Abby hadn't moved out of your life, then this vast turf at school couldn't have opened up to you.

Zeffi: Yeah, I would've only had one option. Or I would've had tons of options, but I would only want to be with Abby.

Katie: Well, this is all starting to make sense. Have you heard me say that if I lose anyone or anything, I've been spared?

Zeffi: Yes.

Katie: Yes, that seems to be the case with you, too. You've been spared this limitedness, and this whole school zone opens up for you.

Zeffi: Yes. Should I read my next statement?

Katie: Good.

Zeffi: *I want Zoë to leave Abby alone and find someone else to like.*

Katie: You want Zoë to leave Abby alone—is that true?

Zeffi: No.

Katie: Wow!

Zeffi: Because then, as you said, I wouldn't have that many options.

Katie: Boy, honey, you're ready for a big world, aren't you?

Zeffi: I guess so.

Katie: So let's turn that around.

Zeffi: Okay. *[Pauses.]* Hmm.

Katie: "I want me . . ."

Zeffi: I want *me* to leave Abby alone and find somebody else to like. Yeah, that's true. I already did!

Katie: That's right. Okay, let's move on to the next statement, number three.

Zeffi: *Zoë shouldn't interfere with my relationship with Abby.*

Katie: So Zoë interferes with your relationship—is that true?

Zeffi: No.

Katie: Okay, let's skip inquiry for this one. Can you turn it around?

Zeffi: I shouldn't interfere with Zoë's and Abby's relationship.

Katie: Now give me an example of why you shouldn't interfere with their relationship.

Zeffi: Well, they're just like "Oh, well, yeah . . ." And so it's not very fun.

Katie: That's a very good reason.

Zeffi: Yeah, I'd rather go play with the first graders or somebody. Yeah.

Katie: The next statement?

Zeffi: *I need Zoë to give Abby and me a break.*

Katie: You're doing so well, sweetheart. Let's skip inquiry here, too, and go right to the turnarounds.

Zeffi: I don't need Zoë to give Abby and me a break. That's actually truer.

Katie: Good. Can you find another turnaround?

Zeffi: Okay. I need me to give Abby and Zoë a break.

Katie: Yes.

Zeffi: Yes, I do. I keep on sort of trying to get in, and then they're giving me a clear message, "No, no, no."

Katie: You know what I love about people who don't want me? They show me who *not* to be with!

Zeffi: Yeah!

Katie: You don't have to guess. They give you a shortcut. Can you find another turnaround? Put you on all of it.

Zeffi: I need to give me a break. Yeah, I do. I'm really bothering me with this. *[Laughter from the audience.]*

Katie: Yes, I love to hear that. "I need to give me a break."

Zeffi: Yes.

Katie: Let's move to the next one, number five.

Zeffi: *Zoë is always poking her nose into everything.*

Katie: Is that true?

Zeffi: No. She doesn't poke her nose into my relationship with the first grade or Ian or the boys or Miss Watson or you or my sister or my mom or Gail or everybody else.

Katie: This is good. So how do you react, what happens, when you believe the thought "I want her to stop poking her nose into everything"?

Zeffi: I feel like if it hadn't been for her, then Abby and I would be best friends and everything. And I walk into Abby's house and see a picture of a newspaper cutout of Abby and Zoë selling lemonade, and a big bubble of anger comes up and it doesn't feel good at all.

Katie: Yes, you see pictures and you superimpose your thought onto it.

Zeffi: And like, I was driving yesterday with my mom and my sister and my brother, and I saw Sara, Abby's mom, walking out of Zoë's house. And it really annoyed me.

Katie: Yes, because *you* imagined—what?

Zeffi: Them having a playdate without me. Except it doesn't really matter, because me and Abby have playdates without Zoë, and Zoë and me have playdates without Abby. So why shouldn't they have playdates without me?

Katie: That works. Okay, can you find another turnaround?

Zeffi: I'm always poking my nose into everything. Well, yeah, I'm poking my nose into their relationship. And me and Abby still have a relationship, so Zoë isn't doing anything. I'm the one who's poking my nose into *their* relationship.

Katie: Very good—and very painful. Nice to know where the suffering's coming from, isn't it?

Zeffi: Yes.

Katie: It's not coming from them. It's coming from your thoughts about them. You know, there's another place where you may be poking your nose into their relationship. You see a lemonade ad, and you poke your nose into the way you're not the person there.

Zeffi: Yeah.

Katie: You poke your nose into the ad.

Zeffi: And actually they were in the ad, *they* were the ones selling lemonade. But I mean, maybe they invited me but I was sick—or maybe I was off on vacation or something. I don't know. I don't really remember.

Katie: Good. Who knows? Let's look at the last statement.

Zeffi: *I don't ever want to experience Zoë taking a friend away from me.*

Katie: "I'm willing to . . ."

Zeffi: I'm willing to experience Zoë taking a friend away from me. And she didn't even take a friend away from me!

Katie: Yes. And that's why we can become so willing to experience something like that again. Because you have the ability to wake yourself up from that kind of nightmare that you're living with. "I look forward to . . ."

Zeffi: I look forward to Zoë taking a friend away from me. And yeah, it will give me a chance to do The Work. *[Laughter and applause from the audience.]*

Katie: That's right. I'm with you. Have you found any problem that you can't Work through?

Zeffi: No. Not ever, ever, ever, ever.

Katie: Wonderful. Okay, my little heart, let's look at the sidebar now. That was the concept that we wrote down. They don't really want you there—is that true?

Zeffi: Yes.

Katie: They don't really want you there—how do you react when you believe that thought?

Zeffi: Well, I feel like I'm there for no reason, and then I start telling myself stories that don't even have anything to do with Abby and Zoë, like I'm too bossy and so that's why they don't want me there.

Katie: So you begin to attack yourself.

Zeffi: Yes.

Katie: Who would you be without the thought "They don't want me there"?

Zeffi: I would just say, "Hi, Abby and Zoë!" and they would say, "Hi, do you want to play with us?" "Um, actually, I'm going to play with Ian, but thanks for offering!"

Katie: So "They don't want me there"—turn it around.

Zeffi: Okay, they're fine with me being there. Or they *do* really want me there.

Katie: Who knows? Everything could have changed.

Zeffi: I know! Sometimes they do want me to play with them.

Katie: So when they do, what fun! And when they don't, what fun!

Zeffi: Yeah, I can just go play with another friend.

Katie: So why is it more fun to play with the first graders?

Zeffi: Because I'm older than them and they adore me and they all want to play with me and they want me to help them chisel the ice and they want to wrestle me off a swing, and they want to make me climb a tree and they want to make me jump down.

Katie: They sound a lot more fun than—

Zeffi: And play Uncle Sam.

Katie: I can see that. Good old Zoë, yeah. So you may want to thank her, and Abby, too. Okay, sweetheart, can you find another turn-around for "They don't really want me there"?

Zeffi: I don't really want them there. I don't really want to play with them. Yeah, yeah! I can see that they're sort of like "Yeah, well . . . hmm, hmm." And so I'm "Have it your own way!" And so I go and play with my really good friends who really want me there.

Katie: Who are really a lot of fun. I think that's what play is all about.

Zeffi: Uh-huh. Why play with somebody who doesn't want you and you don't want them?

Katie: Yes, it doesn't sound like play.

Zeffi: It sounds like argument. And of course we would probably get into an argument. Yeah. Thanks, Katie.

Katie: You are very welcome, sweetheart. It was wonderful to do The Work with you.

"I don't know"
is my favorite
position.

9

Doing The Work
on Underlying Beliefs

Beneath the judgments that we've written, we can often find other thoughts that we've believed for years and that we use as our fundamental judgments of life. I call these thoughts *underlying beliefs*. Underlying beliefs are broader, more general versions of our stories. They're like religions that we unconsciously live.

Suppose you have written down a trivial-sounding thought like "George should hurry up so we can go for a walk." Inquiry might bring to your awareness several unexamined thoughts that may be linked to "George should hurry up," such as:

The present is not as good as the future.

I'd be happy if I had my way.

It's possible to waste time.

Attachment to these underlying beliefs will make life painful for you in situations in which you're waiting or you perceive other people as moving too slowly. If any of these beliefs seem familiar to you, the next time you're waiting for someone, I invite you to write down the thoughts that underlie your impatience and see if they're really true for you. (You'll find suggestions below for doing this.)

Underlying beliefs are the building blocks of your concept of heaven and your concept of hell. They show exactly how you think you would improve reality if you had your way and how bad reality could look if your fears came true. To watch it all collapse—to discover that the painful beliefs we've carried around for years are not true for us, that we've never needed them at all—is an incredibly freeing experience.

Here are some examples of the kind of statements you may find yourself working with:

It's possible to be in the wrong place at the wrong time.

Life is unfair.

It's necessary to know what to do.

I can feel your pain.

Death is sad.

It's possible to miss out on something.

If I don't suffer, it means that I don't care.

God will punish me if I'm not good.

There is life after death.

Children are supposed to like their parents.

Something terrible could happen to me.

Parents are responsible for their children's choices.

It's possible to make a mistake.

There is evil in the world.

You may want to do The Work on any of these statements that seem like obstacles to your freedom.

Whenever you notice that you're feeling defensive in conversations with your friends or family or whenever you're sure that you're right, you may want to jot down your own underlying beliefs and do

The Work on them later. This is wonderful material for inquiry if you really want to know the truth and to live without the suffering these beliefs cause.

One of the best ways of discovering your underlying beliefs is to write out your "proof of truth" for question 1. Rather than moving immediately to the awareness that you can't really know anything, allow yourself to stay in the story. Stay in the place where you really do believe that what you have written is true. Then write down all the reasons that prove it's true. From this list, a wealth of underlying beliefs will become evident.

The following is an example of using the "proof of truth" exercise to discover underlying beliefs.

Using "Proof of Truth" to Discover Underlying Beliefs

Original statement: *I am angry at Bobby, Ross, and Roxann because they don't really respect me.*

Proof of truth:

1. They ignore me when I ask them to put their things away.
2. They fight noisily when I am on the telephone with a client.
3. They make fun of things I care about.
4. They walk in unannounced and expect immediate attention when I am working or even in the bathroom.
5. They don't eat or appreciate the food I prepare for them.
6. They don't remove their wet shoes before they come into the house.
7. If I correct one of them, they tease that one and fight.
8. They don't want me to be with their friends.

Underlying beliefs:

1. They ignore me when I ask them to put their things away:
   Children should respect adults.
   People should respect me.
   People should follow my directions.
   My direction is best for other people.
   If someone ignores me, that means they don't respect me.
2. They fight noisily when I am on the telephone with a client:
   There is a time and a place for everything.
   Children have the self-control to be quiet when the phone rings.
   Clients are more important than children.
   What people think about my children matters to me.
   It's possible to gain respect through control.
3. They make fun of things I care about:
   People shouldn't have fun or be happy at my expense.
   Children should care about what their parents care about.
4. They walk in unannounced and expect immediate attention when I am working or even in the bathroom:
   There are appropriate times to ask for what you want.
   Children should wait for attention.
   The bathroom is sacred ground.
   Other people are responsible for my happiness.
5. They don't eat or appreciate the food I prepare for them:
   Children shouldn't make their own decisions about what to eat.
   I need to be appreciated.
   People's tastes should shift when I say so.
6. They don't remove their wet shoes before they come into the house:
   I am overworked and not appreciated.
   Children should care about the house.
7. If I correct one of them, they tease that one and fight:

I have the power to cause war.
War is my fault.
Parents are responsible for their children's behavior.

8. They don't want me to be with their friends:
   Children should see their parents the way they see their friends.
   Children are ungrateful.

When you discover an underlying belief, apply the four questions to it and then turn it around. As with self-judgments, the most pertinent turnaround is often the one to the opposite polarity, the 180-degree turnaround. The undoing of one underlying belief allows whole families of related beliefs to surface and therefore to become available for inquiry.

Now let's walk through a common underlying belief. Take your time and listen as you ask yourself the questions.

"My Life Should Have a Purpose"

"My life should have a purpose" might at first seem like an odd subject for inquiry. You might think that this underlying belief couldn't possibly cause people pain or problems, that a statement like "My life *doesn't* have a purpose" might be painful enough to warrant inquiry, but not this one. It turns out, though, that this apparently positive belief is just as painful as an apparently negative belief—and that the turnaround, in its apparently negative form, is a statement of great relief and freedom.

Underlying belief: My life should have a purpose.

Is it true? Yes.

Can I absolutely know that it's true? No.

How do I react, what happens, when I believe the thought? I feel fear, because I don't know what my purpose is, and I think I should know. I feel stress in my chest and head. I may snap at my husband and children, and this eventually takes me to the refrigerator and the television in my bedroom, often for hours or days. I feel as if I'm wasting my life. I think that what I actually do is unimportant and that I need to do something big. This is stressful and confusing. When I believe this thought, I feel great internal pressure to complete my purpose before I die. Since I can't know when that is, I think that I have to quickly accomplish this purpose (which I don't have a clue about). I feel a sense of stupidity and failure, and this leaves me depressed.

Who or what would I be without the belief that my life should have a purpose? I have no way of knowing. I know I'm more peaceful without it, less crazed. I would settle for that! Without the fear and stress around this thought, maybe I'd be freed and energized enough to be happy just doing the thing in front of me.

The turnaround: My life should *not* have a purpose. That would mean that what I've lived has always been enough, and I just haven't recognized it. Maybe my life shouldn't have a purpose other than what it is. That feels odd, yet it somehow rings truer. Could it be that my life as it's already lived *is* the purpose? That seems a lot less stressful.

Applying Inquiry to an Underlying Belief

Now write down a stressful underlying belief of your own and put it up against inquiry:

Is it true?

Can you really know that it's true?

How do you react, what happens, when you believe that thought? (How much of your life is based on it? What do you do and say when you believe it?)

Who would you be without the thought?

Turn the underlying belief around.

The dialogues that follow could have been included in chapter 4 ("Doing The Work on Couples and Family Life") and chapter 6 ("Doing The Work on Work and Money"). They have been placed here because they are good examples of doing The Work on underlying beliefs that can affect you in many areas of your life. If you believe that your happiness depends on someone else, as Charles did before inquiry, that belief will undermine all your relationships, including your relationship with yourself. If, like Ruth in the second dialogue, you believe that you need to make a decision when you're not ready to, life will seem like a succession of bewildering responsibilities. Charles thinks that the problem is his wife; Ruth thinks that it's her money. But as these experts will teach us, the problem is always our uninvestigated thinking.

She Was Supposed to Make Me Happy

Charles is sure that his happiness depends on his wife. Watch as this amazing man discovers that even his worst nightmare—his wife's affair—turns out to be what he really wants for her and for himself. In an hour or so, by investigating his own thinking, he changes his whole world. Happiness may look entirely different from the way you imagine it.

Notice also how in this dialogue I sometimes use the turnarounds without the four questions. I don't recommend that people new to The Work do it this way, because they could experience shame and guilt if they turn statements around without inquiring first. But I didn't see Charles experiencing the turnarounds that way, and I wanted to walk with him through as many statements as possible in our limited time together, knowing that after the session he could go back and give himself as intricate a surgery as he wanted in any areas that may have been missed.

Charles: *I'm angry at Deborah because she told me the night before she left for a month that I repulse her—I repulse her when I'm snoring, and I repulse her because of my overweight body.*

Katie: Yes. So have you ever been repulsed? Have you experienced that?

Charles: I've been repulsed by myself.

Katie: Yes, and what else? Someone in your past, maybe: a friend, your parents at some time or other?

Charles: By people who beat children in airports and things like that.

Katie: Yes. So could you stop feeling repulsed at the time?

Charles: No.

Katie: Okay. Feel it. Look at yourself in that situation. Whose business was your repulsion?

Charles: Obviously mine.

Katie: Whose business is it what repulses Deborah? Is she your wife?

Charles: Yes.

Katie: Whose business is it what repulses her?

Charles: I get into some heavy "shoulds" about what a beloved soulmate should think and feel about me.

Katie: Oh, well! That's a good one! *[Laughter from the audience.]* I love how you don't answer the question.

Charles: It's not my business.

Katie: Whose business is her repulsion?

Charles: Hers.

Katie: And what happens when you're mentally in her business? Separation. Could you stop being repulsed when you witnessed the child abuse at the airport?

Charles: No.

Katie: But *she's* supposed to stop being repulsed? Because of the soulmate mythology you have going?

Charles: I've been carrying this "should" about how she should be with me for my whole life, and right now I'm at the point where I'm losing that "should."

Katie: Okay, sweetheart. How do you treat her when you believe the thought that wives are supposed to see their husbands as not repulsive?

Charles: I put her in a prison. I two-dimensionalize her.

Katie: How do you treat her *physically*? How does it look? How does it sound? Close your eyes and look at yourself. Look at how you treat her when you believe the thought that she's supposed to stop being repulsed and she doesn't stop. What do you say? What do you do?

Charles: "Why are you being that way with me? Don't you see who I am? How can you not see?"

Katie: So when you're doing that, how does it feel?

Charles: It's a prison.

Katie: Can you see a reason to drop the story that your wife shouldn't be repulsed by you?

Charles: Absolutely.

Katie: Can you see a stress-free reason to keep the story?

Charles: No, not anymore. When it comes to keeping our family together, and honoring what I know to be true for us as souls—

Katie: Oh. Is it the soulmate thing?

Charles: Yeah. I'm really caught there.

Katie: Yes. So read the part about her being your soulmate.

Charles: You're not ridiculing me now, are you?

Katie: I'm doing whatever you say I'm doing. I am your story of me—no more and no less.

Charles: Okay. Fascinating.

Katie: Yes. When you sit on this couch, your concepts are meat in the grinder, if you really want to know the truth. *[Laughter from the audience.]*

Charles *[laughing]*: Okay. Ground round, here I am. *[More laughter.]*

Katie: I'm a lover of truth. And when someone sits on this couch with me, I am clear that he is, too. I love you. I want what you want. If you want to keep your story, that's what I want. If you want to answer the questions and realize what's really true for you, that's what I want. So, sweetheart, let's continue. Read the part about soulmates.

Charles: I don't have that written down. It would be like "She doesn't accept me for who I am."

Katie: "She doesn't accept me for who I am"—turn it around.

Charles: I don't accept me for who I am. That's true. I don't.

Katie: There's another turnaround.

Charles: I don't accept her for who she is.

Katie: Yes. She is a woman who tells herself a story about you that she hasn't investigated and who repulses herself. Nothing else is possible.

Charles: Ahhh. I've been holding her to that for years. Yes. And myself.

Katie: You tell a story about her, and you repulse yourself.

Charles: I do.

Katie: Or you make yourself happy. You tell one story of your wife, and you turn yourself on. You tell another story of your wife, and you turn yourself off. She tells a story of you, and she turns herself on. She tells another story of you, and she repulses herself. Uninvestigated stories often leave chaos and resentment and hatred within our own families. Until we investigate, nothing else is possible. So read the first one again.

Charles: Okay. *I'm angry at Deborah because she told me that I repulse her because of my snoring and my overweight body.*

Katie: Yes. So turn it around. "I'm angry at myself . . ."

Charles: I'm angry at myself because . . .

Katie: "I told Deborah . . ."

Charles: I told Deborah . . .

Katie: "That she . . ."

Charles: That she repulses me.

Katie: Yes. For her what?

Charles: For her willingness to dispose of the relationship so easily.

Katie: Yes. So you have everything in common with her. You snore, she's repulsed. She leaves, you're repulsed. What's the difference?

Charles: I *am* repulsed by that. *[There are tears in his eyes.]* Oh, my God!

Katie: There's no way she can't be a mirror image of your thinking. There is no way. There's no one out there but your story. Let's look at the next one. "I'm angry at myself for . . ." what?

Charles: For being self-righteous, for thinking that she should be the way I want her to be.

Katie: Whose business is it who you live with?

Charles: Mine.

Katie: Yes. You want to live with her. It's your business who you want to live with.

Charles: Right.

Katie: So this is exactly a turnaround. She wants to live with someone else. You want to live with someone else.

Charles: Oh, I see. I want to be with someone else—someone who doesn't exist, the woman I want her to be. *[Charles bursts into tears.]*

Katie: Good, sweetheart. *[She passes Charles a box of tissues.]*

Charles: That's true. That's true. I've been doing that for a long time.

Katie: Let's look at the next statement.

Charles: *I want Deborah to be grateful for life as it is.*

Katie: She is or she's not. Whose business is it?

Charles: It's her business.

Katie: Turn it around.

Charles: I want me to be grateful for life as it is.

Katie: Yes. You know that thing you preach to her? You know that thing you preach to your children? *You* live it.

Charles: Yeah.

Katie: But as long as you're trying to teach us, there's no hope. Because you're teaching what you don't know how to live yet. How can a person who doesn't know how to be happy teach someone how to be happy? There's no teacher there of anything but pain. How can I end my spouse's pain or my child's pain if I can't end my own? Hopeless. Who would you be without your story of pain? You might be someone without pain, selfless, a listener, and then there would be a teacher in the house. A Buddha in the house—the one that lives it.

Charles: I hear you.

Katie: This is actually the sweetest thing to know. It gives you an internal responsibility. And that's where realization is born into the world and how we find our freedom. Rather than being Deborah-realized, you can be self-realized. Let's look at the next one.

Charles: *I want her to own her own power.* I mean, this is just such bullshit!

Katie: You've come a long way since you wrote this statement, angel. Can you hear the arrogance? "Excuse me, dear, but you should own your own power." *[Laughter from the audience.]*

Charles: But it's so ironic, because she's the one who has the power in the family. I've given her that. I've abdicated my own power.

Katie: Yes. So turn it around.

Charles: I want me to own my own power.

Katie: And stay out of her business and experience the power of that. Yes?

Charles: Mmm. *I want her to understand that there are consequences to her temper.*

Katie: Oh! My, my, my!

Charles: So much self-righteousness here I can't even believe it.

Katie: Honey, are you good! This is self-realization. We are so clear about our partners, but when it hits *here,* it's like "Whoa!" *[Laughter from the audience.]* We begin now. This now is the beginning. It's where you can meet yourself with new understanding. So let's look at the next statement of mind on paper.

Charles: *Deborah shouldn't*—oh, my God!

Katie: There are some people in the audience saying, "Read it anyway." Obviously they're the ones who need it. So "Read it anyway" means "I want some freedom here."

Charles: *Deborah shouldn't fall in love with a fantasy.* She's meeting another man in Europe right now.

Katie: Oh. She's doing everything *you* wanted to do. *[Laughter from the audience.]*

Charles: It's everything I *have* done. I've been in love with a fantasy.

And fighting and hitting my head against Deborah and being repulsed that she doesn't match the fantasy.

Katie: Yes. Welcome home.

Charles: And every single one of the things I wrote here is . . . I'm rubbing my face in self-righteousness. *Deborah should see how incredibly thoughtful, considerate, and loving I am.* I've been hanging myself with that story my whole life. And I've coupled that with beating myself up for not being better. That self-importance/self-rejection thing has been dancing right through my life.

Katie: Yes, sweetheart.

Charles: So I want myself to see how thoughtful and considerate and loving I am.

Katie: Yes.

Charles: And how thoughtful and considerate and loving she is.

Katie: Yes.

Charles: Because she *is*.

Katie: Yes. And you love her with all your heart. That's the bottom line. There's nothing you can do about that. No condemning is going to move that in you. You love her.

Charles: I do.

Katie: Yes. So let's continue.

Charles: *Deborah should*—it's all self-righteousness—*be grateful for all the years I've been the sole breadwinner.*

Katie: So you gave her your money because you wanted something from her.

Charles: Absolutely.

Katie: What was it?

Charles: Her love. Her approval. Her appreciation. Her acceptance of me as is. Because I couldn't give it to myself.

Katie: So you gave her nothing. You gave her a price tag.

Charles: Right.

Katie: Yes. And that's what you feel.

Charles: And I'm repulsed by that.

Katie: Yes, angel. Yes.

Charles: I really did feel I could buy that.

Katie: Yes. Isn't it *fine* that you're seeing that now? So the next time you try to buy your children or her or anyone else, you have this wonderful life experience. You can call on the expert: you. The next time you give your children money or give her money, you can know that the receiving is in the moment you give it. That's it!

Charles: Can you say that another way?

Katie: The getting, the receiving, is experienced in the moment you give something away. The transaction is complete. That's it. It's all about you. One day, when my grandson Travis was two years old, he pointed to a huge cookie in a store window. I said, "Honey, are you sure that's the one you want?" He was sure. I asked him if we could share it, and he said yes. I bought it and took his little sweet hand, and we walked to a table. I took the cookie out of the bag and broke off a small piece, and I held up both pieces. He reached for the small one and looked very shocked as I moved it away and put the large piece in his hand, and his face lit up as he began to move the cookie to his mouth. Then his eyes caught mine. I felt so much love that I thought my heart would burst. He smiled and took his huge cookie from his lips, gave it to me, and took the small piece. It's natural in us. The giving is how we receive.

Charles: I see.

Katie: Giving is spontaneous, and only the story of a future, a story about what they owe you for it, would keep you from knowing your own generosity. What comes back is none of your business. It's over. So, sweetheart, let's look at the next statement.

Charles: *I need Deborah to love me as I am, warts and all. To love my strengths and weaknesses, to understand my need to actualize myself as an artist and spiritual being, to give me room to go through this major midlife passage and try to find more meaning in what I'm doing.* So with all that, I should just focus on one, shouldn't I?

Katie: Yes. Keep it simple, and just turn it around.

Charles: I need Deborah to—

Katie: "I need me . . ."

Charles: I need me to love myself as I am, warts and all. I haven't been loving myself that way. But I'm starting to.

Katie: And it's the story you tell of the wart that keeps you from loving it. The wart just waits for a sane mind to see it clearly. It doesn't do any harm. It's just there like—like a leaf on a tree. You don't argue with a leaf and say, "Yo! Let's talk. Look at your shape. You need to do something about it." *[Charles and the audience laugh.]* You don't do that. But you focus here *[pointing to her hand]*, on a wart, you tell a story about it, and you repulse yourself. A wart is . . . God. It is reality. It is "what is." Argue with that.

Charles: I've been feeling so needy. Needing her to stay at home for the children's sake, too.

Katie: Your children would be much better off with her at home—can you absolutely know that that's true?

Charles: No, I can't know that it's true.

Katie: Isn't that amazing?

Charles: And that's the thing that's caused the most pain—the thought of not living together.

Katie: Yes.

Charles: But I don't know that it's true that my daughter wouldn't thrive without us being together.

Katie: Yes. Your daughter's path would be much richer with her mother at home—can you absolutely know that that's true? *[Charles begins to cry.]* Sweetheart, take all the time you need. What's the sound of it?

Charles *[bursting out]*: I don't want to be separated from my kids! I want to be a twenty-four-hour, seven-days-a-week dad!

Katie: Yes. That's the truth of it, isn't it?

Charles: But my devotion to my work and being in the studio has taken me away a lot. So there's a contradiction in that. I want to wake up with my daughter, you know?

Katie: Yes, I do.

Charles: And I have the picture of a family together. That picture is really embedded.

Katie: Yes, you do.

Charles *[crying and laughing]*: *Donna Reed* was my favorite TV show. *[Katie and the audience laugh.]* It really was!

Katie: So her leaving is not the problem. It's the death of *your* mythology.

Charles: Oh, God! Yes. Absolutely. I've been lying about that.

Katie: Yes. She's messing with your dream.

Charles: Big time! And I'm so grateful to her for this.

Katie: Yes, sweetheart. So what I'm hearing is that she really did give you a gift.

Charles: Yes, she did.

Katie: Good. Let's look at the next one.

Charles: Okay. *I need Deborah to hold our relationship and family sacred so she won't fall in love or sleep with another man.*

Katie: Is it true that that's what you need?

Charles: It's my myth. I don't need her to do anything that isn't her truth. And I love her a lot. I want her to do her truth.

Katie: And how do you treat her and how do you talk to her and how are you with your daughter when you believe this story—the one you just read?

Charles: Selfish, needy, wanting her to give me, give me, give me.

Katie: To give you a phony her that doesn't exist other than in your myth. You want her to be a lie for you. So, angel, close your eyes. Look at her. Watch how you treat her when you believe that story.

Charles: Ahhhhh.

Katie: Okay, now look at her and tell me who you would be, in her presence, if you didn't believe your story?

Charles: A strong, talented, sexy, powerful man.

Katie: Whoa! *[Laughter, whistles, and applause from the audience.]* Oh, my goodness!

Charles: That's my secret. That's what I've been—

Katie: Yes, honey, welcome to the power of ownership. No one can touch that. Not even you. This is your role. You've just been pretending not to see these qualities in you. It didn't work.

Charles: Forty-five years of it.

Katie: Yes, sweetheart. Did you feel the shift from repulsive to sexy and powerful? *[To audience]* How many felt the shift? *[Applause.]* And nothing happened but awareness.

Charles: I closed my eyes and saw it.

Katie: Teach *that* by the way you live.

Charles: I want to.

Katie: Yes. Let it come through your music, and live it with your daughter. And when she says something about her mother that *you* have taught her, you can let her know that you used to feel that way, too.

Charles: You mean in a negative way?

Katie: Yes.

Charles: I don't do that to my daughter.

Katie: Not in words.

Charles: Ahhh.

Katie: The opposite of this empowered, sexy man, this empowered composer. You've taught her the opposite by the way that you live. You've taught her how to react, how to think, how to be.

Charles: I've been a total wuss.

Katie: That's what you've been teaching her about how to react when someone leaves her. You can tell her what your experience has been, and you can begin to live what you know now. And watch as she learns to live the way you live. That's how it shifts in our families, and we don't have to give them The Work unless they ask. We *live* it. That's where the power is. You *live* the turnarounds. "She's wrong to leave"—the turnaround is "I'm wrong to leave," especially in this moment. I left my own life to mentally travel to Europe. Let me come back to my life here now.

Charles: Good.

Katie: There's a story I like to tell. Roxann, my daughter, called me one day and said she wanted me to attend my grandson's birthday party. I told her that I had a commitment that day to be doing a public event in another city. She was so hurt and angry that she hung up on me. Then, maybe ten minutes later, she called me back and said, "I am so excited, Momma. I just did The Work on you, and I saw that there is nothing you can do to keep me from loving you."

Charles: Wow!

Katie: Okay, let's look at the next statement.

Charles: *I don't ever want to have her light into me with verbal abuse.*

Katie: Yes. So "I'm willing . . ." Because you may have that picture in your mind again. Or it may be someone else.

Charles: How do you turn it around?

Katie: "I'm willing . . . ," and you read it just the way you wrote it.

Charles: I'm willing to be abused. Oh. Because it's what happens. Okay.

Katie: All of a sudden, there's nothing unexpected.

Charles: I'm willing to have her light into me with verbal abuse. Oh, my! Okay.

Katie: "I look forward to . . ."

Charles: I look forward to having her light into me . . . Oh . . . I look forward to her verbal abuse. Wow! *That* is a turnaround. Especially for self-righteous stuff. That's a big one.

Katie: Yes.

Charles: Okay. *I don't ever want to hear her say that she's in love with someone she hasn't seen except for one day in fourteen years.* All right. So . . .

Katie: "I'm willing . . ."

Charles: I'm willing to hear her say that she's in love with someone she hasn't seen except for one day in fourteen years.

Katie: "I look forward to . . ."

Charles: I look forward to it. Wow! Okay.

Katie: And if it still hurts—

Charles: Then I've got more work to do.

Katie: Yes. Isn't that fine?

Charles: Because I'm arguing with the truth—with reality.

Katie: Yes.

Charles: So, Katie, I have a question about this. I've been wanting to stay, rather than leave the house, probably because of my investment in the Donna Reed myth.

Katie: I would drop the word *probably*.

Charles: Okay, definitely. So I have a feeling she's going to come back, wanting to actually try it again. And I have the thought that if I stay and continue to be willing to face somebody that I can't trust, then I'm not the strong, powerful, sexy man with integrity.

Katie: So, sweetheart, do The Work. There's nothing else to do. If she comes back—do The Work. If she stays away—do The Work. This is about you.

Charles: But I don't want to be a doormat anymore.

Katie: Oh, really! Do The Work. Have it for breakfast. You eat The Work, or the thought will eat you.

Charles: But if I leave from a place of self-love, because I choose to leave, because I don't want to do that anymore, I don't want to . . .

Katie: Sweetheart, there's nothing you can do to keep yourself from coming or going. You just tell the story about how you have something to do with it.

Charles: You mean that's my habit? Is that what you're saying?

Katie: If a story arises and you believe it, you may think you have to decide. Investigate and be free.

Charles: So if I find and notice that I'm still there, even though I'm telling myself that the path of integrity would be to finally walk away and start a new life with somebody else, that's okay.

Katie: Honey, the decisions will make themselves for you as you inquire.

Charles: So either I will do it or I won't.

Katie: Yes.

Charles: And I should just trust that.

Katie: It happens whether you trust it or not—haven't you noticed? Again, life is a very nice place to be once you understand it. Nothing ever goes wrong in life. Life is heaven, except for our attachment to a story that we haven't investigated.

Charles: That's *really* being in the moment.

Katie: What is, is. I am not running this show. I don't belong to myself, and you don't belong to yourself. We are not ours. We are the "is." And we tell the story of "Oh, I have to leave my wife." It's just not true. You don't have to leave her, until you do. You are the "is." You flow with that, as that. There's nothing you can do to not let her in. And there's nothing you can do to not leave her. This isn't our show, in my experience.

Charles: Wow!

Katie: She comes, and you tell a story, and the effect is that you get to be a martyr. Or she comes, and you tell the story of how you're grateful, and you get to be a happy guy. You are the effect of your story, that's all. And this is hard to hear unless you inquire. That's why I say, "Have The Work for breakfast." Come to know for yourself what's true for you, not for me. My words are of no value to you. You're the one you've been waiting for. Be married to *yourself.* You're the one you've been waiting for all your life.

I Need to Make a Decision

When you become a lover of what is, there are no more decisions to make. In my life, I just wait and watch. I know that the decision will be made in its own time, so I let go of when, where, and how. I like to say I'm a woman with no future. When there are no decisions to make, there's no planned future. All my decisions are made for me, just as they're all made for you. When you mentally tell yourself the story that you have something to do with it, you're attaching to an underlying belief.

For forty-three years, I was always buying into my stories about the future, buying into my insanity. After I came back from the half-way house with a new understanding of reality, I would often return from a long trip to find the house full of dirty laundry, piles of mail on my desk, the dog dish crusted, the bathrooms a mess, and the sink piled high with dishes. The first time it happened, I heard a voice that said, "Do the dishes." It was like coming upon the burning bush, and the voice from the bush said, "Do the dishes." It didn't sound very spiritual to me, but I just followed its directions. I would stand at the sink and just wash the next dish or sit with the piles of bills and pay the one on top. Just one at a time. Nothing else was required. At the end of the day, everything would be done, and I didn't need to understand who or what had done it.

When a thought appears such as "Do the dishes" and you don't follow it, notice how an internal war breaks out. It sounds like this: "I'll do them later. I should have done them by now. My roommate should have done them. It's not my turn. It's not fair. People will think less of me if I don't do them now." The stress and weariness you feel are really mental combat fatigue.

What I call "doing the dishes" is the practice of loving the task in front of you. Your inner voice guides you all day long to do simple things such as brush your teeth, drive to work, call your friend, or do the dishes. Even though it's just another story, it's a very short story, and when you follow the direction of the voice, that story ends. We are really alive when we live as simply as that— open, waiting, trusting, and loving to do what appears in front of us now.

What we need to do unfolds before us, always: doing the dishes, paying the bills, picking up the children's socks, brushing our teeth. We never receive more than we can handle, and there is always just one thing to do. Whether you have ten dollars or ten million dollars, life never gets more difficult than that.

In the following dialogue, notice how I don't insist on one-syllable, yes-or-no answers to questions one and two. I felt that Ruth was too fragile for strict directions like that. It seemed kinder to let her ramble a bit as she was getting used to inquiry.

Ruth: *I am frightened and panicked to the point of paralysis about making decisions about my money, about whether to stay in the market or get out because of the current volatility and my future depending upon it.*

Katie: Your future depends on your money—can you really know that that's true?

Ruth: No, but a lot of me gets frantic about it.

Katie: Yes, a lot of you would *have* to be frantic about it, because you believe it's true and you haven't asked yourself. Your future depends on the money you have invested—how do you react, how do you live, when you believe that thought, whether or not it's true?

Ruth: In a panicky state. In a high state of anxiety. When there was more of it, I was much more calm, but when it fluctuates, I get into a horrible state.

Katie: Who would you be without the thought "My future depends on the money I have invested in the market"?

Ruth: A much more relaxed person. My body wouldn't be so tense.

Katie: Give me a reason to keep the thought that isn't stressful and doesn't make you panic.

Ruth: There isn't one that's not stressful, but *not* thinking about money is a different kind of stress—like I'm being irresponsible then. So either way, I lose.

Katie: How can you *not* think about something? *It's* thinking *you.* Thought appears. How can *not* thinking about it be irresponsible? You either think about it or you don't. Thought either appears or it doesn't. It's just amazing that, after how many years, you think you can control your thinking. Can you control the wind, too?

Ruth: No, I can't control it.

Katie: What about the ocean?

Ruth: No.

Katie: "Let's stop the waves." Not likely. Except they stop when you're asleep.

Ruth: The thoughts?

Katie: The waves. No thought, no ocean. No stock market. How irresponsible of you to go to sleep at night! *[Laughter from the audience.]*

Ruth: I don't sleep very well! I've been up since five.

Katie: Yes, it's irresponsible. Thinking and worrying will solve all my problems—has that been your experience?

Ruth: No.

Katie: So let's stay awake and get some more of that. *[Ruth and the audience laugh.]*

Ruth: I can't control my thinking. I've been trying for years.

Katie: This is a very interesting discovery. Meeting thought with understanding is as good as it's going to get. It will work. And there's a lot of humor in it, as well as a good night's rest.

Ruth: I need some humor around this. I definitely need some humor around this.

Katie: So without this stressful thinking, you wouldn't make the right decision—can you really know that that's true?

Ruth: It seems that quite the opposite would be true.

Katie: Let's experience how it feels to do a 180-degree turnaround. "My future depends on the money I have invested in the stock market"—how would you turn that around?

Ruth: My future does not depend on the money I have invested in the stock market.

Katie: Feel it. That could be just as true. When you get all this money and you're an absolute success in the market and have more money than you could ever spend, what are you going to have? Happiness? Isn't that why you want the money? Let's take a shortcut that can last a lifetime. Answer this question: Who would you be without the story "My future depends on the money in the stock market"?

Ruth: I would be much happier. I'd be more relaxed. I'd be more fun to be around.

Katie: Yes. With or without the money from the stock market success. You'd have everything you wanted money for in the first place.

Ruth: That's . . . yes!

Katie: Give me a stress-free reason to keep the thought "My future depends on the money I have invested in the stock market."

Ruth: There isn't one.

Katie: The only future you want is peace and happiness. Rich or poor—who cares when we're secure in our happiness? This is true freedom: a mind that is no longer deceived by itself.

Ruth: That was my childhood prayer: peace and happiness.

Katie: So the very thing you seek keeps you from the awareness of what you already have.

Ruth: Yes, I've always been trying to live in the future, to fix it, to make it safe and secure.

Katie: Yes, like an innocent child. We're either attaching to the nightmare or we're investigating it. There's no other choice. Thoughts appear. How are you going to meet them? That's all we're talking about here.

Ruth: We're either attaching to the problem or we're inquiring?

Katie: Yes, and I love it that the stock market is not going to cooperate with you, if that's what it takes to bring peace and true happiness into your life. That's what everything is for. It leaves you to your own solution. So when you get all this money and you're happy, totally happy, what are you going to do? You're going to sit, stand, or lie horizontal. That's about it. And you're going to witness the internal story you're telling now if you haven't taken care of it in the way that it deserves, and that is to meet it with understanding, the way a loving mother would meet her child.

Ruth: I get the sense that's all there is to do.

Katie: Yes. Sit, stand, or lie horizontal—that's about it. But take a look at the story you're telling as you're doing these simple things. Because when you get all this money and you have everything you ever wanted, what appears is what appears in this chair now. This is the story you're telling. There's no happiness in it. Okay. Let's look at the next statement, honey.

Ruth: *I don't want to have to be deciding where to invest, and I don't trust others to do it.*

Katie: You have to decide where to invest—can you absolutely know that that's true?

Ruth: No. I could just leave the money alone. And see what it does. Just leave it alone totally. A lot of me says that's the best way.

Katie: You need to make decisions in life—can you really know that that's true?

Ruth: It feels like I need to, but as you say it, I'm not sure.

Katie: It would have to feel that way, because you believe the thought and therefore you're attached to it.

Ruth: Yes.

Katie: You didn't ask yourself what you really believe. It has all been a misunderstanding.

Ruth: The thought of not having to make decisions sounds glorious.

Katie: That's my experience. I don't make decisions. I don't bother with them, because I know they'll be made for me right on time. My job is to be happy and wait. Decisions are easy. It's the story you tell about them that isn't easy. When you jump out of a plane and you pull the parachute cord and it doesn't open, you feel fear, because you have the next cord to pull. So you pull that one, and it doesn't open.

And that's the last cord. Now there's no decision to make. When there's no decision, there's no fear, so just enjoy the trip! And that's my position—I'm a lover of what is. What is: no cord to pull. It's already happening. Free fall. I have nothing to do with it.

Ruth: It was real clear to come here. I didn't have to think, "Should I, shouldn't I, should I?" It was "Mmm, yes. You're available then. Go."

Katie: So how was that decision made? Maybe it just made itself. A moment ago, you moved your head like that. Did you make that decision?

Ruth: No.

Katie: You just moved your hand. Did you make that decision?

Ruth: No.

Katie: No. You need to make decisions—is that true? Maybe things are just moving right along, without our help.

Ruth: That's my insanity, the need to control.

Katie: Yes. Who needs God when *you* are running the show? *[Ruth laughs.]*

Ruth: I don't want to do that, I just don't know how not to.

Katie: Thinking this way, and therefore living this way, is in direct opposition to reality, and it's fatal. It feels like stress, because everyone is a lover of what is, no matter what horror story they believe in. I say let's have peace now, within this apparent chaos. So, sweetheart, how do you react when you believe the thought "I need to make a decision," and the decision doesn't come?

Ruth: Horrible. Just horrible.

Katie: That's a very interesting place to attempt to make a decision from. From that place, we can't even decide to stop or go. That will tell you something. And when you're convinced that you did it, where's your proof? Give me a stress-free reason to keep the thought

"I need to make a decision." I'm not asking you to stop thinking that you make decisions. This Work has the gentleness of a flower opening to itself. Be gentle with your beautiful self. This Work is about the end of your suffering. We're just taking a look at possibilities here.

Ruth: Would it work as an experiment to try not to decide anything for a period of time? Is that craziness, or—

Katie: Well, you just made a decision, and it may change by itself. And then you can say "I" changed my mind.

Ruth: And I'll still be caught in the same ugly loop.

Katie: I don't know. But it's interesting to watch. If I say I won't make a decision, then I've just made a decision. Watch. That's what inquiry is for, to break through stressful mythology. These four questions take us into a world of such beauty that it can't be told. Some of us haven't even begun to explore it yet, even though that's the only world that exists. And we're the last to know.

Ruth: I get glimpses of what it means not to make a decision, and it's feeling like that now against a background of control, trying to do it as an experiment.

Katie: Give me a stress-free reason to keep the thought "I need to make a decision about the stock market."

Ruth: I can't come up with any. I just can't come up with any.

Katie: Who or what would you be without the thought "I need to make a decision"?

Ruth: I wouldn't be like my anxious mother. I wouldn't be becoming more and more insane. I wouldn't feel like I had to isolate myself from people because I was too awful to be around.

Katie: Oh, sweetheart. I love it that you've discovered inquiry.

Ruth: I've been trying so hard at something that doesn't work.

Katie: "I need to make decisions"—turn it around.

Ruth: I don't need to make decisions.

Katie: Yes. Believe me, they will be made. In the peace of that, everything is clear. Life will give you everything you need to go deeper. A decision will be made. If you act, the worst that can happen is a story. If you don't act, the worst that can happen is a story. It makes its own decisions: when to eat, when to sleep, when to act. It just moves along on its own. And it's very calm and entirely successful.

Ruth: Mmm.

Katie: Feel where your hands are. And your feet. This is good. Without a story, it's always good, everywhere you sit. Let's look at the next statement.

Ruth: *I don't want money in the stock market to be so irrational.* Hopeless! Hopeless!

Katie: Money in the stock market is irrational—turn it around, sweetheart. "My thinking . . ."

Ruth: My thinking is irrational.

Katie: Yes. When you see money that way, your thinking is irrational and frightening. Money's irrational, the stock market is irrational—can you really know that that's true?

Ruth: No.

Katie: How do you react when you think that thought?

Ruth: With fear. I get so scared that I leave my body.

Katie: Can you see a reason to drop the thought? And I'm not asking you to drop it. For those of you new to The Work, you *can't* drop it. You may think you can, and then the thought reappears and brings the same fear with it that it did before, possibly even more, because you're a little more attached. So what I'm asking is simply "Can you see a *reason* to drop the thought that the stock market is irrational?"

Ruth: I can see a reason to drop it, but that doesn't mean that I have to drop it.

Katie: Exactly so. This is about realization, not about changing anything. The world is as you perceive it to be. For me, *clarity* is a word for *beauty*. It's what I am. And when I'm clear, I see only beauty. Nothing else is possible. I am mind perceiving my thoughts, and everything unfolds from that, as if it were a new solar system pouring itself out in its delight. If I'm not clear, then I'm going to project all my craziness out onto the world, *as* the world, and I'll perceive a crazy world and think that it is the problem. We've been working on the projected image for thousands of years and not on the projector. That's why life seems to be chaotic. It's chaos telling chaos how to live differently and never noticing that it has always lived that way and that we have been going about it backward, absolutely backward. So you don't drop your thoughts of chaos and suffering out there in the apparent world. You *can't* drop them, because you didn't make them in the first place. But when you meet your thoughts with understanding, the world changes. It has to change, because the projector of the entire world is you. You're it! Let's look at the next statement.

Ruth: *Decisions shouldn't be so difficult or frightening.*

Katie: When you're trying to make them ahead of their time, it's hopeless, as you said. You can't make yourself make a decision ahead of its time. A decision is made when it's made, and not one breath sooner. Don't you love it?

Ruth: It sounds wonderful.

Katie: Yes. You can sit there and feel "Oh, I need to do something with my stocks," and then you can inquire, "Is it true? I can't really know that." So you just let it have you. You just sit there with what your passion is and read and watch the Internet and let it educate you. And the decision will come from that when it's time. It's a beautiful thing. You'll lose money because of that decision, or you'll make money. As it should be. But when you think you're supposed to do something with it and imagine that you're the doer, that's pure delusion. Just follow your passion. Do what you love. Inquire, and have a happy life while you're doing it.

Ruth: Sometimes I can't read. I'm losing pieces of memory and losing the ability to track and—

Katie: Oh, honey, you've been spared! *[Ruth and the audience laugh.]* Have you heard me say that anytime I lose someone or something, I've been spared? Well, that's how it really is. Let's look at your last statement.

Ruth: *I don't ever want to panic over money in the stock market again.*

Katie: "I'm willing . . ."

Ruth: I'm willing to panic over money in the stock market.

Katie: "I look forward to . . ." It could happen.

Ruth *[laughing]*: I look forward to panicking over money in the stock market.

Katie: Yes, because that will put you back into The Work.

Ruth: That's where I want to be.

Katie: That's the purpose of stress. It's a friend. It's an alarm clock, built in to let you know that it's time to do The Work. You've simply lost the awareness that you're free. So you investigate, and you return to what you are. This is what's waiting to be recognized, what is always real.

I don't let go of
my concepts—
I meet them
with understanding.
Then *they* let go of *me*.

10

Doing The Work on Any Thought or Situation

There is no thought or situation that you can't put up against inquiry. Every thought, every person, every apparent problem is here for the sake of your freedom. When you experience anything as separate or unacceptable, inquiry can bring you back to the peace you felt before you believed that thought.

If you aren't completely comfortable in the world, do The Work. That's what every uncomfortable feeling is for; that's what pain is for, what money is for, what everything in the world is for: your self-realization. It's all a mirror image of your own thinking. Judge it, investigate it, turn it around, and set yourself free if freedom is what you want. It's good that you experience anger, fear, or sadness. Sit down, identify the story, and do The Work. Until you can see everything in the world as a friend, your Work is not done.

The Turnaround to "My Thinking"

Once you feel competent in doing The Work on people, you can inquire into issues like world hunger, fundamentalism, bureaucracy, government, sex, terrorism, or any uncomfortable thought that appears in your mind. As you inquire into issues and turn your judgments around, you come to see that every perceived problem appearing "out there" is really nothing more than a misperception within your own thinking.

When your writing on the Worksheet is pointed at an issue, first inquire with the four questions as usual. Then, when you get to the turnarounds, substitute the words "my thinking" for the issue wherever that seems appropriate. For example, "I don't like war because it frightens me" turns around to "I don't like my thinking because it frightens me" or "I don't like my thinking—especially about war—because it frightens me." Is that as true or truer for you?

Here are a few more examples of the turnaround to "my thinking":

Original statement: *I'm angry at bureaucrats for making my life complicated.*

Turnaround: I'm angry at my thinking for making my life complicated.

Original statement: *I don't like my handicap because it makes people avoid me.*

Turnarounds: I don't like my thinking because it makes me avoid people.

I don't like my thinking because it makes me avoid myself.

Original statement: *I want sex to be gentle and loving.*

Turnaround: I want my thinking to be gentle and loving.

When the Story Is Hard to Find

Sometimes when you feel upset, you may find it difficult to identify the thought behind your uncomfortable feeling. If you're having trouble sorting out exactly what thoughts are disturbing you, you might want to try the following exercise:

Start with six blank sheets of paper and somewhere to spread them out.

Number the first page 1, and write across the top "sad, disappointed, ashamed, embarrassed, afraid, irritated, angry." Below that, write "Because" _____.

About halfway down the page, write "And it means that" _____

_____.

Number the next page 2, and write at the top the word *Want*.

Number the next page 3, and write at the top the word *Should*.

Number the next page 4, and write at the top the word *Need*.

Number the next page 5, and write at the top the word *Judge*.

Number the next page 6, and write at the top the words *Never again*.

Spread out the six pages, and let your mind run wild over the upset. Use your thoughts to fan its flames, and note which ones do the best job. If no thought works particularly well, try out new or exaggerated thoughts. Write down the thoughts as simply as you can. It helps to be blunt. There's no need to follow a particular sequence. Here is a guide for using the six pages:

Page 1 is where you describe the situation. Write down what appears as a "fact": for example, "She didn't show up for our lunch date, kept me waiting in the restaurant, never even called." Write "facts" down in the space after "Because." Then circle the relevant emotions: sad, disappointed, and so on. Then, after "And it means that," write your interpretation of the "fact." Try to include your worst-case thoughts: for example, "She doesn't love me anymore" or "She's seeing someone else."

If you catch yourself thinking "I want _____

_____,"

write it down on page 2. Otherwise, use that page to prompt yourself by focusing on exactly how you would improve the situation or person. What would make it perfect for you? Write in the form "I want

_____."

Play God and create your perfection—for example, *want* her to unfailingly appear on time no matter what, *want* to know exactly what she's doing all the time, etc. (When you've almost filled this page, ask yourself if you've written what you *really want;* if not, write that down at the bottom of the page.)

Thoughts in the form of "So-and-so should or shouldn't _____
_____"

go on page 3. If you are unaware of any "shoulds," think about what would restore to the situation your sense of justice and order. Write down all the "shoulds" that would make it "right."

Page 4 is the "I need" page, where you can bring the situation back in line with your sense of comfort and security. Write down your requirements for a happy life. Write down the adjustments that would make things be the way they are supposed to be: for example, "I need her to love me" or "I need to succeed at my job." When you've written a few statements on this page, it can be helpful to ask yourself what you would have then, after all your needs are filled. Write that at the bottom of the page.

On page 5, write your merciless evaluation of the person or situation. Make a list of the person or situation's qualities as they have become apparent to you through this upset.

On page 6, write down the aspect of the situation that you vow or hope you will never have to live through again.

Now underline all the statements that have the highest emotional charge, and do The Work on them, one by one. When you have finished, go back and do The Work on the rest of your statements.

If, after completing the above, you find that you can't look forward to what you wrote on page 6 or that the troublesome story still seems to elude you, another exercise can be very effective. Take several blank sheets of paper and a watch or timer. Focus on the upset and write about it free form for five minutes *without stopping.* When you want to stop, write the last phrase you wrote over and over, until you're ready to continue. Afterward, review what you wrote and underline the phrases that are most painful or embarrassing. Transfer the underlined statements to whichever of the six pages they best fit on. Walk away from your pages for a while, perhaps overnight, and then reread them, underlining all the statements that seem most highly charged. Now you know where to begin doing The Work.

Nothing outside you
can ever give you
what you're looking for.

11

Doing The Work
on the Body and Addictions

Bodies don't think, care, or have any problem with themselves. They never beat themselves up or shame themselves. They simply try to keep themselves balanced and to heal themselves. They are entirely efficient, intelligent, kind, and resourceful. Where there's no thought, there's no problem. It's the story we believe, prior to investigation, that leaves us confused. My pain can't be my body's fault. I tell the story of my body, and because I haven't inquired, I believe that my body is the problem and that if only this or that changed, I would be happy.

The body is never our problem. Our problem is always a thought that we innocently believe. The Work deals with our thinking, not with the object that we think we're addicted to. There is no such thing as an addiction to an object; there is only an attachment to the uninvestigated concept arising in the moment.

For example, I don't care if I smoke or if I don't smoke; it's not about a right or a wrong for me. I smoked heavily, even chain-smoked, for many years. Then in 1986, after my experience in the halfway house, all at once it was over. When I went to Turkey in 1997, I hadn't smoked a cigarette in eleven years. I got into a taxi, and the driver had some wild Turkish music playing on his radio very loud, and he was honking constantly (honking is what they do there; it's the sound of God, and the two lanes are really six lanes merging, and everyone drives around honking at one another, and it's all happening in a perfect flow), and he turned around and with a big smile offered me a cigarette. I didn't think twice; I took it, and he lit a match for me. The music was going full blast, the horns were going full blast, and I sat in the back seat, smoking and loving every moment. It's okay if I do smoke, I noticed, and it's okay if I don't, and I haven't smoked since that wonderful taxi ride.

But here's addiction: a concept arises that says I should or I shouldn't smoke, I believe it, and I move from the reality of the present moment. Without inquiry, we believe thoughts that aren't true for us, and these thoughts are the reasons that we smoke or drink. Who would you be without your "should" or "shouldn't"?

If you think that alcohol makes you sick or confused or angry, then when you drink it, it's as if you're drinking your own disease. You're meeting alcohol where it is, and it does exactly what you know it will do. So we investigate the thinking, not in order to stop drinking but simply to end any confusion about what alcohol will do. And if you believe that you really want to keep drinking, just notice what it does to you.

There's no pity in it. There's no victim in it. And eventually there's no fun in it—only a hangover.

If my body gets sick, I go to the doctor. My body is his business. My thinking is my business, and in the peace of that, I'm very clear about what to do and where to go. And then the body becomes a lot of fun, because you're not invested in whether it lives or dies. It's a projected image, a metaphor of your thinking, mirrored back to you.

On one occasion in 1986, while I was getting a massage, I began to experience a sudden paralysis. It was as if all my ligaments, tendons, and muscles had tightened to an extreme. It was like rigor mortis; I couldn't make even the slightest movement. Throughout the experience, I was perfectly calm and joyful, because I didn't have a story that the body should look a certain way or move fluidly. Thoughts moved through, like "Oh, my God, I can't move. Something terrible is happening." But the inquiry that was alive within me wouldn't allow any attachment to these thoughts. If that process had been slowed down and given words, it would sound like this: "'You're never going to be able to walk again'—sweetheart, can you really know that that's true?" They're so fast, these four questions, that eventually, they meet a thought at the instant of its arising. At some point, after about an hour, my body began to relax and go back to what people would call its normal state. My body can never be a problem if my thinking is healthy.

My Daughter's Addiction

I have worked with hundreds of alcoholics, and I've always found that they were drunk with their thinking before they were drunk with their drinking. Many of them have told me that The Work includes all twelve steps of Alcoholics Anonymous. For example, it gives a clear form to the fourth and fifth steps—"Made a searching and fearless inventory of ourselves" and "Admitted to God, to ourselves, and to another human being the exact nature of our wrongs"— that thousands have wanted to do and haven't known how to.

"Don't necessarily do The Work on drinking," I tell them. "Go back to the thought just prior to the thought that you need a drink, and do The Work on that, on that man or woman, on that situation. The prior thought is what you're trying to shut down with alcohol. Your uninvestigated thinking is the problem, not alcohol. Alcohol is honest and true: It promises to get you drunk, and it does; it promises to make things worse, and it does. It's always true to its word. It's a great teacher of integrity. It doesn't say, 'Drink me.' It just sits there, true to itself, waiting to do its job.

"Do The Work on your uninvestigated thoughts and also go to

twelve-step meetings; share your experience and strength at meetings so that you can hear it yourself. You are always the one you're working with. It's your truth, not ours, that will set you free."

When my daughter, Roxann, was sixteen, she drank very heavily and also did drugs. That had begun to happen before I woke up with the questions in 1986, but I had been so depressed at the time that I'd been totally unaware of it. After inquiry was alive in me, though, I began to notice her actions as well as my thoughts about them.

She used to drive off every night in her new red Camaro. If I asked where she was going, she would give me a furious look and slam the door on her way out. It was a look I understood well. I'd taught her to see me that way. I myself had worn that look on my face for many years.

Through inquiry, I learned to become very quiet around her, around everyone. I learned how to be a listener. I would often sit and wait up for her far past midnight for the pure privilege of seeing her—just for that privilege. I knew she was drinking, and I knew I couldn't do a thing about it. The thoughts that would appear in my mind were thoughts like these: "She's probably drunk and driving, and she'll be killed in a crash, and I'll never see her again. I'm her mother, I bought her the car, I'm responsible. I should take her car from her (but it wasn't mine to take; I'd given it to her; it was hers), she'll drive while she's drunk, and she'll kill someone, she'll crash into another car or drive into a lamppost and kill herself and her passengers." As the thoughts appeared, each one would be met with wordless, thoughtless inquiry. And inquiry instantly brought me back to reality. Here is what was true: woman sitting in chair waiting for her beloved daughter.

One evening, after being gone for a three-day weekend, Roxann came through the door with a look of great misery on her face and, it seemed to me, without any defenses. She saw me sitting there, and she just fell into my arms and said, "Mom, I can't do this anymore. Please help me. Whatever this thing is that you're giving to all these people who come to our house, I want it." So we did The Work, and she joined Alcoholics Anonymous. That was the last time she did alcohol or drugs. Whenever she had a problem after that, she didn't need to drink or drug, and she didn't need me. She just wrote the problem down, asked four questions, and turned it around.

When there's peace here, there's peace there. To have a way to see beyond the illusion of suffering is the greatest gift. I love that all my children have taken advantage of it.

In the next dialogue, you'll meet Charlotte, a woman consumed by her thoughts about her daughter's drug addiction. As you read, consider what *you* might be addicted to. Maybe it's not drugs or cigarettes. Maybe you're addicted to being appreciated, to getting attention, or to being right. Ultimately, you may discover that going outside yourself in order to gain *anything* is painful.

Charlotte: *I'm afraid of my daughter's drug addiction because it's killing her.*

Katie: Can you absolutely know that that's true? And I'm not saying that it's not. This is just a question. Her drug addiction is killing her—can you absolutely know that that's true?

Charlotte: No.

Katie: How do you react when you believe the thought "Her drug addiction is killing her"?

Charlotte: I get very angry.

Katie: And what do you say to her? What do you do?

Charlotte: I judge her, and I push her away. I'm afraid of her. I don't want her around.

Katie: Who would you be, in the presence of your daughter, without the thought "Her drug addiction is killing her"?

Charlotte: I'd be more relaxed, and I'd be more myself and less mean to her, less reactive.

Katie: When this Work found me, my daughter was, in her words, an alcoholic and doing drugs. And the questions were alive in me. "Her addiction is killing her"—can I absolutely know that that's true? No. And who would I be without this story? I would be totally there for her, loving her with all my heart, as long as she lasts. Maybe she'll die tomorrow of an overdose, but she's in my arms now. How do you treat her when you think the thought "Her drug addiction is killing her"?

Charlotte: I don't want to see her. I don't want her around.

Katie: That's fear, and fear is what we experience when we're attached to the nightmare. "Drug addiction is killing her"—turn it around. When you're turning around an issue like drugs, put the words "my thinking" in place of the issue. "My thinking . . ."

Charlotte: My thinking is killing her.

Katie: There's another turnaround. "My thinking is . . ."

Charlotte: Killing me.

Katie: Yes.

Charlotte: It's killing our relationship.

Katie: She's dying of a drug overdose, and you're dying of a thinking overdose. She could last a lot longer than you.

Charlotte: Yes, that's true. The stress is really wearing me down.

Katie: She's stoned, you're stoned. I've been through this one.

Charlotte: Yeah, I get really toxic when it comes up in my face again that she's using drugs.

Katie: "She's using"—turn it around.

Charlotte: *I'm* using?

Katie: Yes, you're using her to stay toxic. She uses drugs, you use her—what's the difference?

Charlotte: Hmm.

Katie: Let's look at your next statement.

Charlotte: *I'm angry and saddened by Linda's drug addiction because I feel that it's endangering my granddaughter Debbie's life.*

Katie: So you think that something will happen, and your granddaughter will die.

Charlotte: Or be molested or—

Katie: So because of your daughter's addiction, something terrible can happen to your granddaughter.

Charlotte: Yeah.

Katie: Is that true? And I'm not saying it's not true. These are just questions; there's no motive here. This is about the end of your suffering. Can you absolutely know that that's true?

Charlotte: No. I can't know that.

Katie: How do you react when you think that thought?

Charlotte: Well, I've been crying for most of the last two days. I haven't slept in forty-eight hours. I've been feeling terror.

Katie: Give me a stress-free reason to believe this.

Charlotte: There is none.

Katie: "My daughter's drug addiction is endangering my granddaughter's life"—turn it around. "My thinking addiction . . ."

Charlotte: My thinking addiction is endangering my life. Yeah. I can see that. That's true.

Katie: Now read it saying "My drug addiction . . ."

Charlotte: My drug addiction is endangering my life?

Katie: Yes, and your drug addiction is her.

Charlotte: Oh. Well, I can see that. My drug addiction is her. I'm so much in her business.

Katie: That's it. She's addicted to drugs, and you're addicted to mentally running her life. She's your drug.

Charlotte: Okay.

Katie: It's insane to mentally be in my children's business.

Charlotte: Even with the baby?

Katie: "She should take care of the baby"—turn it around.

Charlotte: *I* should take care of the baby?

Katie: Yes. *You* do it.

Charlotte: Oh, God! I should do that?

Katie: What do you think? According to you, she's not available.

Charlotte: Well, I'm already raising three of my other daughter's babies from birth, so—

Katie: Well, raise four, raise five, raise a thousand. There are children hungry all over the world! What are you doing sitting here?

Charlotte: I guess my question about that is if I raise the child for her, then I'm enabling her to use drugs. I could be the one to kill her.

Katie: So taking care of the baby is a problem for you? It's the same way for her. This just puts us in a place of humility. Are you doing the best you can?

Charlotte: Yes.

Katie: I believe you. When you think, "My daughter should do something about it," turn it around: "*I* should do something about it." And if you can't, you're just like your daughter. When she says, "I can't," you can understand. But when you get furious at her because you haven't investigated your own thinking, you're both stoned, and you teach your daughter craziness.

Charlotte: Ah.

Katie: "Drug addiction is endangering Debbie's life"—turn it around.

Charlotte: My thinking about Linda's drug addiction is endangering my life.

Katie: Yes.

Charlotte: That's absolutely true.

Katie: Whose business is her drug addiction?

Charlotte: Hers.

Katie: Whose business is your drug addiction?

Charlotte: Mine.

Katie: Take care of *that*. Let's look at the next one.

Charlotte: *My daughter's drug addiction is ruining her life.*

Katie: Can you absolutely know that it's true that your daughter's drug addiction is ruining her life in the long run?

Charlotte: No.

Katie: It all begins to make sense. I love that you answered that question. What I found when I did The Work on my daughter in 1986 was that I had to go deep to find the same thing. And it turned out that because of that addiction, her life today is very rich. The bottom line is that I just can't know anything. I watch the way things are in reality. This leaves me in a position to act sanely and lovingly, and life is always perfectly beautiful. And if she died, I'd still be able to see that. But I can't fool myself. I really have to know the truth. If this path were your only way to God, would you choose it?

Charlotte: Yes.

Katie: Well, that seems to be the case. No mistake. We've been daughter-realized forever; now let's be self-realized. Read the statement again.

Charlotte: *My daughter's drug addiction is ruining her life.*

Katie: How do you react when you think that thought?

Charlotte: I feel hopeless.

Katie: And how do you live when you feel hopeless?

Charlotte: I don't live at all.

Katie: Can you see a reason to drop this thought?

Charlotte: Yes.

Katie: Who would you be without this thought?

Charlotte: Well, I'd certainly be a better mother.

Katie: Good. You're the expert, and here's what I'm learning from you: with the thought, suffering; without the thought, no suffering and you'd be a better mother. So what does your daughter have to do with your problem? Zero. If you think that your daughter is your problem, welcome to The Work. Your daughter is the perfect daughter for you, because she's going to bring up every uninvestigated concept you have until you get a clue about reality. That's her job. Everything has its job. This candle's job is to burn, this rose's job is to blossom, your daughter's job is to use drugs, my job is to drink my tea now. *[Takes a sip of tea.]* And when you understand, she'll follow you, she'll understand. It's a law, because she's your projection. When you move into the polarity of truth, so will she. Hell here, hell there. Peace here, peace there. Let's look at the next one.

Charlotte: It almost seems silly now. Should I read what I wrote anyway?

Katie: You may as well. Thought appears.

Charlotte: *I'm angry, confused, saddened, and afraid*—all of it—*at my daughter Linda's drug addiction because it brings me excruciating pain.*

Katie: Turn it around.

Charlotte: Obviously, my thinking about her is what brings me excruciating pain. Yeah.

Katie: Yes. Your daughter has nothing to do with your pain.

Charlotte: Mmm. That's absolutely true. I can see that. I can feel it.

Katie: I love it when people realize this, because when they see the innocence of their children and their parents and their partners, they come to see their own innocence. This Work is about one hundred percent forgiveness, because that's what you want. That's what you are. Let's look at the next one.

Charlotte: *I'm afraid of Linda's drug addiction because it changes her personality.*

Katie: Turn it around. "I'm afraid of my thinking . . ."

Charlotte: I'm afraid of my thinking because it changes Linda's personality?

Katie: Interesting. Now try "It changes my . . ."

Charlotte: It changes my personality. Yeah, okay.

Katie: And therefore Linda's.

Charlotte: And therefore Linda's.

Katie: Isn't it funny how we're the last place we look? Always trying to change the projected rather than clear the projector. We haven't known a way to do this until now.

Charlotte: Yeah.

Katie: So read it just like that.

Charlotte: I'm afraid of my thinking because it changes my personality.

Katie: Feel it.

Charlotte: Wow! And I can't see her then. That's it! I'm afraid of my thinking because it changes my personality, and then I can't see myself or her. Yeah.

Katie: Have you ever been angry at her and thought, "How can I say that to her? Why am I hurting her? She's my whole life, I love her, and I just treat her like—"

Charlotte: Like shit. It's like I become someone else. I'm so mean to her when she's using.

Katie: Because you're a drug user, and she's your drug. How else can you be a champion of suffering? Parents call me and say, "My child's a drug addict, she's in trouble," and they don't see that *they're* the ones in trouble. Their child is often doing fine, or at least as well as the parent. And when you get clear, your daughter will follow. You are the way. Let's look at the next one.

Charlotte: *I'm angry at Linda's drug addiction because when she uses, I'm afraid of her.*

Katie: Turn it around.

Charlotte: I'm angry at my drug addiction because then I'm afraid of myself. That's exactly what happens when she shows up and she's using. I'm afraid of my own behavior around her.

Katie: You're afraid of her—is that true?

Charlotte: No.

Katie: How do you react, how do you treat her, when you think that thought?

Charlotte: I get angry, volatile, aggressive, and especially I shut her out.

Katie: Like some kind of poison walked into the house.

Charlotte: Yeah, that's exactly what I do.

Katie: And she's your baby.

Charlotte: Yeah.

Katie: And you treat her like some bug that just crawled in.

Charlotte: Right. That's exactly right.

Katie: She's your dearest child, and you treat her like an enemy. That's the power of uninvestigated thinking. That's the power of the nightmare. It has to live itself out. You think, "I'm afraid of her," and you have to live that out. But if you investigate that thought ("'I'm afraid of her'—is it true?"), the nightmare disappears. When she walks into the house and you have the thought "I'm afraid of her," laughter replaces fear. You just put your arms around her, and you can hear how she's afraid of herself. She'll sit there and tell you. There's no listener in your home now; there's just a teacher of fear. That's understandable, because up until now, you haven't asked yourself if your thoughts are true. Let's look at the next statement.

Charlotte: *I need Linda to stay away from me when she's on drugs.*

Katie: Is that true? And I'm not saying it's not.

Charlotte: I feel like it is.

Katie: And does she come to you when she's on drugs?

Charlotte: No, not anymore.

Katie: So that's what you need, because that's what you have. No mistake. If my daughter doesn't come to me, that's how I know I don't need her. If she comes, that's how I know I need her.

Charlotte: And when she does come, I treat her in this horrible way.

Katie: So turn the statement around.

Charlotte: I need myself to stay away from me when I'm on drugs. That's really true.

Katie: One way you can stay away from yourself when you're on drugs, the drug of Linda, is to judge your daughter, write it down, ask four questions, and turn it around. And stay away from who you think you are—this fearful, angry woman—and come back to your beautiful self. It's what you wanted *her* to do, so I know that you can. This is a life's work. You have much more energy when you're just working on yourself.

Charlotte: Yeah, then I would want her around whether she was using or not.

Katie: I don't know.

Charlotte: At least I would be available to her when she's using, instead of shutting off.

Katie: That could be a lot less painful for both of you.

Charlotte: Yeah.

Katie: It's wonderful to realize that. Nice Work, sweetheart.

Everything happens *for* me, not *to* me.

12

Making Friends with the Worst That Can Happen

I have helped people do The Work on rape, war in Vietnam and Bosnia, torture, internment in Nazi concentration camps, the death of a child, and the prolonged pain of illnesses like cancer. Many of us think that it's not humanly possible to accept extreme experiences like these, much less meet them with unconditional love. But not only is it possible, it's our true nature.

Nothing terrible has ever happened except in our thinking. Reality is always good, even in situations that seem like nightmares. The story we tell is the only nightmare we have lived. When I say that the worst that can happen is a belief, I am being literal. The worst that can happen to you is your uninvestigated belief system.

On Forgiveness

The Work is about 100 percent forgiveness. Most people who pray or meditate as a regular practice want to be forgiving—up to a point—because they understand that it hurts not to forgive. But when their identity as the one who was wronged is threatened, they often don't want to let go. Whether or not they're aware of it, their thinking is "I'm the victim here. I'm the one who was wronged. And if I don't suffer, it lets the perpetrator off the hook."

I once met a woman whose brother had been murdered. She had been overwhelmed with grief and hatred toward the murderer and with resentment toward God. After doing a lot of very difficult inner work, she thought she had forgiven the murderer and forgiven God as well. But when the man came up for parole, she was once more flooded with such bitterness that she could hardly get out of bed in the morning. She realized that she hadn't forgiven him at all.

I love how this world is set up for people who want peace of mind. I thought it was beautiful that she wouldn't—couldn't—let herself get away with anything less than freedom. "If the universe is always friendly," I asked her (and for me it is), "why is it a good thing that this man may get out of prison? Why is it good for him, for you, and for the world?" This was a very difficult exercise for her, as you can imagine. You can try to be "spiritual" about it—you can try to summon up all the compassion you *want* to feel—and still you may find yourself waking up in the middle of the night with rage in your heart. Inquiry requires that you find answers that are genuine for you. You can't fake it. Only the real deal will set you free.

When you wake up to go to the bathroom and stub your toe on the corner of the bed in the dark, you may feel a flash of anger. But you don't feel angry at the bed. You don't blame it for stubbing your toe. You don't resent it and vow that you'll never forgive it. You don't conclude that the universe is unfair. The bed is just an object. It was doing its job, just standing there in what, for it, was the right place at the right time. You can't start blaming it without realizing how ridiculous that is. In the end it all comes down to taking responsibility for what you're believing.

Some Buddhists have a forgiveness practice in which they widen their feelings of compassion out from self to friends to nonfriends to enemies and people who have done them wrong. This is a wonderful practice, I hear. But it doesn't go to the root of the delusion. For example, a friend of mine told me about a friend of his who believed the thought "My mother ruined my life." Though that belief caused him a great deal of suffering, it was his whole identity: "I am the man whose mother ruined his life." Whenever he thought he had failed at something—a business venture or a relationship—he would blame his mother. Then he started doing the Buddhist forgiveness meditation, and that really helped him; he felt his heart get lighter after imagining himself sending loving energy to his mother, and he was less angry or abrupt with her when they spoke on the phone. The problem, though, was that he was still "sending love" to the woman who had ruined his life. In other words, he was sending love to his *story* of his mother, not to his mother herself. He was still sitting in a puddle of his own imagination. He hadn't questioned the story.

Later, after he discovered The Work, he was able to question this thought and thoughts like it. "'My mother ruined my life'—is it true?" "Yes" was his first answer. "'My mother ruined my life'—can I absolutely know that it's true?" "No. I can't know that it was my mother who was the principal cause. I can't even know that my life is ruined, for that matter." "'My mother ruined my life'—how do I react, what happens, when I believe that thought?" "I get furious, depressed, and resentful. I feel a heaviness in my heart. I become a victim. I'm rude to my mother. I distrust women." And so on. "'My mother ruined my life'—who would I be if I didn't believe that thought?" "Freer. More responsible for my actions. Less bitter and resentful. A better son. A better lover."

Then he turned the thought around to its opposite, "My mother *didn't* ruin my life," and he found specific examples where the turnaround was true. It was very difficult at first. He couldn't think of a single example, and he was tempted to give up. But every day he kept meditating and trying to find an example, and a few days later he found one: a birthday party she had given for him when he was six years old. On that one occasion, at least, she had been a good, generous mother. Once he found that example, he was able to find others. The examples astonished him. It turned out that the withholding, punishing mother of his imagination was also the mother who had done her best to make him happy. He had cherry-picked his memories and repressed all the good ones.

The examples of how she *hadn't* ruined his life brought him a little humility as well. He found it liberating to see how the opposite of the story he had been believing for two and a half decades might be at least as true as his original story and maybe even truer. After he had done The Work on his mother for a while, he discovered an entirely different woman from the one he thought he had grown up with. He no longer needed to "send her love." The love appeared by itself; it welled up in him spontaneously because there was no story that stood between her and him. As I often point out, forgiveness means realizing that what you thought happened, didn't.

Here is an exercise that will bring to your awareness everything you need to understand about forgiveness: Consider a time when you did something that you knew not to do but did anyway, something that you later deeply regretted. Now get very still, close your eyes, and identify the exact moment of that action. Go into it as deeply as you can, from the perspective of the person you were at the time. Visualize the place where you were, the person or people you were with, your emotions at the time, and the thoughts that gave rise to those emotions. Identify what you were thinking and believing in the moment just prior to the action. As you contemplate that moment, realize how, given what you were believing, you couldn't have done anything different from what you did. How could you have done anything else, considering what you were believing in that moment? With the warped or limited understanding you had, did you really have a choice?

If you go deeply into this exercise, you'll see that nothing else is possible. The possibility that anything else could have happened is just a thought you're having now about a then—an imagined past you're comparing with the real past, which is also imagined. When you realize that your thinking caused your action and you had no choice about believing what you believed, you'll be able to find your innocence.

"But I made a decision to hit my child," a man once told me. "I knew I could hold back, but I just thought 'Screw it' and hit him. And I can't forgive myself for that." He knew he could hold back—is that true? Did *he* make the decision, or was it made *for* him? If he had taken a close look at the thoughts that he was believing at that moment—thoughts like "My son should do what I tell him to do," "He shouldn't defy me," "Children should be respectful," "The only way he'll learn is if I hit him"—he would have realized that in fact there was no conscious decision. Either we believe our stressful thoughts, or we question them. There's no other choice.

We're all like this. We do what we do because we're believing our unquestioned thoughts. That's the only thing we're guilty of. We're all doing the best we can. The realization that there's no choice means that everyone is innocent: I am, you are, the person you're so furious at is, and the murderer and the rapist are as well, as were the Romans who crucified Jesus. Jesus said it himself: They didn't know what they were doing. They couldn't help it.

People aren't people; there is only mind. If you think that someone wronged you, you might want to take that thought to inquiry. I often say, "No one can hurt me—that's *my* job." It's not what *they* said or did that causes our suffering—it's what we *believe* about what they said or did. This is an essential truth. It's life changing. When you understand it, everything about your relationships with yourself, other people, and the world becomes transparent.

My Father Is Going to Beat Me

"Don't go into hell without these four questions," I told Harold at the end of this dialogue, which took place in Switzerland in 2018. His situation as an abused child had truly been a kind of hell. He had discovered The Work just seven days before we talked, and this was his first experience of actually doing it. But even though he was a beginner, he was able to dive deep and find answers that transformed his understanding of his father and of himself.

Harold: *I'm sad about my father because he beat me and abused me.*

Katie: So, sweetheart, what's the situation?

Harold: Well, I experienced terrible things in connection with my father. When I was a child, he beat me many, many times. And now he finally died.

Katie [*pointing to her head*]: But he still lives in here.

Harold: Yes.

Katie: So find a situation when he's actually beating you. As a child.

Harold: I have a situation. He's dragging me to the bathroom, and he's beating me until the walls are red.

Katie: The walls are red?

Harold: The tiles in the bathroom. Red from blood.

Katie: Did he ever beat you before that?

Harold: He constantly beat me, even when I was a very young child.

Katie: Okay. He constantly beat you. And how old were you when he was dragging you to the bathroom?

Harold: Seven or eight years old. The first time was when I was maybe six years old; he did it many times after that.

Katie: Okay. So this particular time he's dragging you to the bathroom. Do you see that in your mind's eye?

Harold: Yes.

Katie: Okay. You're not in the bathroom yet. He's just dragging you there. I'm going to speak to the little seven-year-old you were. He's going to beat you, little boy. Close your eyes. He's dragging you to the bathroom. He's going to beat you—is it true? Can you absolutely know that it's true that he's going to beat you? The answer is either a yes or a no.

Harold: Yes.

Katie: So just feel that. You're that little boy. He's dragging you to the bathroom, and you believe he's going to beat you. Now, with your eyes closed, little boy, as he's dragging you to the bathroom, notice how you react, what happens, when you believe the thought "He's going to beat me."

Harold: I'm terrified. I panic.

Katie: Yes, of course you were terrified. That little boy wasn't safe. But you're safe right here, right now. It's safe now to get really still in that moment. Notice how your mind reacts when you believe the thought "He's going to beat me." Notice the images of the future, even a nanosecond ahead of that moment. What do you see when you believe the thought "He's going to beat me"?

Harold: I'm almost unconscious. I leave my body.

Katie: So before you leave your body, you see an image of what you believe is going to happen in the bathroom.

Harold: I see his hand with the crippled finger.

Katie: And you see him beating you in the bathroom.

Harold: Yes.

Katie: And you're not even in the bathroom yet.

Harold: No, but I've gone through it several times before.

Katie: Yes, you're going through it in your mind in that moment, even though he's not beating you then. Who would you be without the thought "He's going to beat me"?

Harold: I would be relaxed. I would be completely free.

Katie: Yes. You're perfectly fine in that moment, other than what you're imagining—other than your images of a future. It's that leap into a future that's terrifying you. And what the little boy saw came so close to death—"He's going to kill me!"—that the mind lost the ability to project. Identity split out of the body. Identity left the body and looked down at the little boy and the father.

Harold: Could we say that if I hadn't seen what was going to happen before it happened, then it might not have happened?

Katie: No. But you can get still enough to go back there and just experience the trip to the bathroom, the pure experience, without fear—that is, without the story of terror that you put onto it.

Harold: Would you say my ego projected my situation into the future?

Katie: Only totally.

Harold: That's amazing!

Katie: Yes, it's quite a trick. Have you ever seen an apple?

Harold: Of course.

Katie: That's just like "He's going to beat me." Where's your proof that you've ever seen an apple?

Harold: It's only in my mind. It's only my thoughts, and thoughts are flexible.

Katie: So ask me if I've ever seen an apple.

Harold: Katie, have you ever seen an apple?

Katie: Yes. You want my proof? *[Pointing to her head]* It's in here. It's nothing but an image in my head. So a nothing is my proof. Is this image *[pointing to her head]* an apple? *[To the audience]* I'd love that you all understand the difference between reality and imagination. *[In a blithe tone of voice]* Yes, I've eaten an apple. How do I know? I see one in my head. *[Laughter from the audience.]*

Harold: Would you say that everything that's here in my head isn't real? So everything we experience here is a movie?

Katie: I think you're on to something. Yes, I would say that. But I don't have to bother. *You* did.

Harold: So the fact that I'm sitting up here with you is also part of the movie? It has nothing to do with reality, the same as with the apple?

Katie: Do you remember yourself walking up here?

Harold: Yes.

Katie: Where's your proof?

Harold: It's nowhere. It's in the movie; it's in my head. It's not tangible.

Katie: No. Movies aren't real.

Harold: Do you mean we should just let all these thoughts go?

Katie: No. Just notice that they're not real. Who wants to stop the movie? It's not personal.

Harold: So why is it that one person has a difficult life and another person an easy one?

Katie: Well, ask yourself. You seem as awake as I am. And when you really understand, you can see that no one is more awake than anyone else. These four questions and the turnarounds—if you get silent in them, they'll show you what you already know. *[To the audience]* How many of you think you're following this conversation? *[About three-quarters of the audience raise their hands.]* Life is a trick of mind. But only all of it. It's not enough to hear that; you need to experience it. What's left of the dream will come back to test you. And that's a privilege. It's the sweetness of what we call life. Once you understand that life is a dream, the dream belongs on paper, and it deserves a little respect. After all, it conjured you up. That's what's meant by "Mind is the creator of everything." Everything, without exception. And this doesn't have to be a lofty thing. When you argue with your children, your parents, your spouse, just notice that you're out of touch with your true nature. *[To Harold]* And just notice when you remember your father beating you. Be awake to the fact that it's a dream, and if it lingers, put it onto a Judge-Your-Neighbor Worksheet and question it. I'm here to invite you to an intimacy with that, and I love you don't miss it. What was the source of your terror? Was it your father? Or was it what you were believing on the way to the bathroom?

Harold: The imagination of something terrible is worse than what actually happens. But how do you deal with this? I'm asking you personally. I have known The Work only for about seven days, and I would like to know, Katie. Do you ever identify with a thought? Are you ever trapped?

Katie: Well, sweetheart, since you ask me directly, I have to tell you the truth. No. I'm always awake to the dream.

Harold: Do you realize in every moment that this is a dream and then don't identify with the dream but you identify with your true self?

Katie: If I understand the question, it's like asking if I ever think that the apple we were talking about is real. Do I always realize that it's an image in my head? Of course I do! I can say and do anything in this dream. I'm not the doer. *[To the audience]* How many of you just heard me say something? How many of you are hearing my voice right now? What voice? What "now"? You have to go back to a past to experience what I said. *[Pauses.]* How many of you feel a bit lost right now? *[About half the audience raise their hands.]* Oh. Okay, we'll slow it down a little. *[To Harold]* So which statement is truer: "I'm sad about what my father did to me" or "I'm sad about what my thoughts about my father did to me"?

Harold: Probably it's the second.

Katie: I would drop the "probably." *[Laughter from the audience.]* Okay. So let's slow it down for the people who raised their hands. You're sad about what your father did to you—is it true?

Harold: It's not quite as true as it was.

Katie: So let's find a situation where you were sitting in the chair a few moments ago and you were believing the thought "I'm sad about what my father did to me." Now notice how you react when you believe the thought. Notice the images of the past that appear when you believe the thought. You see him dragging you to the bathroom. You see him beating you.

Harold: I now feel that the sorrow is coming from another thought. The sadness is about the fact that I had to become the son of such a father in this incarnation. It's almost like blaming God.

Katie: You know what I love about the past? It's over. *[Laughter from the audience.]* All those dreams that cause sadness and resentment and hurt and disappointment belong on paper or on a screen, so that you can meditate on them with the four questions of The Work. So your father is dragging you to the bathroom, seven-year-old little boy. And how do you react when you believe the thought "He's going to beat me"?

Harold: Pure panic. I'm afraid he'll kill me.

Katie: Now I want you to keep your eyes closed and to understand how you reacted to that thought. Get into that little boy's head in that situation and witness the images of the future that he experiences as his father drags him to the bathroom. Get very present. You're not even in the bathroom yet. What images of the future do you see when you believe that he's taking you to the bathroom to beat you?

Harold: I see the image of an empty bathroom. I see his hand with the crippled finger. And I feel the fear.

Katie: You feel the fear because you see images of him beating you.

Harold: Exactly.

Katie: Get still. Just identify whatever you see as that little boy being dragged to the bathroom.

Harold: I feel like I'm being led to the slaughterhouse.

Katie: Yes. And it's so terrifying that you leave your body.

Harold: Uh-huh.

Katie: So now come back into your body on your way to the bathroom. Who would you be without that thought, little boy?

Harold: I would be less frightened.

Katie: Yes, now look again.

Harold: I'm calmer.

Katie: And look at the trip. Don't miss the trip. It's called life. Can you see the walls, the ceiling, or maybe light coming through a window?

Harold: I see everything. I see the towels. I see everything.

Katie: Yes. So "I'm sad about what my father did to me"—turn it around.

Harold: I'm happy about what my father did to me. Wow! The energy changes immediately.

Katie: He's giving you life now. He's your teacher. He's waking you up.

Harold: You mean he's waking me up from the dream?

Katie: Yes. You're a tough customer. It takes a big teacher for you.

Harold *[looking confused and delighted]*: Hmm. That's an entirely different way of seeing it.

Katie: Well, where's the proof that he ever beat you, other than in your head?

Harold: Only in my mind. Same as with the apple.

Katie: Now, suppose my mother says he beat me, my sister and brother say he beat me, everyone tells me that it's true. That's *their* experience. They could be right. I need more. I need to know what's real for myself and what's not.

Harold: That would mean that we have to let go of all projections, all wishes, all dreams, if we're going to become peaceful.

Katie: It doesn't mean we *have* to, but we certainly have a way to. We can question them all.

Harold: How did you do it?

Katie: Exactly the way we're doing it here. I questioned the thoughts that caused my suffering. I knew it was my job to wake myself up to reality. The fantasy is not pleasant with a mind like yours.

Harold: Let's say I have a thought, and the thought calls for its realization. And then I have the same thought again, and again it gets realized, my whole life. I have romantic relationships that last for about four or five years, and then we break up, and then there's the next one and the next one. It's been like that my whole life. They're never fulfilled.

Katie: Well, I would just begin now. I mean, there's nowhere else to start. This is the time and the place. So go to a time when your father was actually beating you and you were not out of body. Go to a place where he was actually beating you, around that age.

Harold: Um-hmm. Yeah.

Katie: He's going to hit you again. Can you find that place where he hit you and his hand is in the air again and he's going to hit you again?

Harold: I see the images, yes.

Katie: Good. So he's going to hit you again, little boy—can you absolutely know that it's true?

Harold: No, I can't absolutely know that. It's just imagination.

Katie: And yes, his hand's in the air, and yes, he has that look on his face, and now his hand is getting closer and closer. Can you absolutely know that he's going to hit you again?

Harold: No.

Katie: Now notice how you react when you believe the thought "He's going to hit me again." His hand is in the air. Notice what your mind does when you believe the thought. Find the place where you imagine the hit before he hits.

Harold: I'm there.

Katie: Which is more painful? Imagination or when his hand actually hits you?

Harold: Imagination is worse.

Katie: Now notice him hitting you. Notice that the mind is always remembering or anticipating. So what's in the center? The mind is always in the past or the future, either remembering or anticipating. So when he hits you, it's either remembered or anticipated. Now turn it around. "My father beat me." What's an opposite?

Harold: I beat me.

Katie: I beat me. In my mind's eye.

Harold: I did terrible things to myself. I wasn't there for myself.

Katie: No. You were busy remembering and anticipating. In the moment that he was going to hit you again, you anticipated the next hit. And I heard from you that that was more terrifying than the actual hit. So "I beat myself" in my mind's eye. And that was the cause of the terror.

Harold: I beat myself. I abused myself.

Katie: This is not a question of right or wrong, sweetheart. It's just something you do every day, all day long, at whatever level.

Harold: Yes, that's certainly true.

Katie: Can you find another turnaround? "I beat . . ."

Harold: I beat my father?

Katie: Yes, in your mind.

Harold: I can see that. I've been beating him in my mind for all these years.

Katie: What did you write for statement two?

Harold: *I want my father to love me, to understand me, to be there for me, and to be more compassionate toward me.*

Katie: Close your eyes. He's taking you to the bathroom. Look at him. Do you see his face? Is he angry? Is he disturbed?

Harold: Yes, he's both. He's disturbed and angry.

Katie: Look at his face. Look at his state of mind. You want your father to love you, to understand you, to be there for you, and to be more compassionate toward you—is that true? Is it even possible?

Harold: It's impossible.

Katie: Now notice how you react, what happens, when you believe that you want him to love you, to understand you, to be there for you, and to be more compassionate toward you.

Harold: It hurts.

Katie: And you immediately become a victim. At the age of seven.

Harold: Yes. There's a feeling of heaviness and density.

Katie: And aloneness.

Harold: Aloneness also, yes.

Katie: And you're a victim.

Harold: Yes, I feel helpless. The worst is probably that I feel so helpless.

Katie: Who would you be without the thought?

Harold: I would feel free. I see now that it's just a story.

Katie: Yes. That little boy is in a trance. He's in a dream. So let's turn it around to yourself. "I want my father to love me, to understand me, to be there for me, and to be more compassionate toward me"—turn it around. "I want me . . ."

Harold: I want me to love me, to understand me, to be there for me, and to be more compassionate toward me.

Katie: Yes. To be present.

Harold: Can I ask a question?

Katie: Probably. But who knows the future? *[Laughter from the audience.]*

Harold: From your point of view, are the thoughts I'm thinking *my* thoughts, or are they just thoughts that I'm thinking?

Katie: Who cares whose they are, or if they're no one's at all? The fact is that they hurt. I'm only interested in the end of your suffering. But I can tell you that at the stage of learning you're in, these thoughts are like life. They come as needed. They're here to wake you up.

Harold: You mean they have a positive purpose?

Katie: This is a friendly universe. There's nothing that isn't here for your sake. Nothing.

Harold: Hmm. I have to think about whether that's so.

Katie: Well, if you're suffering, there's something out of order, and you can go back and put it in order. Can you find another turn-around? "I want me . . ."

Harold: I want me to love me, to understand me.

Katie: No, we did that one. "I want me . . ."

Harold: I want me to—

Katie: Who else is there? There's you, and there's—

Harold: Ah. I want me to love my father, to understand him, to be there for him, and to be more compassionate toward him.

Katie: Yes, more compassionate toward your father. He's violent; he's dragging you to the bathroom. He's lost in the dream. Look at him. If you were believing what he was believing about you, *you* would drag you to the bathroom, too. We can't stop believing what we're believing in the moment we believe it. We're innocent. So have a little mercy. Look at your father closely. He's tormented. He would have to be tormented, to beat a child.

Harold: Katie, I can't describe what's happening inside me right now, but it feels very good.

Katie: No one can stop me from loving them. They don't have a choice. No one can stop me from connecting with them, however they've treated me. No one can stop me from understanding. Only my unquestioned thinking can cost me that.

Harold: So I am the one who does everything?

Katie: Only totally.

Harold: Only totally? That's pretty—

Katie: Total. *[Harold sits in silence, looking amazed.]* Okay, let's look at statement three, advice to your father.

Harold: *Father should be gentler, more loving, more humane, and more compassionate.*

Katie: Is that true?

Harold: No. He shouldn't. He can't.

Katie: And how do you react when you believe that he should be gentler when he isn't, when he can't be?

Harold: I feel hopeless.

Katie: Who would you be without the thought that your father should be gentler?

Harold: It would be less painful. I'd be more present, more aware of what's actually happening on the way to the bathroom.

Katie: You're more awake now on your trip. So you can turn it around. "In this situation, *I* should . . ."

Harold: In this situation, I should be gentler—

Katie: To yourself. You should be gentler to yourself.

Harold: I should be gentler to myself, more loving to myself, more humane to myself, more compassionate to myself.

Katie: Yes. And in that you can see the difference between reality and imagination. And for all you know, it could be the last breath and moment of your life. You don't want to miss it. No one can cost you that.

Harold: But the turnaround that we just did—isn't it just imagination as well?

Katie: There's nothing that isn't imagination. But it's respectful to be awake to every moment of the dream. The image comes to your mind like an apple. That's okay. But notice what you believe onto the apple: "I hate apples." "Apples are too hard. I prefer bananas." "This apple isn't sweet enough." "Oh, there's only one apple, and there are five of us." The apple, the apple, the apple. Ultimately, everything is a dream. We're in the process of waking up from the dream. The dream of the little boy still belongs to the man. There's something off with that. But as long as this horror is a part of the man, the man deserves an opportunity to take a look. As the boy of your imagination wakes up to that, the man becomes free. The child becomes free, and that child's freedom belongs to the man.

Harold: You said that you're not the doer. But if I can change the imagining or the dream, I am *doing* something, because I'm changing it.

Katie: As long as you think you're doing the sitting in that chair, there's a little Work left.

Harold: Oh. Good. I like that answer.

Katie: Let's find another turnaround. Okay? "I should be gentler to my father . . ."

Harold: I should be gentler to my father, more loving to him, more humane to him, more compassionate to him.

Katie: Now look. Get in touch with your father and his face and his lostness. Look at his face. He's angry. He's confused. "I should be gentler to this tormented man."

Harold: I should be gentler to this tormented man. I should be more loving to him. I should be more humane to him. And I should be more compassionate to him. It feels good somehow.

Katie: You're being everything you wanted *him* to be. You wanted that for him so it could give you peace. We can't change him, but we can see more clearly and free ourselves of our imagined terror.

Harold: It's incredible to see how these images lose their charge when they're questioned!

Katie: Everyone talks about compassion. *This* is compassion. This is not something you're doing. We can't *do* compassion. We can only experience it. Let's look at statement four.

Harold: *I need my father to love me, to acknowledge me, to be a real father to me, and to be there for me.*

Katie: So, little boy, as your father is dragging you to the bathroom, is that what you need to be happy? Do you need him to love you to be happy? Do you need that tormented man to acknowledge you?

Harold: No, I don't need that.

Katie: And he *is* a real father. You need your father to be a real father? *That's* your real father. There are fathers of your imagination, and then there's yours. You know those other fathers in the world that are so kind to their children? That's not *your* father. *This* one is your father. He's a man who beats little boys. He's dragging you to the bathroom. That's the way he's there for you. *[Harold laughs.]* I mean, just in case you missed it, he's right there.

Harold: Yes, he is.

Katie: So is it true you need those things from him?

Harold: No.

Katie: Now notice what happens to your life when you believe these thoughts. What happens to your relationships when you believe these thoughts? "I need them to love me. I need my partner to acknowledge me." What you believe onto your father, you may be believing onto your partner.

Harold: It's very stressful.

Katie: "I need my partner to be a real partner. And to be there for me."

Harold: More and more stressful.

Katie: Then you turn into your father when you believe those thoughts. Not quite so brutal but just enough.

Harold: Crazy.

Katie: Yes.

Harold: It's incredible what we do to ourselves.

Katie: Yes, the dream world is tough. It's good that it's not real.

Harold: That's beautiful. Maybe it's not as real as I thought it was.

Katie: So let's turn it around: "In order to be happy, I need me . . ." And read statement four turned around.

Harold: In order to be happy, I need me to love myself, to acknowledge myself, to be a good father to myself, and especially to be here for myself.

Katie: Yes. You're the father you've been looking for: compassionate, kind, loving. So turn it around again: "I need to love my father . . ."

Harold: I need to love my father.

Katie: Yes. He's asleep. No one would be angry at another human being if they were not asleep.

Harold: But the lady who sold me the book at your bookstore during the break told me that his problem is his problem and my problem is my problem.

Katie: That's a great truth. So "I need to love my father . . ." And continue with statement four.

Harold: I need to love my father, to acknowledge him, to be a father to him, and to be there for him.

Katie: Obviously, he didn't have a father who loved him. It just didn't work out that well. So for you to be gentler with him, more loving with him, more humane and compassionate, is not just to be that way with him, but it's also to father him. And little seven-year-old boys don't know how to do that, especially when they're being dragged to the bathroom and they're projecting what's going to happen when they get there. Your job is to be a real father to him now, to be there for him when he comes to you in your imagination. That's it. People only come to you in your imagination. So the invitation is to deal with those nightmares by questioning your thoughts. Let's look at statement five.

Harold: *Father is bad, evil, cruel, selfish, the Devil incarnate.*

Katie: "In that moment, on my way to the bathroom, my thoughts about my father are . . ." And read it.

Harold: The thoughts that I have about my father are bad, evil, cruel, selfish, the Devil incarnate.

Katie: Okay, close your eyes. Other than what you were believing in the bathroom and on the way to the bathroom, were you okay?

Harold: It's becoming tense again.

Katie: Other than what you're believing, little boy, are you okay?

Harold: I'm not feeling that well anymore.

Katie: Who would you be without those fearful thoughts on the way to the bathroom?

Harold: It's becoming easier again.

Katie: And who would you be in the bathroom when your father raises his hand?

Harold: Who would I be? I can't answer that question.

Katie: I have an answer. Would you like to hear it?

Harold: Yes.

Katie: His hand's in the air. Who would I be without my story of the future? Really grateful that he hasn't hit me yet. Now he hits me. One second later, who would I be without my story of the future and past?

Harold: Completely free.

Katie: The Work is a practice. It's not a quick fix. You can get a lot of freedom from working through all six statements on a Worksheet, and then the ego's job is to override it. If you have come to great awareness through your questioning, the ego's job is to give you another situation where you're believing your stressful thoughts. The awareness that you've experienced in this room—you can never lose it. But your unquestioned thoughts override the awareness that you've experienced today. You don't lose it. It just is overridden by the fake news in your head that you still haven't questioned. It's not enough to say that life's a dream. Life will give you what's next. Let's look at statement six.

Harold: *I never want to experience cruelty, hardness, selfishness, hatred again.*

Katie: "I'm willing to . . ."

Harold: I'm willing to experience cruelty, hardness, selfishness, and hatred again.

Katie: "I look forward to . . ."

Harold: I look forward to experiencing cruelty, hardness, selfishness, and hatred again.

Katie: The next time you're having a wonderful day and you go to sleep at night and then out of nowhere: Father! You're being dragged to the bathroom! You're in the bathroom! If you don't love it, you're not awake to the dream. So it's another Worksheet. Be willing to question the thoughts. That's why we can't sleep at night. We have unfinished business.

Harold: That's the reason why I have trouble sleeping.

Katie: So now you know what to do when you can't sleep. Judge your father, write it down, ask four questions, and turn it around. Or not.

Harold: It's crazy to see that when I look forward to all these things, it actually feels great! *[Applause.]*

Katie: It feels right. There's nothing more exciting than peace.

Harold: I really feel that.

Katie: Here comes a panic attack! It's Father again! Yay! Get still. Go to the situation. Collect the thoughts you were thinking and believing in that situation. Set yourself free, because no one else can do it.

Harold: They're already gone. Thank you, Katie. *[Applause from the audience.]*

Katie *[to the audience]*: Don't go into hell without these four questions. And if you invite these questions into your life, it becomes impossible to go into hell without them. The questions aren't here to wake you up; it's your *answers* to the questions that will wake you up. The questions are the invitation. But only you can answer them. And it does take courage.

Afraid of Death

In the School for The Work, I love to use inquiry to walk people through the thing they fear most, the worst that could possibly happen. For many of them, the worst thing is death: they often believe that they'll suffer terribly not only during the process of dying but also after they die. I take them deep enough into these waking nightmares to dispel the illusion of fear, pain, and suffering.

I have sat with many people on their deathbeds, and after we do The Work, they always tell me that they're fine. I remember one very frightened woman who was dying of cancer. She had requested that I come sit with her, so I did. I sat down beside her and said, "I don't see a problem." She said, "No? Well, I'll show you a problem!" and she pulled off the sheet. One of her legs was so swollen that it was at least twice the size of the normal leg. I looked and I looked, and I still couldn't find a problem. She said, "You must be blind! Look at this leg. Now look at the other one." And I said, "Oh, now I see the problem. You're suffering from the belief that that leg should look like this one. Who would you be without that thought?" And she got it. She began to laugh, and the fear just poured out through her laughter. She said that it was the happiest she had ever been in her life.

I once went to visit a woman who was dying in a hospice. When I walked in, she was napping, so I just sat by her bed until she opened her eyes. I took her hand, and we talked for a few minutes, and she said, "I'm so frightened. I don't know how to die." And I said, "Sweetheart, is that true?" She said, "Yes. I just don't know what to do." I said, "When I walked in, you were taking a nap. Do you know how to take a nap?" She said, "Of course." And I said, "You close your eyes every night, and you go to sleep. People look forward to sleeping. That's all death is. That's as bad as it gets, except for your belief system that says there's something else." She told me she believed in the after-death thing and said, "I won't know what to do when I get there." I said, "Can you really know that there's something to do?" She said, "I guess not." I said, "There's nothing you have to know, and it's always all right. Everything you need is already there for you; you don't have to give it a thought. All you have to do is take a nap when you need to, and when you wake up, you'll know what to do." I was describing life to her, of course, not death. Then we went into the second question, "Can you absolutely know that it's true that you don't know how to die?" She began to laugh and said that she preferred being with me to being with her story. What fun, having nowhere to go but where we really are now.

When the mind thinks of death, it looks at nothing and calls it something, to keep from experiencing what it—the mind—really is. Until you know that death is equal to life, you'll always try to control what happens, and it's always going to hurt. There's no sadness without a story that opposes reality.

The fear of death is the last smoke screen for the fear of love. We think that we're afraid of the death of our body, though what we're really afraid of is the death of our identity. But through inquiry, when we realize that death is just a concept and that our identity is a concept, too, we realize who we are. This is the end of fear.

Loss is another concept. I was in the delivery room when my grandson Race was born. I loved him at first sight. Then I realized that he wasn't breathing. The doctor had a troubled look on his face and immediately started to do something with the baby. The nurses realized that the procedures weren't working, and you could see panic begin to take over the room. Nothing they did was working; the baby wouldn't breathe. At a certain moment, Roxann looked into my eyes, and I smiled. She later told me, "You know that smile you often have on your face, Mom? When I saw you look at me like that, a wave of peace came over me. And even though the baby wasn't breathing, it was okay with me." Soon afterward, breath entered my grandson, and I heard him cry.

I love that my grandson didn't have to breathe for me to love him. Whose business was his breathing? Not mine. I wasn't going to miss one moment of him, whether he was breathing or not. I knew that even without a single breath, he had lived a full life. I love reality, not the way a fantasy would dictate but just the way it is, right now.

Henry: *I'm angry at death because it destroys me. I'm afraid of dying. I can't accept death. Death should let me be reincarnated. Death is painful. Death is the end. I never want to experience the fear of death again.*

Katie: Let's start at the top. Read your first statement again.

Henry: *I'm angry at death because it destroys me.*

Katie: If you want to live in terror, get a future. That's quite a future you've planned, sweetheart. Let's hear the next statement.

Henry: *I'm afraid of dying.*

Katie: What's the worst that could happen when you die? Let's play with that.

Henry: The death of my body.

Katie: And then what will happen?

Henry: I don't know.

Katie: Well, what do you think is the worst that could happen? You think that something terrible could happen. What is it?

Henry: That death is the end and I'm not born again. And that there is no soul.

Katie: And then? You're not born again. There is no soul. So far, there's nothing. So far, the worst that can happen to you is nothing. And then?

Henry: Yes, but it's painful.

Katie: So the nothing is painful.

Henry: Yes.

Katie: Can you really know that that's true? How can nothing be painful? How can it be anything? Nothing is nothing.

Henry: I imagine this nothing as a black hole that is very uncomfortable.

Katie: So nothing is a black hole. Can you really know that that's true? I'm not saying it's not true. I know how you love your stories. It's the old black-hole story.

Henry: I think that's the worst thing that could happen.

Katie: Okay. So when you die, you would go into a big black hole forever.

Henry: Or to Hell. I call this black hole Hell.

Katie: A big black hellhole forever.

Henry: And it is a hellfire.

Katie: A big black hellhole fire forever.

Henry: Yes, and it's turned away from God.

Katie: Totally away from God. Fire and darkness in this big black hellhole forever. I want to ask you, can you absolutely know that that's true?

Henry: No. I can't.

Katie: How does it feel when you believe that thought?

Henry *[crying]*: It's painful. It's horrible.

Katie: Sweetheart, look at me. Are you in touch with what you're feeling right now? Look at yourself. *This* is the dark hole of Hell. You're in it. It doesn't come later; you're living your story of your future death right now. This terror is as bad as it gets. Can you see a reason to drop this story? And I'm not asking you to drop it.

Henry: Yes.

Katie: Give me a reason to keep this story that doesn't feel like being in a dark fire from hell.

Henry: I can't.

Katie: Who or what would you be without this story? You've already been living the worst that could happen. Imagination without investigation. Lost in Hell. No way out.

Henry: Pushed away from God.

Katie: Yes, angel, pushed away from the awareness of God in your life. You can't push yourself away from God; that's not a possibility. You can only push yourself away from the awareness of God within you, for a while. As long as you worship this old idol, this old black-hole story of yours, there's no room for any awareness of God in you. This story is what you've been worshipping like a child, in pure innocence. Let's look at the next statement.

Henry: *I'm afraid of dying.*

Katie: I understand that. But no one is afraid of dying; they're just afraid of their story about dying. Look at what you think death is.

You've been describing your life, not death. This is the story of your life.

Henry: Hmmm. Yes.

Katie: Let's look at the next statement.

Henry: *I can't accept death.*

Katie: Is that true?

Henry: Well, yes. I have a lot of trouble accepting it.

Katie: Can you absolutely know that it's true that you can't accept death?

Henry: It's hard to believe that that's possible.

Katie: When you're not thinking about death, you fully accept it. You're not worrying about it at all. Think of your foot.

Henry: Okay.

Katie: Did you have a foot before you thought of it? Where was it? When there's no thought, there's no foot. When there's no thought of death, there's no death.

Henry: Really? I can't believe it's that simple.

Katie: How do you react, how do you feel, when you believe the thought "I can't accept death"?

Henry: Helpless. Frightened.

Katie: What would you be in your life without this story "I can't accept death"?

Henry: What would my life be without that thought? It would be beautiful.

Katie: "I can't accept death"—turn it around.

Henry: I can accept death.

Katie: Everyone can. Everyone *does*. There's no decision in death. People who know that there's no hope are free. The decision's out of their hands. It has always been that way, but some people have to die bodily to find out. No wonder they smile on their deathbeds. Dying is everything they were looking for in life. Their delusion of being in charge is over. When there's no choice, there's no fear. And in that there is peace. They realize that they're home and that they've never left.

Henry: This fear of losing control is very strong. And also this fear of love. It's all connected.

Katie: It's terrifying to think you could lose control, even though the truth is that you never had it in the first place. That's the death of fantasy and the birth of reality. Let's look at the next statement.

Henry: *Death should let me be reincarnated.*

Katie: You should be reincarnated—can you really know that that's true? Welcome to the story of a future.

Henry: No. I can't know if that's true.

Katie: You don't even like it *this* time around. Why do you want to do it again? *[Henry laughs.]* "Boy, what a dark hole *this* is. Hmm, I think I'll come back again." *[Laughter from the audience.]* "You want to come back again"—is that true?

Henry *[laughing]*: No, it's not. I don't want to be reincarnated. It was a mistake.

Katie: We reincarnate—can you absolutely know that that's true?

Henry: No, I've just heard and read that we do.

Katie: How do you react when you believe that thought?

Henry: I feel anxious about what I'm doing now, because I think I may have to make up for it later and I may even be punished for it or at least have to suffer for many lifetimes because I've hurt so many people in my life. I'm afraid that I've piled up a lot of bad karma and maybe I've blown it this lifetime and I'll have to start over again and again in lower forms of life.

Katie: Who would you be without the thought that we reincarnate?

Henry: Less fearful. Freer.

Katie: Reincarnation may be a useful concept for some people, but in my experience, nothing reincarnates but a thought. "I. I am. I am woman. I am woman with children." And so on ad infinitum. Do you want to end karma? It's simple: "I." "I am"—is it true? Who would I be without this story? No karma whatsoever. And I look forward to the next life, and here it comes. It's called "now." Let's look at the next statement.

Henry: *Death is painful.*

Katie: Can you really know that that's true?

Henry: I can't.

Katie: How does it feel when you believe the thought that death is painful?

Henry: It feels stupid now.

Katie: "Death is painful"—turn it around. "My thinking . . ."

Henry: My thinking is painful.

Katie: Isn't that truer?

Henry: Yes. Yes.

Katie: Death was never that unkind. Death is simply the end of thought. Fantasy without investigation is painful, sometimes. Let's look at the next.

Henry: *Death is the end.*

Katie *[laughing]*: That's a good one! Can you really know that that's true?

Henry: I can't.

Katie: Isn't that one of your personal favorites? *[Laughter from the audience.]* How do you react when you believe that thought?

Henry: Up to now, I've always been afraid.

Katie: "Death is the end"—turn it around.

Henry: My thinking is the end.

Katie: The beginning, the middle, the end. *[Henry and the audience laugh.]* All of it. You know how to die really well. Have you ever just gone to sleep at night?

Henry: Yes.

Katie: That's it. Dreamless sleep. You do it really well. You sleep at night, then you open your eyes, and there's still nothing, there's no one awake. There's never anyone alive until the story begins with "I." And that's where life begins, with the first word you think. Prior to that, there's no you, no world. You do this every day of your life. Identification as an "I" wakes up. "I" am Henry. "I" need to brush my teeth. "I" am late for work. "I" have so much to do today. Before that, there's no one, nothing, no black hellhole, only peace that doesn't even recognize itself as peace. You die very well, sweetheart. And you're born very well. And if things get rough, you have inquiry. Let's look at your last statement.

Henry: *I never want to experience the fear of death again.*

Katie: "I'm willing . . ."

Henry: I'm willing to experience the fear of death again.

Katie: Now you know what to do with it. So give it a shot. "I look forward to . . ."

Henry *[laughing]*: I look forward to experiencing the fear of death again. I'll try my best.

Katie: Good. There's no place, there's no dark hole you can go into where inquiry won't follow. Inquiry lives inside you if you nurture it for a while. Then it takes on its own life and automatically nurtures you. And you're never given more pain than you can handle. You never, ever get more than you can take. That's a promise. Death experiences are just mental experiences. And when people die, it's so wonderful that they never come back to tell you. It's so wonderful, they're not going to bother. *[Laughter from the audience.]* That's what investigation is for. So, sweetheart, look forward to the fear of death. If you're a lover of truth, set yourself free.

Bombs Are Falling

The next dialogue, with a sixty-seven-year-old Dutch man, shows the power of an uninvestigated story, how it can control our thoughts and actions for almost a whole lifetime.

Bombs also fell on a German man who participated in one of my European Schools for The Work. He was six years old when Soviet troops occupied Berlin in 1945. The soldiers took him, along with many other children, women, and old people who had survived the bombing, and put him into a shelter. He remembers playing with one of the live hand grenades that the soldiers had given the children as toys. He watched as another of the little boys pulled the pin; the grenade exploded, and the boy's arm was blown off. Many of the children were maimed, and he remembers their screams, their wounded faces, their skin and limbs flying. He also remembers a girl of six who slept near him being raped by a soldier, and he told me that he could still hear the screams of the women being raped night after night in the barracks. His whole life had been dominated by the experience of a six-year-old, he said, and he had come to the School to go deeper into himself and his nightmares and to find his way back home.

At the same School, there was a Jewish woman whose parents had survived Dachau. When she was a child, her nights, too, were filled with screams. Her father would often wake up in the middle of the night screaming and spend hours pacing back and forth, crying and moaning. Most nights, her mother would wake up, too, and join her father in his moans. Her parents' nightmare became her

nightmare. She was taught that if people didn't have a number tat-
tooed on their arm, they were not to be trusted. She was as traumatized as the German man was.

A few days into the School, after I'd heard their stories, I put
those two people together for an exercise. The Worksheets they had
written out were judgments on the enemy soldiers in World War II
from opposite sides. Each one in turn gave inquiry to the other. I
loved watching these two survivors of thought as they became
friends.

In the following dialogue, Willem investigates childhood terrors
that have been with him for more than fifty years. Although he isn't
yet ready to look forward to the worst that can happen, he does have
some important insights. We can never know how much we have
received when we've finished a piece of honest inquiry or what effect
it will have on us. We may never even be aware of the effect. It's none
of our business.

Willem: *I don't like war because it has brought me a lot of fear and terror.*
It showed me that my existence is very insecure. I was hungry all the
time. My father wasn't there when I needed him. I had to spend
many nights in the bomb shelter.

Katie: Good. And how old were you?

Willem: At the beginning of the war I was six and at the end, twelve.

Katie: Let's look at "It has brought me a lot of fear and terror." So go
to the worst time, to the very worst time you had, with all the hunger
and the fear and no father. How old were you then?

Willem: Twelve.

Katie: And where are you? I'll talk to the twelve-year-old.

Willem: I'm coming home from school, I hear the bombs, so I go
into a house and then the house falls down on me. The roof hits me
on the head.

Katie: And then what happens?

Willem: First I thought I was dead; then I realized that I was alive, and I crawled out of the ruins and ran away.

Katie: So you ran away, and then what happened?

Willem: I ran down the street and into a bakery. And then I left the bakery and went into a church, into the crypt, thinking "Maybe I'll be safer here." And later, I was put onto a truck with other wounded people.

Katie: Was your body okay?

Willem: Yes, but I had a concussion.

Katie: Okay. I'd like to ask the little twelve-year-old boy, What is the worst moment? When you hear the bombs? When the house falls in on you?

Willem: When the house is falling down.

Katie: Yes. And while the house is falling, apart from your thinking, little boy, is it okay? Except for your thoughts, is it okay? In reality?

Willem: Now, as an adult, I can say it's okay, because I know I survived it. But as a child, it was not okay.

Katie: I understand. And I'm asking the twelve-year-old boy. I'm asking you to look at the house falling down. It's coming down. Are you okay?

Willem: Yes. I'm still alive.

Katie: And then when the house falls on you, are you okay? In reality?

Willem: I'm still alive.

Katie: Now you're crawling out of the house. Tell me the truth, little boy. Are you okay?

Willem [*after a long pause*]: I'm alive.

Katie: And again I'm asking the little boy, is anything not okay?

Willem: I don't know whether my stepmother or my brothers are still alive.

Katie: Good. Now except for that thought, are you okay?

Willem [*after a pause*]: I'm alive, and that's okay, given the situation.

Katie: Without the story of your mother and your family, are you okay? I don't mean just alive. Look at the twelve-year-old.

Willem: Although I was in panic, I *can* say this is okay. I was alive and happy that I came out of the house.

Katie: So close your eyes. Now move aside from the little boy. Just watch the little twelve-year-old. Watch him with the house falling in on him. Now watch him crawling out. Look at him without your story, without the story of bombs and parents. Just look at him without your story. You can have your story back later. Just for now, look at him without your story. Just be with him. Can you find the place in you where you knew it was okay?

Willem: Hmm.

Katie: Yes, sweetheart, you tell the story of how the bomb is going to wipe out your family and you, and you scare yourself with that story. Little boys don't understand how the mind works. They can't know that it's just a story that's scaring them.

Willem: I didn't know.

Katie: So the house fell, the roof hit you on the head, you got a concussion, you crawled out, you went to a bakery, you went to a church. Reality is much kinder than our stories. "I need my father. Did a bomb hit my family? Are my parents alive? Will I ever see them again? How will I survive without them?"

Willem: Hmm.

Katie: I'd like to go back and be with that little boy again, because he's still sitting here today. The story "It's going to fall down and kill my family" causes much more terror and pain than the house actually falling on you. Did you even feel it falling on you?

Willem: Probably not, because I was in so much fear.

Katie: So, sweetheart, how many times have you experienced the story? For how many years?

Willem: Very often.

Katie: How many more bombs did you hear?

Willem: Just two more weeks of bombing.

Katie: So you experienced that for two weeks, and you've lived it in your mind for how many years?

Willem: Fifty-five.

Katie: So the bombs have been falling inside you for fifty-five years. And in reality only for part of six years.

Willem: Yes.

Katie: So who is kinder, war or you?

Willem: Hmm.

Katie: Who is making war unceasingly? How do you react when you believe this story?

Willem: With fear.

Katie: And look at how you live when you believe this story. For fifty-five years, you've been feeling fear with no bombs and no houses falling. Can you see a reason to drop this little boy's story?

Willem: Oh, yes.

Katie: Who would you be without it?

Willem: I would be free, free of fear probably, especially free of fear.

Katie: Yes, that's my experience. I want to talk to the little twelve-year-old again. Is it true that you need your father? Is it really true?

Willem: I know that I missed him.

Katie: I understand that fully. And is it true you need your father? I'm asking you for the truth.

Willem: I've grown up without a father.

Katie: So is it really true you needed him? Is it true you needed your mother until you met her again? In reality?

Willem: No.

Katie: Is it true that you needed food when you were hungry?

Willem: No. I didn't starve.

Katie: Can you find a stress-free reason to keep the story that you needed your mother, you needed your father, you needed a house, you needed food?

Willem: So I can feel like a victim.

Katie: That's very stressful. And stress is the only effect of this old, old story, which isn't even true. "I needed my mother." It's not true. "I needed my father." It's not true. Can you hear it? How would you live if you weren't a victim?

Willem: I would be much freer.

Katie: Little twelve-year-old boy in the shelter, can you see a reason to drop the story "I need my mother, I need my father, I need a house, I need food"?

Willem: Yes.

Katie: It's only our story that keeps us from knowing that we always have everything we need. Can you turn your statement around? Read the statement again.

Willem: *I don't like war because it has brought me a lot of fear and terror.*

Katie: "I don't like my thinking . . ."

Willem: I don't like my thinking about war because it has brought me a lot of fear and terror.

Katie: Yes. The worst that happened to you in reality was a concussion. So let's move gently to the next statement.

Willem: *There should only be discussions, instead of war.*

Katie: Can you really know that that's true? You've been having a mental discussion for fifty-five years! *[Willem laughs.]* And it hasn't settled any war—inside you.

Willem: Hmm.

Katie: How do you react when you think the thought "There should be no war"? How have you lived your life for fifty-five years when you think that thought and you read about war in the newspaper?

Willem: It makes me frustrated, disappointed, and angry and sometimes desperate. I struggle to resolve conflicts in a peaceful manner, and I'm not very successful at it.

Katie: So in reality, war keeps breaking out in you and in the world, and in your mind there's a war against reality with the story "There should be no war." Who would you be without that story?

Willem: I could deal more freely with conflicts if I didn't have that idea.

Katie: Yes. You would experience the end of war with reality. You would be someone we could hear, a man of peace, telling the truth about how to end war—someone to be trusted. Let's look at the next statement.

Willem: *International conflicts should be resolved in a peaceful way.* Should I turn it around?

Katie: Yes.

Willem: My inner conflicts should be resolved in a peaceful way.

Katie: Yes, through inquiry. You learn to resolve problems peacefully within yourself, and now we have a teacher. Fear teaches fear. Only peace can teach peace. Let's look at the next statement.

Willem: *War destroys a lot of human lives and wastes huge amounts of material resources. It brings great sorrow and suffering to families. It's cruel, brutal, and terrible.*

Katie: Can you hear the turnaround as you're saying it? Are you experiencing it? Let's see what it sounds like. Turn it around and put yourself on all of it.

Willem: Put me—

Katie: "My thinking destroys . . ."

Willem: My thinking destroys a lot of my human life and wastes huge amounts of my own material resources.

Katie: Yes. Every time you tell the story of war inside you, it diminishes your own favorite resources: peace and happiness. And the next one? Turn it around.

Willem: I bring great sorrow and suffering to my own family.

Katie: Yes. How much sorrow do you bring when you come home to your family with this story inside you?

Willem: That's hard to accept.

Katie: I don't see any bombs falling. No bombs have fallen around you for fifty-five years, except in your mind. There's only one thing harder than accepting this, and that is *not* accepting it. Reality rules, whether we're aware of it or not. The story is how you keep yourself from experiencing peace right now. You needed your mother—is that true?

Willem: I survived without her.

Katie: Let's work with a yes or no and see what that feels like. You needed your mother—is it true in reality?

Willem: No.

Katie: You needed your father—is it true?

Willem: No.

Katie: Feel it. Close your eyes. Look at that little guy taking care of himself. Look at him without your story. *[Long pause. Finally, Willem smiles.]* Me, too. I lost my story, I lost my old pain-filled life. And I found a wonderful life on the other side of terror and internal war.

The war that I made against my family and against myself was as brutal as any bomb that could be dropped. And at a certain point, I stopped bombing myself. I began to do this Work. I answered the questions with a simple yes or no. I sat in the answers, I let them sink in, and I found freedom. Let's look at the next statement.

Willem: *I don't ever want to experience again the bombs falling on my head or being a hostage or feeling hunger.*

Katie: You may experience the story again. And if you don't feel peace or laughter when you hear yourself telling the story of the poor little boy who needed his parents, then it's time to do The Work again. This story is your gift. When you can experience it without fear, then your Work is done. There is only one person who can end your internal war, and that's you. You're the one the internal bombs are falling on. So let's turn it around. "I'm willing . . ."

Willem: I'm willing for the bombs to be falling on my head again.

Katie: If only in your thinking. The bombs aren't coming from out there; they can only come from inside you. So "I look forward to . . ."

Willem: It's hard to say this.

Katie: I look forward to the worst that can happen, only because it shows me what I haven't yet met with understanding. I know the power of truth.

Willem: I look forward to the bombs falling again and feeling hunger. Hunger is not so bad. *[Pauses.]* I don't feel it yet. Maybe I will later.

Katie: You're not supposed to feel it now. It's okay. It's good that you can't quite look forward to the bombs falling; there's some freedom in that admission. The next time the story arises, you may experience something that delights you. The processing that you did today can take you over, days or weeks from now. It may hit you like a sledge-hammer, or you may not even feel it. And just in case, look forward to it. Sit down and write out what's left. It's not easy doing mental surgery on a fifty-five-year-old phantom. Thank you for your courage, sweetheart.

I'm Angry at Sam for Dying

It takes a great deal of strength and courage to see through the story of a death. Parents and relatives of children who have died are especially attached to their stories for reasons that we all understand. Leaving our sadness behind or even inquiring into it may seem like a betrayal of our child. Many of us aren't ready to see things another way yet, and that's as it should be.

Who thinks that death is sad? Who thinks that a child shouldn't die? Who thinks that they know what death is? Who tries to teach God in story after story, thought after thought? Is it you? I say let's investigate, if you're up for it, and see if it's possible to end the war with reality.

Gail: This is about my nephew, Sam, who recently died. I was very close to him. I helped bring him up.

Katie: Good, sweetheart. Read what you've written.

Gail: *I'm angry at Sam for dying. I'm angry that Sam is gone. I'm angry that Sam took such stupid risks. I'm angry that at twenty he's gone in a blink. I'm angry that Sam slipped and fell sixty feet off the mountain. I want Sam back. I want Sam to be more careful. I want Sam to let me know that he's fine. I want the image of his body falling sixty feet off the cliff, landing on his head, to go away. Sam should have stuck around.*

Katie: "Sam should have stuck around"—is that true? This is our religion, the kind of belief that we live by but haven't known how to examine. *[To audience]* You may want to go inside and ask for yourself about the one who divorced you or who died and left you or about your children who moved away, "That person should have stuck around"—is that really true? *[To Gail]* Read it again.

Gail: *Sam should have stuck around.*

Katie: Is that true? What's the reality of it? Did he?

Gail: No. He left. He died.

Katie: How do you react when you think this thought, this concept, that argues with reality?

Gail: I feel tired and sad, and I feel separate.

Katie: That's how it feels to argue with what is. It's very stressful. I'm a lover of reality, not because I'm a spiritual woman but because it hurts when I argue with what is. And I notice that I lose, one hundred percent of the time. It's hopeless. We take these concepts to the grave with us if they're not examined. Concepts *are* the grave we bury ourselves in.

Gail: Yes. It's always stressful when I think that.

Katie: So, angel, who would you be without that thought?

Gail: I'd feel happy again.

Katie: Which is why you want him to live. "If he were alive, then I'd be happy." This is using him for your happiness.

Gail: Right.

Katie: We live; we die. Always right on time, not one moment sooner or later than we do. Who would you be without your story?

Gail: I'd be here, present in my own life, and I'd let Sam do his thing.

Katie: You'd even let him die in his own time?

Gail: Yes. As if I had any choice. I would be here instead of—

Katie: In the grave. Or falling off the mountain with Sam over and over again in your mind.

Gail: Yes.

Katie: So your story is "Sam should stick around." Turn it around.

Gail: *I* should stick around.

Katie: Yes. Your story that Sam shouldn't have died is yourself mentally falling off that cliff he falls off. *You* should stick around instead and mentally stay out of his business. This is possible.

Gail: I understand.

Katie: Sticking around would look like this: woman sitting in chair with friends, present, living her life, not mentally returning to that cliff to watch Sam fall, over and over. There's another turnaround to "Sam should stick around." Can you find it?

Gail: Sam should *not* stick around.

Katie: Yes, angel. He's gone in the way that you knew him. Reality rules. It doesn't wait for our vote, our permission, or our opinion—have you noticed? What I love most about reality is that it's always the story of a past. And what I love most about the past is that it's over. And because I'm no longer insane, I don't argue with it. Arguing with it feels unkind inside me. Just to notice what is is love. And how do I personally know that Sam lived a full life? It's over. He lived it to the end—*his* end, not the end you think he should have had. That's reality. It hurts to fight what is. And doesn't it feel more honest to open your arms wide to it? This is the end of war.

Gail: I can see that.

Katie: Okay, let's look at the next statement.

Gail: *I need Sam back.*

Katie: That's a good one. Is it true?

Gail: No.

Katie: No. It's just a story, a lie. *[To audience]* The reason I call it a lie is that I asked her, "Is it true?" and she said no. *[To Gail]* How do you react when you believe the story "I need Sam back," and he's not back?

Gail: Shut down inside. Anxious. Depressed.

Katie: Who would you be without the thought "I need Sam back"?

Gail: *I'd* be back. I'd be alive again, connecting with what's in front of me.

Katie: Yes. Just as you felt when he was here.

Gail: Right. If I let him go, I'd have what I wanted. Thinking I need him now keeps me from having what I've been wanting ever since he died.

Katie: So "I need Sam back"—turn it around.

Gail: I need *myself* back.

Katie: And another turnaround?

Gail: I *don't* need Sam back.

Katie: Yes. You keep going back to that cliff and falling off with Sam. So come back yourself. You keep thinking, "Oh, I wish he hadn't done that." But *you* keep doing it, over and over, in your mind. You just keep falling off that cliff. So if you need help, turn it around, see how you can help yourself. Let's look at the next statement.

Gail: *I need to know that Sam is totally fine and at peace.*

Katie: He's not fine—can you absolutely know that that's true?

Gail: No. I can't know that he's not fine.

Katie: Turn that one around.

Gail: I need to know that *I'm* totally fine and at peace, with or without Sam's body here.

Katie: Yes. *That's* possible. So how are your toes and your knees and your legs and your arms? How are you, sitting here in this moment?

Gail: They're good. I'm fine.

Katie: Are you in any better or worse shape now than when Sam was here?

Gail: No.

Katie: Sitting here right now, in this moment, do you *need* Sam to come back?

Gail: No. That's just a story.

Katie: Good. You investigated. You wanted to know. Now you do.

Gail: Right.

Katie: So let's look at the next statement.

Gail: *I need God, or someone, to show me the perfection of Sam's dying.*

Katie: Turn it around.

Gail: I need me to show me the perfection of Sam's dying.

Katie: Yes. You don't grieve when the lawnmower cuts the grass. You don't look for the perfection in the grass dying, because it's visible to you. In fact, when the grass grows, you cut it. In the fall, you don't grieve because the leaves are falling and dying. You say, "Isn't it beautiful!" Well, we're the same way. There are seasons. We all fall sooner or later. It's all so beautiful. And our concepts, without investigation, keep us from knowing this. It's beautiful to be a leaf, to be born, to fall, to give way to the next, to become food for the roots. It's life, always changing its form and always giving itself completely. We all do our part. No mistake. *[Gail begins to cry.]* What are your thoughts, sweetheart?

Gail: I really like what you're saying, talking about it as beauty, as part of the seasons. It makes me feel glad and appreciative. I can see it in a bigger way, and I can appreciate life and death and the cycles. It's like a window I can look through and see it differently, see how I could hold it in that way, and how I could appreciate Sam and the way he died.

Katie: Do you realize that he's given you life?

Gail: Yes. He's like the fertilizer or the soil that's growing me right now.

Katie: So that you can give it back and live as appreciation, fully nourished, as you understand our pain and give us the new life you're realizing. Whatever happens, that's what's needed. There is no mistake in nature. Look how painful it is to have a story that won't embrace such beauty, such perfection. Lack of understanding is always painful.

Gail: Until now, I couldn't really see it as beauty. I mean, I've seen beauty come to me from Sam's death, but I couldn't see the actual death—him dying—as beauty. I only saw it as him being a twenty-year-old doing stupid things. But he was just doing it his way.

Katie: Oh, my . . . Who would you be without that story?

Gail: I'd appreciate his death the way you appreciate the leaves. I could appreciate him going out that way, instead of thinking it was wrong.

Katie: Yes, honey. Through self-inquiry, we see that only love remains. Without an uninvestigated story, there's only the perfection of life appearing as itself. You can always go inside and find the beauty that's revealed after the pain and fear are understood. Let's look at the next statement.

Gail: *Sam is gone, dead. Sam is the beloved boy I got to mother. Sam is exquisitely beautiful, gentle, kind, a good listener, curious, brilliant, non-judgmental, accepting, strong, powerful. Sam is riding the crest of a wave.*

Katie: Read the first part of that again.

Gail: *Sam is gone, dead.*

Katie: Is that true? "Sam is dead"—can you absolutely know that that's true?

Gail: No.

Katie: Show me death. Get a microscope and show me. Put the cells of a dead body under the lens, and show me what death is. Is it anything more than a concept? Where does Sam live? *[Touching her head and heart]* Here. You wake up and think of him; that's where Sam lives. You lie down at night; there he is in your mind. And every night when you go to sleep, if you're not dreaming, that's death. When there's no story, there's no life. You open your eyes in the morning, and the "I" begins. Life begins. The Sam story begins. Did you miss him before the story began? Nothing lives but a story, and when we meet these stories with understanding, we *really* begin to live, without the suffering. So how do you react when you think that thought?

Gail: I feel dead inside. I feel terrible.

Katie: Can you see a reason to drop the story "Sam's dead"? And I'm not asking you to drop your story, this idea that you hold so dear. We love our old-time religion, even though it doesn't work. We devote ourselves to it day in and day out in every culture of the world.

Gail: Yes.

Katie: Inquiry doesn't have a motive. It doesn't teach a philosophy. It's just investigation. So who would you be without the story "Sam's dead"? Even though he's mentally living with you all the time.

Gail: He's probably here more now, right now, than he was when he was in his body.

Katie: Who would you be without the story?

Gail: I'd appreciate the fertilizer. And I'd love being where I am rather than living in the past.

Katie: Turn it around.

Gail: *I'm* gone, *I'm* dead, when I go into my story about Sam dying.

Katie: Yes.

Gail: I really see that now. Are we done?

Katie: Yes, sweetheart. And we always begin now.

Terrorism in New York City

After the events of September 11, 2001, our political leaders and the media said that America had begun a war against terrorism and that everything had changed. When people came to do The Work with me, I found that nothing had changed. People like Emily were frightening themselves with their uninvestigated thoughts, and after they found the terrorist inside them, they could return to their families, to their normal lives, in peace.

A teacher of fear can't bring peace on Earth. We have been trying to do it that way for thousands of years. The person who turns inner violence around, the person who finds peace inside and lives it, is the one who teaches what true peace is. We are waiting for just one teacher. You're the one.

Emily: *Ever since the terrorist attack on the World Trade Center last Tuesday, I've been terrified that I'll be killed in the subway or in my office building, right near Grand Central and the Waldorf. I keep thinking how scarred my sons would be if they lost me.* They're only one and four years old.

Katie: Yes, sweetheart. So terrorists could attack you in the subway.

Emily: Uh-huh.

Katie: Can you absolutely know that that's true?

Emily: That it's possible or that it will happen?

Katie: That it will happen.

Emily: I can't know that it will happen, but I do know that it's possible.

Katie: And how do you react when you think that thought?

Emily: I feel terrified. I already feel sad about my loss, for myself, my husband, and my kids.

Katie: And how do you treat people on the subway when you think that thought?

Emily: I feel shut down, very shut down.

Katie: How do you treat yourself when you think that thought and you're on the subway?

Emily: Well, I try to repress the thought, and I focus a lot on reading and doing what I'm doing. I'm tight.

Katie: And where does your mind travel when you're tight and you think that thought as you're reading on the subway?

Emily: I just keep picturing my children's faces.

Katie: So you're in your children's business. You're reading a book on the subway full of people, and in your mind you're seeing the faces of your children with you dead.

Emily: Yes.

Katie: Does this thought bring stress or peace into your life?

Emily: Definitely stress.

Katie: Who would you be on the subway without that thought? Who would you be if you were incapable of thinking the thought "A terrorist could kill me on the subway"?

Emily: If I couldn't think the thought—you mean if my mind wouldn't do it? *[Pauses.]* Well, I would be like I was last Monday, before the attack happened.

Katie: So you'd be a little more comfortable on the subway than you are.

Emily: Much more comfortable. I grew up on the subways. I'm actually quite comfortable on the subway without that thought.

Katie: "A terrorist can kill me on the subway"—how would you turn that around?

Emily: I can kill myself on the subway?

Katie: Yes. The killing is going on in your mind. The only terrorist on the subway in that moment is you, terrifying yourself with your thoughts. What else did you write?

Emily: *I am furious at my family*—my husband, my parents, all of us live here in New York City—*for not helping me make a contingency plan in case the terrorism here gets worse, finding a place where we can all meet outside the city, getting our passports updated, some money out of* *the bank. I'm furious at them for being so passive, for making me feel crazy for trying to make a plan.*

Katie: So *I am furious at my family*—let's just turn that one around. *I'm furious . . .*

Emily: I'm furious at myself for not helping me make a contingency plan?

Katie: Can you see that? Quit being so passive. Get a contingency plan, not just for you and your children and husband, for your whole family in New York. Get a plan for everyone.

Emily: I am trying, but they're making me feel like I'm nuts for doing that. I'm angry about that.

Katie: Well, apparently they don't need a plan. And they don't want a plan. You're the one who needs a contingency plan, so make a contingency plan for the evacuation of New York.

Emily *[laughing]:* That sounds so funny.

Katie: I know. I find that so often self-realization leaves us only with laughter.

Emily: But I'm still angry that they made me feel like a nut.

Katie: Can you find it, that part of you that *is* a nut?

Emily: Well, I did do the same thing with Y2K, so I guess they've been through this with me before. I *am* a bit on the paranoid side.

Katie: So they're right, according to their world. They have a point. You could work on your contingency plan in peace, not expecting them to want to go.

Emily: I'll make my kids go.

Katie: Because they're small and you can put them both under your arms and run for it. Buckle them in the car and just drive.

Emily: I think I'd better learn how to drive. I don't have a driver's license.

Katie *[laughing]*: You're angry at your family because they don't have a contingency plan, and you don't have a driver's license?

Emily *[laughing]*: Now, that is ridiculous. I can see that. I'm judging them, and I can't even drive if I need to. How could I not have seen this?

Katie: Now, let's say you have the license and the tunnels and bridges are all closed. You need to get another plan. You need to get five more jobs so you can buy a private helicopter.

Emily *[laughing]*: Okay, okay.

Katie: But they wouldn't let those fly, either.

Emily: No. Definitely not.

Katie: So there you are. Maybe that's why your family doesn't bother with a contingency plan. They notice that the tunnels were shut down; planes weren't allowed in the air last week; there was no way out. Maybe they understand that. Maybe you're the last to know.

Emily: That really could be.

Katie: So it just leaves us to find peace from where we are. To make a contingency plan work, from what I've seen of reality, you need to be psychic so you can know ahead of time when to evacuate and where to go that would be safe.

Emily: Part of me thinks I should get out now. But then of course the problem is where is safe? Talk about needing to be psychic . . .

Katie: So you need to work on your psychic abilities. And from what I've seen, psychics don't win the lottery.

Emily: That's true.

Katie: So you need a contingency plan—is that true? Can you absolutely know that that's true?

Emily: I guess I can't know that that's true anymore. It's kind of a relief.

Katie: Oh, honey, just feel it. Maybe that's what your family knows.

Emily: I think I'm not such a good planner after all. There is no plan to have.

Katie: Of course not. You can't outsmart reality. Where you are, right now, might be the safest place in the world. We just don't know.

Emily: I honestly never thought of that.

Katie: So who would you be without the thought "I need a contingency plan"?

Emily: Less anxious, less on alert, lighter. *[Pauses.]* But also more upset. *[Crying]* Sad. Very, very sad. All those people died. My city changed. There's nothing I can do.

Katie: Okay, so that's the reality of it. There's nothing you can do. That's humility. For me, that's a sweet thing.

Emily: I'm just so used to being proactive, to making things happen, at least for the people close to me, to protecting them.

Katie: And feeling in control. It works for a while. But then reality catches up with us. But if we take all that amazing ability, that proactiveness, and mix it with humility, then that's really something. Then we can be clear and helpful. "I need a contingency plan"—turn it around.

Emily: I don't need a contingency plan.

Katie: Feel it. Can you see how that could be just as true? How it could even be truer?

Emily: Could be. I can see that it could be truer.

Katie: Oh, sweetheart. Me, too. That's why I'm always so comfortable where I am. When you run in fear, it's square into the wall. Then you look back at where you were, and you see that it was much safer. And without a contingency plan, when something happens, it just comes to you what to do. You can find everything you need to know right where you are. And in reality, you already live that. When you need a pen, you reach over and you take it. If there's not a pen there, you go get one. And that's what it's like in an emergency. Without fear, what to do is just as clear as reaching and picking up a pen. But fear isn't so efficient. Fear is blind and deaf. Let's hear what else you've written.

Emily: Okay. *I think the terrorists are so ignorant in their hatred and their need to feel powerful. They are so desperate to hurt us. They'd do anything—why not poison or car bombs? They're evil, ignorant, and yes, they're successful and powerful. They can destroy this country. They're like locusts, everywhere, hiding, waiting to hurt us, disrupt us, kill us.*

Katie: So these terrorists are evil.

Emily: Yes.

Katie: Can you absolutely know that that's true?

Emily: I think I can know that they are ignorant. They're ignorant about the effects of violence on us.

Katie: Can you absolutely know that that's true? That they're ignorant about that? This is a good one, sweetheart. Can you know that they're ignorant about pain and death and suffering?

Emily: No. They're not ignorant about that, because they've probably experienced it. I can't know that that's true, but I think they probably have. And that's what they're reacting to. But they're still ignorant about the fact that violence never works.

Katie: Or they're not ignorant. They believe a thought that's the opposite of yours: that violence works. That's what they think the whole world has taught them. They are in the grip of that thought.

Emily: But it doesn't work, really. To hurt another person, you either have to be ignorant, confused, or a psychopath.

Katie: You could be right, and a lot of people would agree with you, but what we're looking at here is not the right or wrong of it. So let's go back to what you read and turn it around.

Emily: *I think the terrorists are so ignorant in their hatred and their need to feel powerful.*

Katie: Turn it around.

Emily: I am so ignorant in my hatred and my need to feel powerful. That's true. I needed my contingency plan to make me feel powerful.

Katie: Yes, and how does it feel to hate?

Emily: Well, it does empower me for the moment. I mean, it makes me feel less helpless.

Katie: And then what happens when you hate?

Emily: I'm stuck. I can't get past it, and it's consuming.

Katie: And you have to find a way of defending that position. You have to prove that you're right about your hatred. That it's valid and worthwhile. And how does it feel to live that way? How do you react when you believe the thought that they're evil and ignorant?

Emily: In the context of what we're saying, it feels pretty false, actually. I'm not sure that I even feel that way anymore.

Katie: But from their position, their hatred is absolutely valid. They're willing to die for it. It's a matter of right. That's what they believe. They're crashing their lives into buildings.

Emily: Yes.

Katie: Their hatred is no obstacle to them. That's what it's like when we're attached to a concept. And that concept is "You are evil, and I'll die to take you out." It's for the good of the world.

Emily: I can see that.

Katie: So continue with the turnaround.

Emily: I am evil in my ignorance—

Katie: Of where these people are coming from. They know the suffering it's going to bring to their families when they kill themselves intentionally.

Emily: Okay.

Katie: They're not ignorant on one level, and on another level of course they are, because their thoughts just leave more suffering. So continue to turn around what you wrote after the evil and their ignorance.

Emily: *They're evil, ignorant, and yes, they're successful and powerful.*

Katie: "And I . . ."

Emily: I am evil, ignorant, successful, and powerful?

Katie: Yes. In all your righteousness.

Emily: Oh, okay. My contingency plan is right, and other people just don't get it.

Katie: So let's continue. "They're like locusts"—turn it around.

Emily: I am like locusts, everywhere, hiding, waiting to hurt me, disrupt me, kill me?

Katie: Yes.

Emily: My thoughts are like locusts.

Katie: Exactly. Your uninvestigated thoughts.

Emily: Right.

Katie: I don't see any terrorists in this moment except the one you live with: yourself.

Emily: Yes. I see that.

Katie: I live in peace, and that's what everyone deserves. We all deserve to end our own terrorism.

Emily: I can understand the arrogance of doing what I've been doing.

Katie: That's where I see the possibility of change. Otherwise, we're like ancient, primitive beings—all willing to die for a cause.

Emily: How are we all willing to die for a cause?

Katie: Well, sweetheart, if someone comes after your children—just watch it.

Emily: Okay. Yes.

Katie: I mean, you're even angry with your parents because they won't get a contingency plan. And feel what it feels like to go to war against your own family.

Emily: Yes.

Katie: What's the matter with them? You would grab them, with them screaming "I just want to be left alone." You grab them and haul them out—to where? For all you know, you move them to the very community that gets hit.

Emily: That's true. That's arrogant, too. Crazy, even.

Katie: What else did you write?

Emily: *I don't ever want to see an ash-covered person again as I did that day walking home. I don't ever want to see another face mask or a look of shock.* Part of the problem is that the media kept showing images of the towers falling over and over again. It felt like it was happening for a whole week.

Katie: "Part of the problem was that the media kept showing it over and over"—turn it around.

Emily: I kept showing it over and over.

Katie: Yes. "I want the media to stop"—turn it around.

Emily: I want me to stop.

Katie: So work on you. Your mind is the media.

Emily: I'm not sure how.

Katie: You could begin by putting those images in your mind up against inquiry. Because in reality there's no one in front of you covered with ash right now. It's not happening here, except in your mind. *[Long pause.]* Okay. Let's go back and take a look. Describe the ash-covered person in your mind. Describe the one who has the most charge for you. The person you actually saw.

Emily: Well, the one who has the most charge for me was the man who walked by my office building when I was sitting outside waiting for my husband a couple of hours after the World Trade Center towers fell. I work in Midtown, so the guy had walked more than sixty blocks. We saw a lot of other ash-covered people when we walked home, but this guy was dressed in an expensive, well-fitted business suit, carrying his briefcase, and he was wearing one of those breath masks that you see on television. And he was absolutely gray—his entire head, his suit, his shoes, his briefcase were covered in ash. The ash was untouched. He was like a zombie, just walking, not looking around. He must have been in shock. He had obviously walked all the way from what was the World Trade Center. Everything was sunny, and everything here in Midtown seemed normal, and then this ghost walked by. That hit me harder than any other image that day. It hit me hard. I thought, "Now it's entering my world. It's here."

Katie: Good, sweetheart. Now I want to look at it with you. "He was like a zombie"—is that true?

Emily: He certainly looked like it.

Katie: Of course he did: Look who's telling the story. The man had his briefcase with him. He thought to take it. Maybe he was simply walking home. There were no subways running. Maybe he wanted to get to his family to let them know he was all right.

Emily: Yes.

Katie: He was being perfectly intelligent. He had on a breath mask. You didn't.

Emily: Hmm.

Katie: So for all you know, he was doing better than you were.

Emily *[after a pause]*: That could be. I was nowhere near the disaster, sitting there feeling incredibly stressed out and afraid.

Katie: "The man was like a zombie"—how do you react when you believe that thought?

Emily: I feel horror, as if the world were ending.

Katie: And who would you be, watching that man, without the thought "He is like a zombie"?

Emily: I'd just think, "There's a man covered in ash. I hope he's close to home."

Katie: A really *smart* man. Not a zombie. He may have been on his way home when the towers fell, and he held on to his briefcase. Or he may have gotten out of the building with his briefcase. What to do came to him in an instant. I don't think he had a contingency plan: "If the plane hits and if I get out, I think I'll pick up my briefcase as a contingency plan and walk home."

Emily: He had walked sixty blocks or whatever it was. I guess he was an instant symbol in my mind of what had happened.

Katie: Yes, but he could just as easily be a reminder of how efficient you can be when some disaster happens. He had his briefcase. He'd made it for sixty blocks. But how were *you* doing when you saw him?

Emily: I actually felt like I was going into shock.

Katie: Yes. He was doing fine. You were like a zombie, and you projected it onto him. If you needed someone in a pinch and you saw yourself standing there and him standing there, who would you go to for help?

Emily *[laughing]*: I'd go to him. Amazing. But I'd definitely go to him.

Katie: Okay, sweetheart. So gently, let's turn it around: "I'm willing . . ."

Emily: I'm willing to see another ash-covered person.

Katie: Yes, even if only in your mind—because you haven't seen anyone since then walking around like that, except inside you. So reality and the story never match; reality's always kinder. And it's going to be fun to watch how this plays out in your life, especially with your children. They'll learn from you that they don't have to be on guard and have a plan; they'll learn that they'll always know what to do. They'll see that where they are is okay and anywhere they're going is fine. And without the fearful story "I need a contingency plan," various good moves might come to you: a place to meet up with your husband in case the phones don't work. Learning to drive might be useful as your kids get past the toddler stage. Who knows what a calm mind will come up with?

Emily: Thank you, Katie. I see that.

Katie: Oh, honey, you're welcome. I love how you don't settle for anything but the pure truth of it.

You move totally
away from reality
when you believe
that there is a
legitimate reason
to suffer.

13

Questions and Answers

When people ask me questions, I answer them as clearly as I can. I'm glad when they tell me that these answers are helpful, but I know that the truly helpful answers are the ones they find by themselves.

Q: I feel overwhelmed by the number of judgments I have. How could I ever possibly have time to investigate all my beliefs?
A: Don't worry about undoing all of them. Just investigate the belief that's causing you stress now. There is never more than one. Undo that one.

If you really want to know the truth, there is no idea that can't be met with understanding. We're either attaching to our concepts or investigating them. How do I know which one to work with? Here it comes now.

One of the things that I understood about the thoughts appearing inside me was that I was someone to be trusted with them. I was the vessel that they could appear in and finally be met with unconditional love. The same thoughts also came to me through my children when they were free to tell me how they felt. They came through every other form of communication. They couldn't come fast enough for me, because I knew what to do with them. From my children's mouths or from my mind, I wrote them down, and I inquired. I treated them as what they were: visiting friends, neighbors I had misunderstood who were kind enough to knock on my door again. Everyone is welcome here.

Judge your neighbor, write it down, ask four questions, and turn it around—just one at a time.

Q: Does freedom always come right after you do The Work?
A: It does in its own way, but you may not recognize it. And you may not necessarily notice a change on the particular issue you've written about. For example, you may have written a Worksheet on your mother, and the next day you find that your obnoxious neighbor— the one who's been driving you crazy for years—no longer annoys you, that your irritation with her has completely disappeared. Or a week later, you notice that for the first time in your life, you love to cook. It doesn't always happen in one session. I have a friend who did The Work on being jealous of her husband because their little boy preferred him to her. She felt a small release after doing The Work. But the next morning, while she was in the shower, she felt every-thing give way and began to sob, and afterward all the pain around the situation was gone.

Q: What does it mean if I keep needing to do The Work on the same thing over and over again?
A: It doesn't matter how often you need to do it. You're either at-taching to the nightmare or investigating it. There's no other choice. The issue may come back a dozen times, a hundred times. It's always a wonderful opportunity to see what attachments are left and how much deeper you can go.

Q: I've done The Work many times on the same judgment, and I don't think it's working.
A: "You've done The Work many times"—is that true? Could it be that if the answer you think you're looking for doesn't appear, you simply block anything else? Are you frightened of the answer that

might be underneath what you think you know? Is it possible that there's another answer within you that could be as true or truer?

When you ask "Is it true?" for example, you may not really want to know. It could be that you'd rather stay with your statement than dive into the unknown. Blocking means rushing the process and answering with your conscious mind before the gentler polarity of mind (I call it "the heart") can answer. If you prefer to stay with what you think you know, the question is blocked and can't have its life inside you.

Notice if you move into a story before letting yourself fully experience the answer and the feelings that come with it. If your answers begin with "Well, yes, but . . . ," you're shifting away from inquiry. Do you really want to know the truth?

Another possibility is that you're inquiring with a motive. Are you asking the questions to prove that the answer you already have is valid, even though it's painful? Do you want to be right more than you want to know the truth? It was the truth that set me free. Acceptance, peace, and less attachment to a world of suffering are all *effects* of doing The Work. They're not goals. Do The Work for the love of freedom, for the love of truth. If you're inquiring with other motives, such as healing your body or solving a problem, your answers may be arising from old motives that never worked for you, and you'll miss the wonder and grace of inquiry.

You might also be doing the turnaround too quickly. If you really want to know the truth, wait for the new answers to surface. Give yourself enough time to let the turnarounds find *you*. If you choose, make a written list of all the ways that the turnaround applies to you. The turnaround is the reentry into life, as the truth points you to who you are without your story. It's all done for you.

Are you letting the realizations you experience through inquiry live in you? Live the turnarounds, report your part to others so that you can hear it again, and make amends for the sake of your own freedom. This will certainly speed up the process and bring freedom into your life now.

Finally, can you really know that inquiry is not working? When the thing you were afraid of happens and you notice that there is little or no stress or fear—that's when you know it's working.

Q: When I'm doing The Work myself and I sense that I'm blocking inquiry, what can I do?
A: Continue doing The Work if you're up for it. I know that if even one small honest answer or turnaround is allowed to surface from inside you, you will enter a world that you don't even know exists. But if your intention is to be right rather than to know the truth, why bother continuing? Just realize that the story you're sticking to is more valuable to you now than your freedom and that that's okay. Come back to inquiry later. You may not be suffering enough, or you may not really care, even though you think you do. Be gentle with yourself. Life will bring you everything you need.

Q: What if my suffering is too intense? Should I still do The Work?
A: Suffering is caused by attachment to a deeply embedded belief. It's a state of blind attachment to something that you think is true. In this state, it's very difficult to do The Work for the love of truth, because you're invested in your story. Your story is your identity, and you'd do almost anything to prove that it's true. Inquiry into self is the only thing that has the power to penetrate such ancient concepts.

Even physical pain isn't real; it's the story of a past, always leaving, never arriving. But people don't know that. My grandson Racey fell down once when he was three years old. He scraped his knee, and there was some blood, and he began to cry. And as he looked up at me, I said, "Sweetheart, are you remembering when you fell down and hurt yourself?" And immediately, the crying stopped. That was it. He must have realized, for a moment, that pain is always in the past. The moment of pain is always gone. It's a remembering of what we think is true, and it projects what no longer exists. (I'm not saying that your pain isn't real for you. I know pain, and it hurts! That's why The Work is about the end of suffering.)

If a car runs over your leg and you're lying in the street with story after story running through your mind, chances are that if you're new to The Work, you're not going to think "'I'm in pain'—is it true? Can I absolutely know that it's true?" You're going to scream, "Get the morphine!" Then later, when you're in a comfort zone, you can sit down and do The Work. Give yourself the physical medicine and then the other kind of medicine. Eventually, you can lose your other leg, and you won't see a problem. If you think there's a problem, your Work isn't done.

Q: There are thoughts that I feel I shouldn't be thinking—nasty, perverted, and even violent thoughts. Can The Work help me stop having these thoughts?
A: How do you react when you believe that you shouldn't think certain thoughts and you do? Ashamed? Depressed? Now turn it around—you *should* think them! Doesn't that feel a bit lighter, a bit more honest? Mind wants its freedom, not a straitjacket. When the thoughts come, they aren't meeting an enemy who is opposing them, like a child who comes to her father, hoping that he'll listen, and instead the father screams at her, "Don't say that! Don't do that! You're wrong, you're bad!" and punishes her when she approaches. What kind of father is that? This is the internal violence that keeps you from understanding.

I can't meet you as an enemy and not feel separate, from you and from myself. So how could I meet a thought within me as an enemy and not feel separate? When I learned to meet my thinking as a friend, I noticed that I could meet every human as a friend. What could you say that hasn't already appeared within me as a thought? The end of the war with myself and my thinking is the end of the war with you. It's so simple.

Q: Is inquiry a process of thinking? If not, what is it?
A: Inquiry appears to be a process of thinking, but actually it's a way to *undo* thinking. Thoughts lose their power over us when we realize

that we aren't doing the thinking anyway. Thoughts simply appear in the mind; they're not personal. What if there is no thinker? Are you breathing yourself, too? Through The Work, instead of escaping or suppressing our thoughts, we learn to meet them with unconditional love and understanding.

The mind can find its true nature only by thinking. What else is there? How else is it going to find itself? It has to leave clues for itself, and it comes to realize that it has dropped its own breadcrumbs. It has come out of itself, but it hasn't realized that yet. Inquiry is the breadcrumbs that enable it to return to itself. The everything returns to the everything. The nothing returns to the nothing.

Q: My answer to "Can I absolutely know that it's true?" is always "No." Is there anything we can know for certain?
A: No. Experience is just perception. It's ever changing. Even "now" is the story of a past. By the time we perceive it, it's already gone.

From the moment we attach to a thought, it becomes our religion, and we keep attempting to prove that it's valid. The harder we try to prove what we can't know is true, the more we experience depression and disappointment.

When you ask yourself question 1, your mind begins to open. Even to consider that a thought may not be true will let a little light into your mind. If you answer, "Yes," then you may want to ask yourself question 2, "Can you absolutely know that it's true?" Some people get very agitated, even angry, when they say, "No, I can't absolutely know that!" And then I might ask them to be gentle with themselves and just experience that understanding for a moment. If they sit with their answer, then it does become gentle, and it opens to infinite possibilities, to freedom. It's like stepping out of a narrow, smoky room into open space.

Q: How can I do The Work if no one around me is doing it? Won't other people see me as detached and uncaring? How will my family be able to adjust to my new way of thinking?

A: No one around me was doing The Work when I began; I did it alone. And yes, your family might see you as detached and uncaring. As you come to see what isn't true for you and as you experience question 3 ("How do you react, what happens, when you believe that thought?"), there is such a shift inside you that you may lose the most essential agreements with your family. "Charlie should brush his teeth"—is it true? No, not until he does; you have ten years of proof that he hasn't been brushing his teeth regularly. How do you react? For ten years, you've gotten angry, you've threatened him, you've given him "the look," you've gotten frustrated, you've laid guilt on him. Now the whole family is telling Charlie to brush his teeth (just as you've taught them to do through your example), and you're no longer participating. You're betraying the family religion. When they look to you for consent, you can't give it. So now they may begin to shame you for not shaming him the way you taught them to do. Your family is an echo of your own past beliefs.

If your truth now is kind, it will run deep and fast within the family and will replace betrayal with a better way. As you continue to find your own way in inquiry, sooner or later your family will come to see as you yourself do. There's no other choice. Your family is a projected image of your thinking. It's your story; nothing else is possible. Until you love your family without conditions even as they shame Charlie, self-love is not a possibility, and therefore your Work is not done.

Your family will see you as they see you, and that will leave you to work on them all. How do you see *yourself*? That's the important question. How do you see *them*? If I think that they need The Work, then *I* need The Work. Peace doesn't require two people; it requires only one. It has to be you. The problem begins and ends there.

If you want to alienate your friends and family, go around saying, "Is it true?" or "Turn it around" if they're not asking you for help. You may need to do that for a while in order to hear it for yourself. It's uncomfortable to believe that you know more than your friends do and to represent yourself as their teacher. Their irritation will lead you either deeper into inquiry or deeper into your suffering.

Q: What do you mean when you say, "Don't be spiritual—be honest instead"?
A: I mean that it's very painful to pretend yourself beyond your own evolution, to live a lie, any lie. When you act like a teacher, it's usually because you're afraid to be the student. I don't pretend to be fearless. Either I am, or I'm not. It's no secret to me.

Q: How can I learn to forgive someone who hurt me very badly?
A: Judge your enemy, write it down, ask four questions, turn it around. See for yourself that forgiveness means discovering that what you thought happened, didn't. Until you can see that there is nothing to forgive, you haven't really forgiven. We're all innocent; we hurt others because we believe our unquestioned thoughts. No one would ever harm another human being unless he or she was confused. So whenever you suffer: inquire, identify the thoughts you're thinking, write them down, question them, and allow the answers from within to set you free. Be a child. Start from the mind that knows nothing. Take your ignorance all the way to freedom.

Q: I've heard you say, "When you're perfectly clear, what is is what you want." Suppose I save all month to go to a good restaurant so I can eat grilled lemon sole, and the waiter brings me braised ox tongue. What is is not what I want. Am I confused? What does it mean to argue with reality?
A: Yes, you're very confused. If you were clear, what you'd want is braised ox tongue, because that's what the waiter brought. That doesn't mean you have to eat it. How do you react when you think that he shouldn't have brought you braised ox tongue? Until you project that you have to eat it or that you don't have enough time to

reorder or that you have to pay for what you didn't order or that there has been any kind of injustice, there's no problem. But when you believe that he shouldn't have brought it, you might become angry at him or feel some form of stress. Who would you be without your story as you face the waiter? Who would you be without the thought that there's not enough time or that the waiter made a mistake? You might be a person loving the moment, loving the apparent mistake. You might even be calm enough to repeat your original order with clarity and amusement. You might say, "I appreciate you, and what I ordered was grilled lemon sole. My time is limited, and if you can't serve me the grilled lemon sole and have me out of here by eight, I'll need to go elsewhere. I prefer to stay here. What do you suggest?"

Arguing with reality means arguing with the story of a past. It's already over, and no thinking in the world can change it. The waiter has already brought you the braised ox tongue. There it is, sitting in front of you, staring you in the face. If you think that it shouldn't be there, you're confused, because there it is. The point is, how can you be most effective in this moment, given that what is is? Seeing reality clearly doesn't mean that you're going to be passive. Why would you be passive when you can be clear and have a wonderful, sane life? You don't have to eat the braised ox tongue; you don't have to keep from clearly reminding the waiter that you ordered grilled lemon sole. Seeing reality clearly means that you can act in the kindest, most appropriate, and most effective way.

Q: What do you mean by "There are no physical problems—only mental ones"? What if I lose my right arm and I'm right-handed? Isn't that a huge problem?

A: How do I know I don't need two arms? I have only one. There's no mistake in the universe. To think in any other way is fearful and hopeless. The story "I need two arms" is where the suffering begins, because it argues with reality. Without the story, I have everything I need. I'm complete with no right arm. My handwriting may be shaky at first, but it's perfect just the way it is. It will do the job in the way I need to do it, not in the way I thought I needed to do it. Obviously, there needs to be a teacher in this world of how to be happy with one arm and shaky handwriting. Until I'm willing to lose my left arm, too, my Work's not done.

Q: How can I learn to love myself?
A: "You're supposed to love yourself"—is that true? How do you treat yourself when you believe the thought that you're supposed to love yourself and you don't? Can you see a reason to drop the story? And I'm not asking you to drop your sacred concept. Who would you be without the story "You're supposed to love yourself"? What's the direct opposite? "You're *not* supposed to love yourself." Doesn't that feel a little more natural? You're not supposed to love yourself yet—not until you do. These sacred concepts, these spiritual ideas, always turn into dogma.

Q: What do you mean when you say that you are my projection?
A: The world is your perception of it. Inside and outside always match; they are reflections of each other. The world is the mirror image of your mind. If you experience chaos and confusion inside, your external world has to reflect that. You have to see what you believe, because you are the confused thinker looking out and seeing yourself. You are the interpreter of everything, and if you're chaotic, what you hear and see has to be chaos. Even if Jesus, even if the Buddha, were standing in front of you, you would hear confused words, because confusion would be the listener. You would hear only what you thought he was saying, and you'd start arguing with him the first time your story was threatened.

As for my being your projection, how else could I be here? It's not as though I had a choice. I am the story of who you think I am, not who I really am. You see me as old, young, beautiful, ugly, honest, deceitful, caring, uncaring. I am, for you, your uninvestigated story, your own myth.

I understand that who you think I am is true for you. I was innocent and gullible also, but only for forty-three years, until the moment when I woke up to the way things really are. "It's a tree. It's a table. It's a chair." Is it true? Have you stopped to ask yourself? Have you ever become still and listened as *you* asked *you*? Who told you it was a tree? Who was the original authority? How did they know? My entire life, my entire identity, had been built on the trust and uninquiring innocence of a child. Are you this kind of child? Through this Work, your toys and fairy tales are laid aside as you begin to read the book of true knowledge, the book of yourself.

People tell me, "But, Katie, your happiness is all a projection," and I say, "Yes, and isn't it beautiful? I love living this happy dream. I'm having a wonderful time!" If you lived in heaven, would you want it to end? It doesn't end. It can't. That is what's true for me, until it's not. If it should change, I always have inquiry. I answer the questions, the truth is realized within me, and the doing meets the undone, the something meets the nothing. In the balance of the two halves, I am free.

Q: You say that The Work will leave me without stress, without problems. But isn't that irresponsible? What if my three-year-old child is starving? Won't I see her from a position of no stress and think, "Well, that's reality," and just let her starve?

A: Oh, my! Sweetheart, love is kind; it doesn't stand still and do nothing when it sees its own need. Do you really think that violent thoughts, such as the ones that come with problems, are necessary to feed a child? If your three-year-old is starving, feed her, for *your* sake! How would it feel to provide for a starving child without stress or worry? Wouldn't you be clearer about how and where to find the food that is available, and wouldn't you feel elation and gratitude for it? Well, that's how I live my life. I don't need stress to do what I know to do; that's not efficient, the way peace and sanity are. Love is action, and in my experience, reality is always kind.

Q: How can you say that reality is good? What about war, rape, poverty, violence, and child abuse? Are you condoning them?

A: Of course not! I'm not crazy. I simply notice that if I believe they shouldn't exist when they do exist, I suffer. They exist until they don't. Can I just end the war in me? Can I stop raping myself and others with my abusive thoughts? If not, I'm continuing in myself the very thing that I want to end in the world. Sanity doesn't suffer, ever. Can you eliminate war everywhere on Earth? Through inquiry, you can begin to eliminate it for one human being: you. This is the beginning of the end of war in the world. If life upsets you, good! Judge the war makers, write it down, inquire, and turn it around. Do you really want to know the truth? All suffering begins and ends with you.

Q: Always accepting reality sounds like never wanting anything. Isn't it more interesting to want things?

A: My experience is that I do want something all the time. What I want is what is. It's not only interesting, it's ecstatic! What I want is what I already have.

When I want what I have, thought and action aren't separate; they move as one, without conflict. If you find anything lacking, ever, write down your thought and inquire. I find that life never falls short and doesn't require a future. Everything I need is always supplied, and I don't have to do anything for it.

What do I want specifically? I want to answer your question, because that's what's happening right now. I respond to you, because that's what love does. It's an effect of the original cause: you. I love this life. Why would I want something more or less than what I have, even if it's painful? What I see, where I am, what I smell and taste and feel—it's all so fine. If you loved your life, would you want to change it? There is nothing more exciting than loving what is.

Q: You sometimes say, "God is everything, God is good." Isn't that just one more belief?

A: *God,* as I use the word, is another name for what is. I always know God's intention: it's exactly what is in every moment. I don't have to question it anymore. I'm no longer meddling in God's business. It's simple. And from that basis, it's clear that everything is perfect. The last truth—I call it the last judgment—is "God is everything, God is good." People who really understand this don't need inquiry. Ultimately, of course, even this isn't true. But if it works for you, I say keep it and have a wonderful life.

All so-called truths eventually fall away. Every truth is a distortion of what is. If we investigate, we lose even the last truth. And that state, beyond all truths, is true intimacy. That is God-realization. And welcome to the reentry. It's always a beginning.

Q: If nothing is true, then why bother? Why go to the dentist, why treat myself for illness?

A: I go to the dentist because I like to chew. I prefer it when my teeth don't fall out. Silly me! If you're confused, inquire and find what's true for you.

Q: How can I live in the now?

A: You do. You just haven't noticed.

Only in this moment are we in reality. You and everyone can learn to live in the moment, *as* the moment, to love whatever is in front of you, to love it as you. If you keep doing The Work, you will see more and more clearly what you are without a future or a past. The miracle of love comes to you in the presence of the uninterpreted moment. If you are mentally somewhere else, you miss real life.

But even the now is a concept. Even as the thought completes itself, it's gone, with no proof that it ever existed other than as a concept that would lead you to believe it existed, and now that one is gone too. Reality is always the story of a past. Before you can grasp it, it's gone. Each of us already has the peaceful mind that we seek.

Q: I find it very hard to tell the truth because it's always changing for me. How can I be consistent in speaking honestly?

A: Human experience is constantly changing, though the place of integrity never moves. I say let's begin from where we are. Can we just tell the truth as it appears now, without comparing it to what was true a moment ago? Ask me again later, and I may have a different truthful answer. "Katie, are you thirsty?" No. "Katie, are you thirsty?" Yes. I always tell what my truth is right now. Yes, no, yes, yes, no. That's the truth.

My cousin once called me at two in the morning, very depressed, and said that he was holding a loaded pistol to his head and the hammer was cocked. He said that if I didn't give him one good reason why he should stay alive, he would blow his head off. I waited for a long time. I really wanted to give him a reason, and no good reason came to me. I waited and waited, with him on the other end of the phone line. Finally, I told him that I couldn't find one. And he burst into tears. That was evidently the truth he needed. He said it was the first time in his life that he had ever heard integrity and that was what he was looking for. If I had concocted some reason because I believed that he shouldn't kill himself, I would have given him less than the only thing I really have to give, which is my truth in the moment.

I have noticed that people who do The Work for a while get really clear about the truth as they see it. It becomes easy to stand in it and easy to be flexible and change their minds. Being honest in the moment becomes a very comfortable thing.

Do you know anyone who hasn't changed his mind? This door was a tree, then it will be firewood for someone, then it will return to air and earth. We're all like that, constantly changing. It's simply honest to report that you've changed your mind when you have.

When you're afraid of what people will think if you speak honestly—that's when you become confused.

Q: Is it true that I can't hurt another person?
A: It's not possible for me to hurt another person. (Please don't try to believe this. It's not true for you until you realize it for yourself.) The only person I can hurt is myself. If you ask me point-blank for the truth, I'm going to tell you what I see. I want to give you everything you ask for. The way you receive my answer is the way you hurt yourself with it or help yourself with it. I'm just giving you what I've got.

But if I think that saying something to you would cause you to hurt your own feelings, I don't say it (unless you tell me that you really want to know). If I think I'm unkind to you, I'm not comfortable within myself. I cause my own suffering, and I stop for my own sake. I take care of myself, and that way you, too, are taken care of. My kindness ultimately has nothing to do with you. We're all responsible for our own peace. I could say the most loving words, and you might take offense. I understand that. What I realize is that the story you tell yourself about what I say is the only way you can hurt yourself. You're suffering because you didn't ask four questions and turn it around.

Q: So many people, so many souls, are becoming enlightened now. There seems to be a universal collective hunger for this, a common awakening, as if there is only one organism, one being, waking up. Is this your experience, too?
A: I don't know anything about that. All I know is that if it hurts, investigate. Enlightenment is just a spiritual concept, just one more thing to seek in a future that never comes. Even the highest truth is just one more concept. For me, the experience is everything, and that's what inquiry reveals. Everything painful is undone—now, now, now. If you think you're enlightened, you'll love having your car

towed away. That's it! How do you react when your child is sick? How do you react when your husband or wife wants a divorce? I don't know about people collectively waking up. Are you suffering, now? That's my interest.

People talk about self-realization, and this is it! Can you just breathe in and out happily? Who cares about enlightenment when you're happy right now? Just enlighten yourself to this moment. Can you just do that? And then eventually, it all collapses. The mind merges with the heart and comes to see that it's not separate. It finds a home, and it rests in itself, as itself. Until the story is met with understanding, there is no peace.

Q: I've heard that people who are free don't have any preferences, since they see everything as perfect. Do you have preferences?
A: Do I have preferences? I'm a lover of what is, and what is is what I always have. "It" has its own preferences: the sun in the morning and the moon at night. And it appears that I always have a preference for the thing happening now. I prefer the sun in the morning, and I prefer the moon at night. And I prefer to be with the person in front of me now. As soon as someone starts asking questions, I'm there. He is my preference, and there's no one else. Then when I'm talking to another person, she's the one, and there's no one else. I discover my preferences by noticing what it is that I'm doing. Whatever I'm doing, that's my preference. How do I know? I'm doing it! Do I prefer vanilla over chocolate? I do, until I don't. I'll let you know as we place our order at Ben & Jerry's.

Q: Do all beliefs need to be undone?
A: Investigate all the beliefs that cause you suffering. Wake yourself up from your nightmares, and the sweet dreams will take care of themselves. If your internal world is free and wonderful, why would you want to change it? If the dream is a happy one, who would want to wake up? And if your dreams aren't happy, welcome to The Work.

There is only one problem, ever: your uninvestigated story in the moment.

14

The Work in Your Life

Beginners sometimes ask me what will happen if they do The Work on a regular basis. They are afraid that without a story, they won't be motivated to act and won't know what to do. The experience of those who do The Work is that the opposite is true. Inquiry naturally gives rise to action that is clear, kind, and fearless.

When you begin to meet your thinking with understanding, your body follows. It begins to move by itself, so you don't have to do anything. The Work is about noticing our thoughts, not about changing them. When you work with the thinking, the doing naturally follows.

If you sit in a chair and have a great insight, is that the end of it? I don't think so. Doing The Work is only half the process; the other half happens when the insights come to life. Until they live as action, they're not fully yours.

The Work will show you where you've got your happiness backward. When you think that people should be kind to you, the reverse is true: you should be kind to them and to yourself. Your judgments about others become *your* prescription for how to live. When you turn them around, you see what will bring you happiness.

The advice you've been giving your family and friends turns out to be advice for you to live, not us. You become the wise teacher as you become a student of yourself. It stops mattering if anyone else hears you, because *you're* listening. You are the wisdom you offer us, breathing and walking and effortlessly moving on as you make your business deal, buy your groceries, or do the dishes.

Self-realization is the sweetest thing. It shows us how we are fully responsible for ourselves, and that is where we find our freedom. Rather than being other-realized, you can be self-realized. Instead of looking to us for your fulfillment, you can find it in yourself.

We don't know how to change; we don't know how to forgive or how to be honest. We're waiting for an example. You're the one. You are your only hope, because we're not changing until you do. Our job is to keep coming at you as hard as we can with everything that angers, upsets, or repulses you until you understand. We love you that much, whether we're aware of it or not. This whole world is about you.

To put The Work into action, begin with the voice inside you that's telling you what we should do. Realize that it's actually telling *you* what to do. When it says, "He should pick up the socks," listen to the turnaround "I should pick up the socks," and just do it. Stay in the flow that's effortless and unending. Pick them up until you love it, because it's your truth. And know that the only important house to clean is your mind.

There is no peace in the world until you find peace within yourself in this moment. Live these turnarounds, if you want to be free. That's what Jesus did, what the Buddha did. That's what all the famous great ones have done and all the unknown great ones who are just living it in their homes and communities, happily and in peace.

At some point, you may want to go to the deepest pain inside you and clear it up. Do The Work until you see your part in it. Then go to the people you've judged, and apologize; tell them what you've seen about yourself and how you're working on it now. It's all up to you. Speaking these truths is what will set you free.

You may be afraid to go deeper into The Work because you think that it's going to cost you something valuable. My experience is the opposite: without a story, life only gets richer. Those who stay in The Work for a while discover that inquiry is not serious and that investigating a painful thought just turns it into laughter.

I love that I'm free to walk in the world without fear, sadness, or anger, ready to meet anything or anyone in any place, at any time, with arms and heart wide open. Life will show me what I haven't undone yet. I look forward to it.

Just keep coming home to yourself. You are the one you've been waiting for.

Appendix: Self-Facilitation

The following are examples of self-facilitated Work written by people who were upset by their thoughts about a friend or a lover. They illustrate the depth inquiry can go to when you take the time to write your answers thoroughly and honestly.

My Boyfriend's Handicap or Mine?

The written statement: *I'm saddened and angry because Allen can't walk and we can't do normal "couple" things together.*

Is it true? Yes.

What's the reality? The reality is that Allen is in a wheelchair and he can't walk.

Rewritten statement (arrived at with the prompt "What would I have if Allen could walk?"): "My life would be better if Allen could walk."

Can I really know that that's true? No.

How do I react, what happens, when I believe the thought that my life would be better if Allen could walk? I feel like a martyr. I feel sorry for myself. I feel envious of other couples. I feel cheated and panicky. I feel like a part of my life is never lived out—especially sexually. I long for things that are difficult or impossible for us to do, like travel to nonhandicap places. I worry needlessly and endlessly that somehow I'm making a mistake loving this man as I do. I doubt God, even though Allen is the man he puts in front of me over and over again to love.

What does it feel like to believe the thought? Crazy, alone, a freak, constant addictive thinking that constipates me. My chest physically hurts so much that it feels like someone is standing on it. I get mad. We stand out. We're strange and abnormal—never the ideal.

How do I treat Allen when I believe that my life would be better if he could walk? I'm cold and distant. I'm uncomfortable. I hold back loving thoughts, things that I really want to share with him. I don't make love to him. I expect him to do all the work sexually. I act like I know more than he does about how to take care of himself.

How do I treat myself? I think I'm crazy, that there's something wrong with me because I love a man in a wheelchair. The worst thing I do is I don't let myself love him fully. I tell myself I'm co-dependent. I get so distracted that I drink. I read too much, or I don't read at all. I try to work some angle with another man, usually in my head and sometimes with a real man. I tear myself up with dual thinking: "Is it right? Isn't it right?" I can't sleep. I act like it doesn't really bother me to my family and friends, and I get defensive and hard. I won't let myself think about all the wonderful things we have together. I look for theories to prove I'm right—astrology, double-Capricorn stuff, metaphysical bullshit. I feel ashamed of myself for not following my heart. I won't go with him to New Mexico because of my brilliant career, my fabulous house, and my cats.

Can I see a reason to drop the thought that my life would be better if Allen could walk? Yes. All of the above reactions.

Can I find one stress-free reason to keep the thought? Not one.

Who would I be without the thought that my life would be better if Allen could walk? A woman in love with a man named Allen.

Rewritten statement turned around: "My life would not be better if Allen could walk." That feels just as true.

Original statement turned around: "I am saddened and angry because I can't walk." Yes. Sometimes I stop myself from going places, and then I blame Allen. I get angry thinking that I can't get up and walk where I want to. We *can* do normal "couple" things together. True. What Allen and I do is normal for us. So I stop us from enjoying our normal "couple" things by comparing us to other couples and thinking that their normal should be our normal.

Janine Shouldn't Lie to Me

The written statement: *I don't like Janine because she lies to me.*

Is it true? Yes.

What is my proof that this is true? She told me that the class would be limited to thirty people. There were fifty-five people. She told me that she would send me tapes by the end of the week. She sent them a month later. She told me that she felt sure she could arrange an earlier ride to the airport. When the time came, she said that there was no ride available for me.

Does any of this proof really prove that she lies to me? Yes.

Can I absolutely know that it's true that Janine lies to me? Yes.

How do I react when I believe the thought that Janine lies to me? I feel out of control and helpless. I can't believe anything she says. I feel frustrated. I get very uptight whenever I am with her or even thinking about her. I am always thinking of how I would do her job better than she does.

Rewritten statement (arrived at with the prompt "What's the 'should'?"): "People shouldn't lie."

Is it true? No—they do!

How do I treat Janine when I believe the story that people shouldn't lie, and she does? I see her as phony, unreliable, incompetent, and uncaring. I treat her with mistrust and coldness. I see everything about her—words, gestures, actions—as lies. I am short with her. I don't like her, and I want her to feel my dislike and disapproval.

How does that feel? It feels out of control. I don't like myself. I feel guilty and wrong.

Who would I be (in the presence of Janine) without the story that people shouldn't lie? I would see Janine as doing her best and actually doing very well, considering the huge amount of information she is handling for so many people. I would be more caring and helpful to Janine. I might take the time to chat with her and get to know her. When I close my eyes and see her without that story, I really like her and want to be her friend.

Rewritten statement turned around: "People should lie." Yes, they should, because they do.

Original statement turned around: "I don't like myself because I lie to Janine." That's true. I told her that I couldn't get a later flight. That airline was sold out, but I didn't try the waiting list or another airline. The truth is that I lied. I wanted to take an earlier flight. "I don't like Janine because I lie to myself [about Janine]." Yes, that's truer. I tell myself a lot of lies about Janine when I draw conclusions about everything she says and does. It's not Janine that I don't like—it's the stories, the lies that I tell myself about her that I don't like. "I do like Janine because she doesn't lie to me." That's true also. I really don't believe she has ever intentionally told me anything that was not true. She is passing along information she's been given, and she can't know if it will change or not. And I really do like her.

I am the cause of my own suffering—but only all of it.

Contact Information

To find out more about The Work of Byron Katie, please visit thework.com.

Questions? Email info@thework.com.

Byron Katie International, Inc.
P.O. Box 1206
Ojai, CA 93024
USA
1-805-444-5799
International 001-805-444-5799

When you visit the website, you'll be able to read detailed instructions about The Work; watch video clips of Katie facilitating people on a wide variety of issues; view Katie's calendar of events; download free materials; register for an upcoming nine-day School for The Work, a No-Body or Forgiveness Intensive, or an online course; find out about how to call the free *Do The Work* helpline; learn about the Institute for The Work and its Certified Facilitators; download Judge-Your-Neighbor Worksheets; listen to archived radio interviews; download apps for your iPhone, iPad, or Android; subscribe to the free newsletter; and shop in the online store. We also invite you to Katie's Facebook, Twitter, Google+, and Pinterest pages. For video, visit TheWorkofBK YouTube channel; and for live streaming events, visit livewithbyronkatie.com.

If you would like to help our work in prisons and VA hospitals and support scholarships for the School, the Work Foundation will gratefully accept your tax-deductible gift. The Work Foundation is a 501(c)(3) not-for-profit organization. Make a secure online donation at theworkfoundationinc.org or mail your donation to:

The Work Foundation

P.O. Box 638

Ojai, CA 93024

USA

For a large selection of audio and video recordings of The Work, visit www.thework.com, where you can also find the audio version of this book on compact disk.

The School for The Work

This is the ultimate inner adventure. Unlike every other school on Earth, this one isn't for learning; it's for unlearning. You'll spend nine days losing the fear-based stories you've innocently clung to all your life. The curriculum at the School is a living, evolving process, changing with the needs of the participants and on the basis of past students' experiences. Each exercise is led directly by Katie and is tailored to meet the needs of the participants attending—no two Schools are the same. And after nine days with Katie, you won't be, either. "Once the four questions are alive inside you," Katie says, "your mind becomes clear, and therefore the world you project becomes clear. This is more radical than anyone can possibly imagine."

Notes to the Introduction

page xiii   **"The more clearly you understand yourself and your emotions, the more you become a lover of what is"**: Baruch Spinoza, *The Ethics*, Book 5, Proposition 15. Here's a more literal translation: "He who clearly and distinctly understands himself and his emotions loves God, and does so the more, the more he understands himself and his emotions." Spinoza's term *God*—he often says "God-or-nature"—actually means "ultimate reality" or simply "what is."

page xiv   **"we are disturbed not by what happens to us, but by our thoughts about what happens"**: Epictetus, *Encheiridion*, V. Two other relevant statements: "Nothing external can disturb us. We suffer only when we want things to be different from what they are." (*Encheiridion*, V) "No one has the power to hurt you. It is only your own thinking about someone's actions that can hurt you." (*Encheiridion*, XX)

page xv   **"To realize your true nature, you must wait for the right moment and the right conditions"**: Quoted in a Dharma talk by the great Chinese Zen master Pai-chang (720–814). See *The Enlightened Mind: An Anthology of Sacred Prose,* edited by Stephen Mitchell (New York: HarperCollins, 1991), 55. I have been unable to identify the sutra.

page xviii   **Katie often says that the only way to understand The Work is to experience it:** This paragraph was written by my friend and literary agent Michael Katz, who also wrote the section in chapter 10 called "When the Story Is Hard to Find" and edited many passages in this book.

page xviii   **"Perhaps the most important revelation":** Antonio Damasio, *The Feeling of What Happens: Body and Emotion in the Making of Consciousness* (New York: Harcourt, Brace, 1999), 187.

page xviii   **"The left brain weaves its story":** Michael Gazzaniga, *The Mind's Past* (Berkeley: University of California Press, 1998), 26.

page xix   **"Considering that, all hatred driven hence":** From "A Prayer for My Daughter," in *The Collected Works of W. B. Yeats,* vol. 1: *The Poems,* edited by Richard J. Finneran (New York: Scribner, 1997), 192. The second line of the stanza reads: "The soul recovers radical innocence."

page xxx   **Step aside from all thinking:** From Seng-ts'an, "The Mind of Absolute Trust," in *The Enlightened Heart: An Anthology of Sacred Poetry,* edited by Stephen Mitchell (New York: HarperCollins, 1989), 27.

ABOUT THE AUTHORS

Byron Katie experienced what she calls "waking up to reality" in 1986, and since then she has introduced The Work to hundreds of thousands of people throughout the world, at her public events, at Schools for The Work, and in business settings, universities, schools, churches, prisons, and hospitals. She is also the author of *I Need Your Love—Is That True?*, *A Thousand Names for Joy*, and *A Mind at Home with Itself*. Her other books are *Question Your Thinking, Change The World*; *Who Would You Be Without Your Story?*; and, for children, *Tiger-Tiger, Is It True?* and *The Four Questions*. On her website, thework.com, you will find basic information about Katie and The Work, free materials to download, audio and video clips, a schedule of events, and a free helpline with a network of facilitators.

Stephen Mitchell's many books include the bestselling *Tao Te Ching, Gilgamesh, The Gospel According to Jesus, Bhagavad Gita, The Book of Job, The Second Book of the Tao, The Iliad, The Odyssey, Beowulf, The Way of Forgiveness*, and *The First Christmas*. You can read extensive excerpts from all his books on his website, stephenmitchellbooks.com.

It's always a
beginning.